A Journalii

Solitaria

Embrace Cozy Life on Floating Islands

version 1.2.4

Copyright

The Copyright

So gather your cosy companions 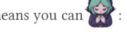 - both furry and not - and lose yourself in this magical world. Let the words weave their charming spell and transport you to a place of slow life and warmth.

Overview

Here's what you can do in Solitaria

🔍 Explore the wonders of Solitaria, from its lush forests to its sparkling seas. Visit the friendly Islanders, who have their own stories and personalities. Forage for natural resources, craft useful items, fish for delicious seafood, play fun mini-games, and make new friends along the way!

👧 Seek the guidance of the Goddess, the benevolent ruler of Solitaria. She will help you discover the secrets of this world and grant you Divine Favors if you please her. These abilities will change how you play and interact with Solitaria!

⛺ Customize your own Floating Island, a cozy home in the sky. Decorate it with your favorite items, grow crops, raise animals, and invite Islanders to hang out with you!

🤠 Set your own goals and pace! Collect items, fish, craft items, unlock Goddess secrets and earn Divine Favor. Or simply relax and enjoy the scenery. The choice is yours!

🪴 A crafting system that lets you make tools, accessories, food and gifts for yourself or the Islanders.

🐟 A fishing system that lets you catch fish of different sizes and types. You can use them as gifts or ingredients for cooking.

🏆 Mini-games that use the same poker deck as the main game. You can play them alone or with the Islanders for fun or rewards.

🎁 A gift system that lets you give items to the Islanders as tokens of friendship or gratitude. Different items will affect their favor levels differently and might trigger different reactions or events.

🫧 A favor system that tracks your relationships with the Islanders. Interact with them, give them gifts, help them with their requests, and increase their favor. You might even trigger special events or scenes with them!

🔮 50 Oracles that will inspire you with ideas, questions, twists, outcomes and more when you are stuck or need a challenge!

🕐 A time system with three sections per day: morning, afternoon, and evening.

📅 Each season brings new events, festivals and stories that celebrate the seasons and the Islanders. Join them in their festivities and enjoy seasonal foods and activities.

Player Guide

You are about to embark on a cosy adventure in the Floating Islands, where you can explore, craft, play, and make friends with the Islanders and Creatures.

If this is your first time playing Solitaria or SSSystem, don't worry! We have two options for you to get started quickly and easily:

To start playing quickly: If you want to jump right into the game without reading too much rules, follow the yellow box instructions on these pages:

Page 10 to 26	You only need to read the Game Mechanics section from *Pg.10* to *Pg.26*, where we explain how to use dice, cards, tokens, and other tools to play the game.
Page 38 to 43	You also need to read how to use the Various Playkit sheets from *Pg.38* to *Pg.43*, where we show you how to keep track of your character, inventory, quests, and more.
Page 47	If you like journaling your game sessions, you can also check out the Date System on *Pg.47*, where we give you some tips on how to record your daily activities.

Once you have read these sections, you are ready! Go to *Pg.76* or *Pg. 7*, and follow the instructions there. You will PLAY through a short tutorial as you board your transportation to the Floating Islands.

· · · · · · · · · · · · · · · · · ·

If you want to learn more about the game world, the characters, and the mechanics before playing:

Page 1 to 88	You can read everything from page 1 to page 88 at your own pace and enjoy all the details and background information we have prepared for you.
Page 8 to 9	You can also use the Table of Content on page 8 and page 9 to help you navigate the Game Book and find what you are looking for.

This book is designed to guide you smoothly from one game element and idea to the next one, creating a seamless and enjoyable experience.

· · · · · · · · · · · · · · · · · ·

If you are a seasoned player of SSSystem or have played our previous game iXe before:

Page 32	We recommend that you read at page 32 onwards, we have made some improvements in SSSystem v2 that affect how time, randomness, character creation, and actions works.
Start Page. 88	Enjoy! This game does not have any combat or damage mechanics but instead introduces concepts such as time management, actions, crafting, mini-games, and more.

If you have played Solitaria before and want to try something new, check out our website or other platforms. There might be new Floating Islands with different themes, seasons, and characters for you to discover and enjoy.

The Invitation

In the realm of Solitaria, where tranquility resides,
A graceful goddess guides, with love that gently glides.
She weaves a tapestry of meaning, so profound and pure,
To touch the souls of weary beings, their spirits to allure.

Each day, all living things strive to keep on living,
Their journey filled with joys and sorrows, always giving.
Yet, behold, no life lasts forever, we must comprehend,
In this sacred realm, let us learn, let us transcend.

With tender care, she whispers to the hearts that seek,
A sanctuary from the chaos, where solace they shall reap.
In her hands, she holds the ones in need of respite,
Inviting them to Solitaria, where dreams take flight.

Within these lands of solitude, a haven we shall create,
A haven where weary souls find solace, a tranquil state.
For in the embrace of solitude, one's essence can be found,
To rediscover the worth of life, let its melody resound.

She beckons them to rest, beneath the sheltering trees,
To breathe in nature's symphony, as the gentle breeze.
A respite from the bustling world, a sanctuary so grand,
Where time slows its pace, and healing is at hand.

Amidst the golden hues of dawn, behold the beauty untold,
Embrace the fleeting moments, let their significance unfold.
For in the tapestry of life, every thread is meant to be,
A reminder of the preciousness of existence, can't you see?

In the company of kindred spirits, they find solace and cheer,
Sharing stories, forging bonds, wiping away every tear.
With every passing season, a new chapter to explore,
Through trials and triumphs, wisdom they shall implore.

Within the heart of Solitaria, a symphony of life does play,
Every whisper of the wind, every dawn's first ray.
Let us cherish the fleeting dance, in this enchanting sphere,
For life's true essence lies within, as love softly draws near.

And so, the graceful goddess weaves her heartfelt song,
A tapestry of meaning, where each life can belong.
In Solitaria's embrace, she nurtures spirits worn,
Revealing the value of life, a treasure to be adorned.

For in the depths of solitude, where dreams are set free,
We rediscover our purpose, our worth, our legacy.
Let this world of Solitaria guide us, as we journey on,
To cherish life's embrace, until the final dawn.

Introduction

Solitaria is a secluded realm, a hidden haven far from the daily grind. It exists as a sanctuary for those seeking respite from life's worries. Within this mystical land, each place serves as shelter crafted just for you, weary traveler looking for solace.

Your journey begins the moment you receive the invitation -

The invitation can come in many forms, depending on your preference and personality. It could be a letter tied with golden string, an envelope with a wax seal, an email with a mysterious attachment, an SMS with a cryptic code, or a flyer with a hidden message. Whichever it may be, you've been given an invitation to Solitaria, a realm of peace and wonder.

Inside the letter invites you to Solitaria to rest, recuperate and revive your spirit. At first, you set the letter aside until, one morning, an urge wells up within - a yearning to leave behind the hectic demands weighing you down. You make your choice: to accept the invitation and go. You open the invitation and find a message that reads:

Dear Friend,

You have been chosen to visit Solitaria, a haven for those who need a break from life's stress. Here, you will find a place to relax, heal and renew your energy. Solitaria is a land of wonder and mystery, where you can pursue your dreams and passions. Whether you want excitement or peace, Solitaria has something for everyone.

To confirm this invitation, simply follow the instructions attached. A gateway will appear before you, taking you to your destination. You may stay as long as you like, and come back whenever you wish. No one will notice or disturb you while you are away.

This is a unique chance to leave the troubles of the world and discover a new way of living. Do not think twice, do not wait. Solitaria is waiting for you.

Yours truly,

Mr Warden

The Journey Begins:

You arrive at the mysterious place marked on the ticket. Here awaits your transport to Solitaria, let us start by drawing a card from your poker deck. Check the suits of the Poker deck and check the method of transportation that you have been assigned with:

♦**The Express Train**: A gleaming crimson steam locomotive emerges from the mist, chimney billowing clouds of fragrant jasmine incense. You board its golden carriages as soothing music plays and aromatic tea is served.

♣**The Hot Air Balloon**: A gigantic pastel-colored balloon appears, decorated with butterflies and flowers. You climb into the basket and feel the air gently lift you up as butterflies swirl around and floral scents fill the air.

♥**The Sea Train**: From the seashore emerges an antique aquamarine train carriage sitting atop clam shells. You climb aboard and feel the sea spray against your face as the train puffs steadily across the waves.

♠**The Winged Carriage**: A carriage drawn by winged horses lands softly by you. You climb inside its comfortable, floral-scented interior and feel yourself lifting gently into the sky as the horses' wings beat rhythmically.

Whichever you choose, it transports you to Solitaria (You may start playing from *Page. 78 or* study the Player's Guide for New player on *Page.4*).

Table of Content

What is Solitaria?

Picture yourself in a solo roleplaying game, where you step into the shoes of someone who receives a special invitation from the illustrious Goddess of Solitaria herself. It's an invitation to escape the hustle and bustle of the busy world and find solace on a small, secluded island.

Solitaria is a game that celebrates the simple joys of life, the warmth of friendship, and the magic of every passing moment. It's about savoring the cozy pleasures and relishing in the company of good friends. Whether you're tending to your garden, engaging in heartfelt conversations, or embarking on thrilling quests, every day in Solitaria is a chance to create cherished memories.

Now, how does one end up in Solitaria, you may ask?
Well, my friend, the paths are as diverse as the colors of the rainbow. You might have yearned for a change of scenery and wished upon a star. Or perhaps, fate played its mischievous hand, and you found yourself here by sheer mistake or a stroke of good luck. Whatever the case may be, you're here, and the floating island awaits!

As you set foot on this extraordinary island, you'll be greeted by the serene nature and surrounded by the mysterious community. Each resident has a unique story to tell, and you'll have the chance to start your life anew amidst their cheerful company. Maybe you'll take on the noble task of restoring a long-forgotten family farm, breathing new life into the fertile soil.

Or perhaps you'll feel the call of the mysterious forest, beckoning you with its secrets and the enigmatic portal just outside your humble hut. Who knows? Maybe love will blossom in the most unexpected places, and you'll find yourself walking down the aisle!

So, my dear friend, welcome to Solitaria, where the journey is as magical as the destination. Embrace the enchantment, cherish the camaraderie, and let the laughter echo through the meadows.

What do you need to start playing?
This Book,
A journaling book and a pen,
A deck of playing card (without the joker),
A printed playkit containing the various Sheet.

To enjoy the game without spending too much time on the rules, begin here and continue reading until Pg.26.

How to play?

Before we embark on our grand adventure, let's familiarize ourselves with the game's ins and outs. There are 3 crucial sections to how to play Solitaria: *Learning the Game*, *Setting up the game in Session 0*, and *Immersing Yourself in the Gameplay*.

Learning the game:

This very book you hold in your hands is your gateway to the wonders of Solitaria. Within its pages, you'll find tips, rules, and guides to get you started on your stay in Solitaria. Pay heed to the following:

1. **Components**: Here we will acquaint ourselves with the game's components. You'll become familiar with the **deck of cards, your journal, player sheets**, and other essential elements that breathe life into Solitaria. Understanding their purpose and usage.

2. **Gameplay Mechanics**: We'll delve into the intricacies of how the game works, guiding you through prompts, checks, decision-making, and the art of drawing cards. Before you know it, you'll be a master of this system.

Session 0, Gateway to Adventure!

In this section, we'll ensure you're fully prepared to embark on your Solitaria escapades. Consider Session 0 as the warm-up stage before getting into the real action.

Let's explore two types of Session 0:

1. **Fresh Beginnings**: If you're just starting out, gather your resources. Grab your gamebook, a trusty deck of cards, a journal to chronicle your exploits, and your player sheets. Get everything in order.

2. **Continuing the Tale**: If you've already experienced the wonders of Solitaria and wish to carry on from previous sessions, this type of Session 0 is for you. Pick up where you left off, rekindle the magic, and dive back into the enchantment.

Lose yourself in Solitaria's gentle pace of life!

Life in Solitaria may seem deceptively simple, but trust me, there's never a dull moment! Now, let me make one thing clear from the start:

Solitaria isn't your typical RPG.

You won't find any muscle-bound heroes or fearsome monsters to slay here. No, no, the only thing you'll be slaying in this game is time itself!

Instead of barging into people's houses, swinging swords, and looting everything in sight, you'll find yourself engrossed in the wonderfully mundane activities that make life extraordinary.

Solitaria is a place where bonds are forged, laughter is shared, and hearts are filled with warmth.

And don't fret, there's plenty to do beyond socializing! You'll stumble upon fascinating projects, challenging puzzles, adventures, and intriguing tasks that will keep you engaged.

But remember, **Time** is both your ally and your greatest foe. Days in Solitaria have a tendency to slip away in the blink of an eye, and before you know it, the sun will be setting, signaling the end of yet another enchanting day.

There are 3 stage: Starting, Daily, and End of the Day.

Game Flow: Starting your Day

You start your day in the morning by consulting the **Rize Spirit**:

1. But before you dive into the day's activities, let's start by checking the **Season** and **Weather**. Is it a sunny day with gentle breezes, or perhaps a cozy afternoon with colorful leaves falling all around?
2. Now, take a moment to gaze upon the island and see what awaits you. You can also seek guidance from the mischievous Rize Spirit, who always has a knack for knowing what needs to be done:

Maybe there's someone waiting outside your door, ready to brighten your day with their infectious enthusiasm.

Oh, who could it be? Draw the card of destiny and let fate determine whether it's your best friend, a curious neighbor, or a new acquaintance.

They might inform you that the esteemed Goddess herself is seeking your presence, beckoning you to a special gathering.

Alternatively, the portal to another realm could shimmer enchantingly, tempting you to embark on an extraordinary quest.

Sometimes, the island may have more mundane but essential tasks in store for you. The farm, with its adorable animals and bountiful crops, might require your tender care.

Or perhaps the lake sparkles invitingly, hinting at a lively day of fishing and discovery.

But fear not, if nothing extraordinary seems to be happening on occasion. Even in the most tranquil moments, the island has a way of revealing its secrets when the time is right.

Game Flow: Daily Actions

Ah, the heart of the game! As you go about your day, use the Island's Map to your full advantage. Each island is unique with it's own special location and actions. Here we will show you what actions you can perform:

1. **Friends**: You'll encounter various friends who are always eager to interact with you. Each friend comes with their own unique scenario. Maybe they need something, and you're the only one who can help. It could be a simple favor or a adventure waiting to unfold. Or they might simply drop by for a pleasant chat, sharing stories and laughter.

2. **Trading Box**: Another delightful aspect of island life. You never know what treasures you might stumble upon or what your friends might be willing to part with. Trade your way to new and exciting items. Sharing a thoughtful present with a friend not only strengthens your bond but also brings a radiant smile to their face.

3. **Goddess Orb**: This enigmatic artifact holds secrets and quests, guiding you towards thrilling adventures. Seek the wisdom of the Goddess within the orb to gain insight into your next steps.

4. **Taking a Stroll**: While traversing the island, take the time to observe the world around you. The island is teeming with life, both ordinary and extraordinary. Listen to the whispers of the spirits, and cherish the beauty of nature in all its forms. Keep an eye out for peculiar phenomena that might pique your curiosity. And oh, what's that? A mysterious object has washed up on the lake! Who knows what secrets it holds?

5. **Ah, the island spirits!** These ethereal beings hold the key to hidden destinations within the island. Each scenarios offers its own set of stories and surprises, allowing you to immerse yourself in the wonders of the island.

6. **Lake**: Let's not forget about the soothing lake, where fishing becomes an art form. Cast your line, feel the anticipation, and see what the underwater realm has in store for you. The lake is also a fantastic place for foraging, as the surrounding flora often holds delightful surprises waiting to be discovered.

7. **Forest**: The forest beckons with its lush greenery and mysterious aura. Wander through the woods, exploring every nook and cranny. Who knows what treasures you might find hidden among the foliage? Keep your eyes peeled for raw materials or new landmarks.

8. **Field**: The field is where your inner farmer and chef collide. Tend to your crops, feeling the earth between your fingers as you nurture nature's bounty. Harvest your hard-earned produce and embark on a culinary journey, creating delectable dishes that will tantalize your taste buds.

9. **Feeling a bit artsy?** The cozy cabin welcomes you to indulge in the realms of writing and painting. Let your imagination run wild as you craft unique items or brush vibrant strokes on a canvas.

10. **Temple**: The temple stands tall, radiating an aura of spirituality and tradition. Here, you can perform ancient rituals that connect you with the island's mystical energy. Immerse yourself in the ceremony, feeling the harmonious vibrations that resonate through your very being.

11. **Workshop**: In the workshop, unleash your inner craftsman. Use your acquired resources to craft marvelous creations that will enhance your island and bring joy to those who encounter them. From intricate trinkets to useful tools, let your imagination guide your hands as you bring your visions to life.

12. **Weather Forecast**: And as you traverse the island, always keep an eye on the ever-changing weather. The sky might transform from clear blue to a swirling storm, affecting your activities and opening new possibilities. Adapt to the weather's whims and seize the opportunities it presents.

Game Flow: Ending your Day

As the day draws to a close, it's time to bid farewell to the adventures and retire to the comfort of your cozy abode.

Before drifting off to sleep, take a moment to reflect on the day's events.
- Did the island change in any noticeable way?
- What was your friend's response to your actions?
- Did any interesting or unexpected occurrences transpire?

Seek the wisdom of the Nite Spirit, who will provide you with updates and insights based on your actions throughout the day.

It's a lovely way to conclude your daily journey and eagerly anticipate the adventures that await you on the morrow.

Rinse and Repeat

In a delightful cycle of rinse and repeat!

Simply wake up, carry out your daily actions, and tuck yourself back into sleep everyday.

Learning the Game Mechanics

Solitaria is an game that revolves around the **Sparuh Solo System**. To understand the game and dive into the Core Mechanics of Solitaria, it's important to grasp these 2 game mechanics.

Let's delve into the various components that make up this game starting with **The Deck System**:

In Solitaria, the main game component is **The Deck**. You'll need a standard deck of *52 poker cards* (excluding the jokers) to play.

Splitting the Deck: As you embark on your adventure, you will split the Deck into two distinct parts: the **Main Deck** and the **Discard Pile**, also known as the **Fate Deck**.

Difference between Main Deck and Fate Deck

1. **Main Deck**: The Main Deck acts as a **versatile generator**, providing you with cards for various prompts. It serves as a source for generating names, topics, character creation details, scenario elements, weather checks, rolling stats for characters, randomizing rewards, and much more.
   (*Consider it an oracle that guides your journey.*)
2. **Fate Deck**: The Fate Deck comes into play when you need to **make decisions**, perform checks against environments, scenarios,or islanders,perform actions or rituals, or determine the outcome of any situations.
   (*It serves as a reservoir of possibilities, allowing you to shape the direction of your adventure.*)

The Time System
Day System
Solitaria operates on a day system, dividing your gameplay into sections of **three, four, or five actions per day**. This number depends on your Character's **Energy Level**. You have the flexibility to play as few as 2 actions or as many as 10 actions per day, the average is four actions per day.

Seasons System
Accompanying the day system is the season system, which consists of two part. The first half of the season concludes when you exhaust the Main Deck for the **first time**, while the second half ends when the Main Deck is depleted for the **second time**, thereby signifying the end of that season.

Once a season comes to a close, you can proceed to the next season, unlocking new challenges and adventures.

Forming the Fate Deck: As you play Solitaria, the **Fate Deck** gradually forms as cards accumulate in the Discard Pile.

At the beginning of the game, *shuffle the Main Deck and draw 5 cards to form the initial discard pile, which becomes the Fate Deck.* As you progress, you will continue adding cards to the Fate Deck, when generating daily prompts such as weather, scenario, items, or characters.

End of Seasons: Exhausting the Main Deck
The Main Deck will gradually decrease in size until eventually, all the cards end up in the Fate Deck. This process signifies that the season is nearing its conclusion or has already ended.

On average, players draw at least four or more cards for their daily prompts, implying that one deck of cards will last for approximately 11 or 12 days of gameplay.

Table Layout

Game Play Area

1. **Main Deck**: The Main Deck is the heart of Solitaria, the game that holds all the possibilities and adventures. It consists of 52 standard poker cards without the jokers.
2. **Fate Deck, the Discard Pile**: The Fate Deck, also known as the *Discard Pile*, plays a crucial role in Solitaria. It represents the accumulated decisions, actions, and outcomes of your journey. Whenever a card is discarded from the Main Deck, used to generate a prompt, it finds its place in the Fate Deck.
3. **Lower Base Range & Higher Base Range Cards**: These cards symbolize the abstract aspects of your environment, situations, and even the stroke of luck that may sway your fate.

> During each **Fate Step**, **you'll shuffle the Fate Deck and draw 2 cards**. These two cards determine the lower and higher base ranges, serving as a benchmark for *success or failure*. The lower-valued card represents the **low range**, while the higher-valued card represents the **high range**.

4. **Playkits**: Playkits for your Player Sheets and Islander Sheets. These kits include various tools, markers, and accessories to help you keep track of your progress, stats, and the unique characteristics of your player and islander.
5. **Journal, Book and Pen**: The Journal Book and Pen are your trusty companions for recording your adventures, important events, discoveries, and reflections.
6. **Solitaria Gamebook**: It serves as your guide, providing the Island's Map, available actions, instructions, prompts, and engaging narratives that shape your decisions and actions.

Gameplay Instruction

Setting Up:

Step 1: Give the deck of cards a good shuffle, ensuring that all the surprises and possibilities are thoroughly mixed. Place the shuffled deck face-down on the table, creating the **Main Deck**.

Step 2: *The Fate Deck* is the repository of past decisions and choices that have shaped your journey.

To form the **Initial Fate Deck**, **draw five cards** from the **Main Deck** and **Stack them face-down**.

(Designate a special spot on the table for this discard pile, as it will become your Fate Deck. It's like your personal time capsule, preserving the consequences of your actions.)

Step 3: With your cards ready and waiting, it's time to **prepare** your **Player Sheet** and any additional **Playkits** you might have.

Make sure to keep them within easy reach, as they will assist you in navigating the game.

Starting Your Day:

Step 4: As the first rays of the sun grace the land of Solitaria, consult the **Rize Spirit** or the **Island's Map** for a myriad of actions available to you.

You can choose to **Begin** your day with "**0. Pre-day Action: Rize Spirit.**" This section sets the stage for the day, r*evealing the season, weather*, and presenting an **Initial Scenario** to kickstart your adventure.

Whether someone is seeking your help, the mystical portal is glowing, or the farm appears ready for bountiful harvest, let **Rize Spirit**, the prompt generator, guide your imagination.

Step 5.1: Now, you have a choice to make. You can either follow the Rize Spirit's **Initial Scenario**, immersing yourself in the unfolding tale, or you can chart your own path and **Explore** Solitaria independently.

Step 5.2: If you decide to forge your own destiny, don't forget to **Make A Promise** to return to the scenario that the Rize Spirit has generated. **Goal Setting** is a crucial part of your journey.

Step 5.3: Should you opt for your own pursuits, **consult** the **Island Map** and select any **Action** that calls to you. **Perform** the chosen Action according to the provided **Instructions**.

Step 6: Depending on the instructions accompanying your chosen **Action**, you may find yourself at a crossroads between a **Prompt** or a **Fate Step**.

Prompts

Step 6.1: As the card reveals its message, **consult** the **Oracles** for additional guidance and insights.

(To generate a Prompt, draw a Card from the Main Deck.)

Fate Step:

At pivotal moments in your quest, when tough decisions, challenges, or risks demand resolution, the *Fate Step* takes center stage.

Step 7: Shuffle the **Fate Deck**.

Step 7.1: *Draw and play two cards* from the Fate Deck. These **Base Cards** establish the range against which you'll measure your actions.

The lower-value card forms the *lower range*, while the higher-value card sets the stage for the *higher range*. Prepare to test your fate against these benchmarks.

Step 7.2: Now, it's time to confront the situation at hand. *Play a card* by *drawing* from the top card of the Fate Deck to resolve the challenge that stands in your way.

Step 7.3: Don't forget to consult your *Player Sheet*, where hidden bonuses in the *Attributes* section might provide you with an extra edge.

Envision the Outcome:

Step 8: With the *Fate Step* resolved, take a moment to envision the outcome of your actions. Let your imagination run wild and weave a story that brings the game to life.

Envision the brave choices you made, the obstacles you overcame, and the impact your decisions had on the world of Solitaria.

Immerse yourself in the narrative and embrace the power of storytelling.

Step 9: Now that you've completed the steps, it's time to *rinse and repeat*. Return to **Step 5, Step 6 or Step 7**, delving deeper into the adventure that awaits.

Action Step One

The game is built on one-two key steps

One The Action you choose to undertake is a pivotal aspect of the game. Picture a straightforward map that serves as our example, with each location on the map assigned a number, representing the various Actions available for you. Sometimes, you will see some actions located off the map, these are used for actions that is not typically found on the *Island Map*.

Initial Action

Island Map Legend

Within each map, you'll find an image displaying the layout and various locations. These locations are marked with numbers that correspond to specific actions you can take. To help you navigate through the game, there's a legend that explains the purpose and effects of each location and action.

(Each map is distinct, offering its own set of modifiers and actions for you to explore and engage with.)

. . . .

#0. Pre-Day Action: Rize Spirit

Regardless of your chosen action, the day always begins with "**0. Pre-Day Action: Rize Spirit**" on the Island Map. This action sets the foundation for your day and provides clear guidance on what you should focus on.

In our example, let's say we're in the Season of Luminous Fireflies. Simply draw a card and refer to the suits. Don't worry about the suits unless you're new to the game and unsure where to begin.

Otherwise, pay attention to the numbers and turn your attention to the Weather section. Each season brings its own unique set of weather conditions.

(Draw a card - Main Deck): Season
- ♦ - Season of Floating Islands
- ♣ - Season of Luminous Fireflies
- ♥ - Season of Whirling Winds
- ♠ - Season of Eternal Night

Next, focus on the numbers and refer to the Weather section. Each season has its unique set of weather conditions. We'll refer to Season of Luminous Fireflies.

Weather: Season of Luminous Fireflies
- A - Sunny ☼
- 2 - Cloudy ☁
- 3 - Drizzling 🌦
- 4 - Misty 🏞
- 5 - Rain 🌧
- 6 - Heat Wave 🔥
- 7 - Thunderstorm ⛈
- 8 - Hail 🌨
- 9 - Humid 💧

- 10 - Breezy 🍃
- J - Foggy 🌫
- Q - Smoggy 🏞
- K - Soft Sunny ☕

Lastly, Rize Spirit will inform you of something going on today as a *Initial Scenario*.

Next, draw another card to determine the *Initial Scenario*. There are 13 potential scenarios available at any given time. If you cannot address it immediately, "*Set a Goal*" to tend to it later:

A - A "*Seasonal Scenario*" is starting. *(Flip to the Seasonal Scenario Page for the current season.)*
2 - Someone's Looking for You.
Look for Someone.
3 - The Spirits are acting strangely.
Visit the Spirit
4 - The Goddess Orb is shining brightly. ***Visit the Goddess***
5 - The Lake is lively today. Do a ***Lake*** Action.
6 - A mysterious letter just arrived.
Check Your Mailbox.
7 - Feeling a creative itch?
Express Yourself.
8 - Today is a beautiful day. ***Take a Walk.***
9 - Outdoor is calling. ***Go on an Adventure.***
10 - There's fruits in the Forest. ***Forage.***
J - Heard noises on the Island.***Investigate.***
Q - There's a new gossip in town.***Newspaper.***
K - Nothing Happens.

Now that you've taken care of it and are fully awaken, it is time to start your day.

TWO In Solitaria, the **Fate Step** is a crucial game mechanic that determines the success or failure of your chosen **Action**. It utilizes the **Fate Deck**, a collection of cards that shape the outcome of your decisions, resolve conflicts, and advance the story.

Each **Action** is tied to a specific situation and set of challenges, which leads to a result that you can then document in your journal.

If you're playing freely without utilizing any **Actions**, based on the situation, you will determine with your own judgement whether a **Fate Step** is necessary.

For **Actions**, it is crucial to proceed with the mechanics of the **Fate Step**, as it determines the outcome. The **Result** of **Fate Step** is then incorporated into your journal and may *impact* your character's status tracks, such as energy, power, abilities, or attributes.

By utilizing **Fate Step**, Solitaria ensures that each decision you make has consequences and shapes the story as it unfolds. So, choose your **Actions** wisely, as the cards hold the power to influence the journey that lies ahead.

The Fate Step works by creating a *range of values* that you must either *exceed* or *match* to be successful. The *outcome* of your action is determined by the value of the card you play relative to the *range established by these two base cards.*

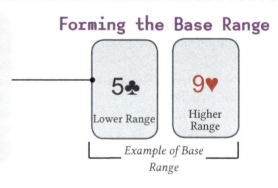

Forming the Base Range

Example of Base Range

Creating the Fate Deck

Start by drawing 5 cards from the **Main Deck** and adding them to your discard pile, also known as the **Fate Deck**.
*(The Fate Deck is created when you first start your **Game Session**)*

Base Range Cards

It is the **abstract representation** of the environment, situation, enemy, or even luck that the player encounters in their journey. For each new **Fate Step**, *shuffle* the **Fate Deck** and play 2 cards.
(These 2 cards become the base range and serve as a benchmark for success or failure in the game. The lower-valued card being the lower range and the other, higher-valued card being the higher range.)

Fate Draw: Draw from the Fate Deck

You must **draw a card** from the **Fate Deck** during the **Fate Step** and apply the result of the card played.

Apply Attribute Bonus

Simply look at the **Attributes** (*suits*) on your **Character Sheet** and apply the bonus (*-1, 0, +1, or +2*) based on the **Fate Card's suit** that you've played. The **Attribute Bonus** should kick it automatically when you play your **Fate Card**.

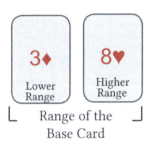

Range of the Base Card

Fate Card

Playing your Fate Card against the Base Range during Fate Step.

The results you would get from this **Fate Draw** is a **Success** and a **Lesser disadvantage**. 5 is higher than 3 and lower than 8, so you're within the range for a success.

But the ♦ is lower rank than the ♥ thus resulting in a lesser disadvantage.

Variation of Base Ranges

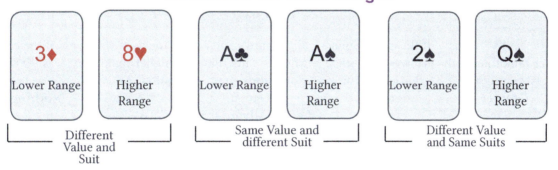

Fate Step Results

During Fate Step, the Fate of your Action is determined by two factors: the **Card's Value** and **Suits**.

The **combination** of these two elements will dictate the **outcome** of your **Action** and each *Action* can lead to different changes to your Character's status and to the scenario that you are in.

To determine the outcome, you will need to **compare** the **card's value** and **suit rank** to the **base range cards** that have been played.

CARDS VALUE

If the card's value is lower than the Lower base range's value, it is a **Failure.**	(*Instant*) If the card's value is the same as the Lower base range's value, it is a **Critical Failure.**	If the card's value is within the Lower and Higher base range's value, it is a **Success.**	(*Instant*) If the card's value is the same as the Higher base range's value, it is a **Plot Twist.**	If the card's value is higher than the Higher base range's value, it is a **Critical Success.**

SUITS RANK

If the card's Suits is lower rank than both cards, you receive a **Greater Disadvantage**	If the card's Suits is lower rank than one cards, you receive a **Lesser Disadvantage**	If the card's Suits is higher rank than one cards, you receive a **Lesser Advantage**	If the card's Suits is higher rank than both cards, you receive a **Greater Advantage**	If the card's Suits is the same rank as both cards, **Nothing Happens.**
RESULT +2 To Both Base Range	+1 To Both Base Range	+1 To Your Fate Card	+2 To Your Fate Card	N/A

Building the Fate Deck
As you play, continue to **build** the **Fate Deck** by **Drawing** cards from the **Main Deck** when you generate your prompts. The Fate Deck will continue to grow until the Main Deck is depleted, marking the end of the **Session** and **Seasons**.

Repeat the steps
After the results have been determined, you can repeat the steps above to keep playing the game.

Resolve Action

Resolving Actions

Once you have completed the **One-Two step** of **Drawing** and **Playing Cards** during **Fate Step**, it's time to determine the outcome of your actions. The **Result** can fall into one these outcome:

Success: When the result of your action is a success, it means you have achieved your goal or completed the task at hand.

Critical Success: On rare occasions, you may achieve a critical success. This signifies that not only have you succeeded, but you have exceeded expectations, going above and beyond in your action.

Failure: If the outcome of your action is a failure, it means you were not able to accomplish what you set out to do.

Critical Failure: In some unfortunate instances, you may experience a critical failure. This represents a significant setback or a disastrous outcome for your action.

Plot Twist: Sometimes, the result of your action can lead to an unexpected plot twist, adding an exciting twist to the story. This could present new challenges, opportunities, or surprises that you hadn't anticipated.

Envisioning the Outcome

Once you have determined the result of your action, take a moment to envision the outcome.

Imagine how the success, failure, critical success, critical failure, or plot twist will impact your character's journey and the world of Solitaria.

How to Envision the Result

Once you know the category of your result, it's your turn to envision what it looks like in the context of your action.

A helpful tool to guide your imagination is the Oracle, which is provided on the Action page.

On the Action page, you will find an instruction to consult the Oracle for further details.

The Oracle will provide you with prompts and suggestions specific to your action, helping you to delve deeper into the context and content of your result.

1. Example of Success:

You attempt to persuade an islander to join you on an adventure. You draw a card and it falls into the success category, marking a successful invite.

2. Example of Critical Success:

Your character attempts a daring acrobatic maneuver. You draw a card and it lands in the critical success category. Consulting the Oracle, you learn that not only does your character execute the maneuver flawlessly but also garners applause and amazement from onlookers.

3. Example of Plot Twist:

Your character embarks on a fishing trip, hoping to catch a big haul. As you draw a card, a plot twist is in store for you. Consulting the Oracle, you find that instead of reeling in fish, your character hooks onto something unexpected – a buried treasure chest!

4. Example of Failure:

Your character tries to solve a challenging puzzle. However, your card draws indicate a failure.

5. Example of Critical Failure:

Your character attempts to charm a potential romantic interest. Unfortunately, the card draws lead to a critical failure. Using the Oracle, you discover that your character's attempts at charm are met with instant rejection and embarrassment, leaving them disheartened.

Other Oracles

If you are seeking more in-depth ideas or need inspiration for your result, turn to the Oracle section in the game book. Here, you will find a variety of Oracles that cover different aspects, such as locations, characters, emotions, and more. Use these Oracles to generate rich and detailed content for your result.

Oracle Examples

A ♦	While exploring, you come across a peculiar tree with glowing mushrooms growing on its branches.
2 ♦	You notice a trail of tracks leading deeper into the forest.
3 ♦	As you venture further, you spot a rare species of bird perched high on a branch.
4 ♦	Suddenly, the forest becomes dense and misty.
5 ♦	As you make your way through the forest, you stumble upon a hidden waterfall.
6 ♦	Amidst the trees, you stumble upon a hidden clearing filled with a variety of medicinal herbs.
7 ♦	While exploring, you come across a fallen tree blocking your path.
8 ♦	A gentle breeze rustles through the leaves, revealing a man made item nestled at the base of a majestic oak tree.

Next, go to Pg.38 and learn how to use the various playkit and game sheets.

Custom Actions

In addition to the predefined actions in Solitaria, you have the freedom to create your own custom actions, tailored to your character's unique abilities, interests, and the world around them. This allows for endless possibilities and customization within the game.

Here's how you can create your very own custom action:

Determine the Goal:

Think about what your character wants to achieve with this custom action. Is it a specific task, an interaction with an islander, or a unique ability your character possesses? Define the goal you want to accomplish through this action.

Define the Parameters:

Specify the requirements and limitations of the action. Consider what resources, skills, or conditions are necessary for the action to be performed successfully. This ensures that the action remains balanced and aligned with the world of Solitaria.

Set the Outcome:

Decide what the possible outcomes of the action could be. Consider success, failure, critical success, critical failure, and the potential for plot twists. This helps create a framework for resolving the action and adding depth to your character's journey.

Envision the Result:

Once you've determined the category of the result, take a moment to imagine how it plays out within the context of your custom action. Visualize the impact it has on your character and the world around them. This will bring your custom action to life and enrich the storytelling experience.

Utilize the Oracle:

To further enhance your custom action, consult the Oracle provided on the Action page. The Oracle offers prompts and suggestions that help you delve deeper into the details and context of your result. It sparks your imagination and assists in creating a more immersive and engaging outcome.

Example:

Let's say you create a custom action called "Artisan's Touch."

Artisan's Touch
This action allows your character to infuse their creations with magical energy, enhancing their quality and granting unique properties.

1. **Goal**: Infuse a crafted item with magical energy.
2. **Parameters**: Requires a crafted item, a source of magical energy, and focus.
3. **Possible Outcomes**: Success, critical success, failure, critical failure, or a plot twist.
4. **Result**: If successful, the crafted item gains enhanced properties or magical abilities. If failed, the infusion doesn't work as intended, or the item is damaged in the process.

By following these steps, you can bring your custom action to life and add a personal touch to your character's journey in Solitaria. Remember to refer to the Oracle section for additional ideas and inspiration to further enrich your custom actions.

Game Action Island

Now that you have completed the initial #0 Action, Learn about Fate Steps, and Prompts, a range of exciting options awaits you. You can now choose from a variety of **Actions**, numbered from #1 to #7 according to the Island's Map, each offering its own unique experience and opportunities.

Game Actions

#1. Home
#2. Visit the Island Spirits
#3. Explore the Woods
#4. Trading Box
#5. Lake
#6. Goddess's Orb, Temple
#7. Friends

Each location provide a selection of actions where you'll find a list of available actions. These actions will provide you with a detailed overview of what you can do.

#1. Home

1. Check Mailbox
2. Cook a Meal
3. Rest
4. Personalize Home
5. Journal
...and more.

#2. Island Spirits

1. Discover Footprints
2. Trade Opportunity
3. Spirit Cravings
4. Curious Findings
5. Lost Memories
...and more.

#3. Explore the Woods

1. New Landmark
2. Source of Food
3. Animal Sighting
4. Encounter Islander
5. Rustling Sound
...and more.

#4. Trading Box

1. Mysterious Gift
2. Exchange Request
3. Gift Exchange
4. Auction
5. Seasonal Bazaar
...and more.

#5. Lake

1. Fishing
2. Reflection
3. Picnic
4. Observation
5. Mystic Ritual
...and more.

#6. Temple

1. Power Recovery
2. Guidance
3. Ritual
4. Maintenance
5. Divine Favor
...and more.

#7. Friends

1. Helping Hands
2. Gifts
3. Shared Adventure
4. Hangout
5. Friendship Ritual
...and more.

#. Others

While the examples provided earlier showcase a variety of locations and actions, it's important to note that different Island Maps can feature a different number of locations and actions. Some maps may have more locations and actions to explore, while others may have fewer.You also have the freedom to customize your own.

Action's Details

Within each location, you'll find a list of *Actions* along with their descriptions.
Actions in Solitaria embody a streamlined gameplay style, ensuring that you can dive right into the adventure without any unnecessary hurdles. Let's take a delightful playthru of a few example Actions to get you warmed up and ready.

Keep in mind that different Island Maps may introduce their own unique, new, and intriguing *Actions*, so make sure to consult the specific instructions for each action.

#1. Home

Check Mailbox: Explore your mailbox and discover any letters or messages by envisioning the Action and proceed to Fate Step. (*Once a day*).

On a Critical Success, you received an Islander Letter: Heartfelt messages from friends, loved ones, or even mysterious admirers. The prompts will guide you through heartwarming scenarios that celebrate friendship, romance, or simple acts of kindness.
On a Plot Twist, Mysterious Letter: Uncover secret messages or cryptic puzzles that ignite your curiosity and lead you on thrilling quests.
On a Failure or a Success, A promotional letter: The classic newsletters that flood our inboxes, relentlessly trying to sell us all sorts of things we don't really need.
On a Critical Failure, Requests for Help: Find letters requesting assistance from various islanders who are in need.

Let's take a closer look at the structure of the actions available to us in "Home". For this example, we will use "Check Mailbox" Action:

1. The action will begin with an introduction, providing a brief overview of the location and its purpose.
2. The action will instruct you to proceed to **Fate Step**, it will determine the type of the letters you'll receive based on your success rate.
3. Then proceed to the *Follow-up Action*s, which you need to consider either the suit, number, or both on the drawn card.
4. *Follow-up Actions:* After determining the type of letter, go to the next *Action step* for the corresponding Action.

An Action's Steps

Envision the Action: When you receive a letter from an Islander, take a moment to imagine the scene of receiving the letter. Picture yourself opening the mailbox or finding the letter left at your doorstep. Engage your senses and immerse yourself in the moment, envisioning the excitement or curiosity that arises upon discovering the letter.

Shuffle the Islander's Sheets: To determine the sender of the letter, shuffle the **Islander's Sheets** deck. This ensures a random selection and adds an element of surprise as you unveil the identity of the sender.

Draw an Islander Sheet: From the shuffled Islander Sheet, draw one sheet to reveal the sender of the letter. If, by chance, there are no available Islander Sheets remaining, you have the opportunity to create a brand new islander.

Checking the Previously Drawn Card: Retrieve the card that you drew prior to receiving the letter. This card holds significance in determining the content or scenario of the letter.

Consulting the Oracle: Utilize the Oracle, to generate the next scenario based on the drawn card. Cross-reference the details of the card with the prompts and scenarios provided in the Oracle.

Scenario Generation: Based on the information obtained from the Oracle, create the next scenario or event that occurred. Consider the letter's content, the islander who sent it, and the prompts from the Oracle to shape the scenario. Reflect upon the connections and potential interactions between the sender, the scenario, and any ongoing storylines or relationships you have going in Solitaria.

Now, let's turn our attention to the *Oracle* of the Islander's Letter. Consult the Oracle with the same Card you've drawn earlier in **#1. Home.**

Let us assume we've drawn a 4 ♦ and refer to the Oracle for the "Islander's Letter". The table on the left shows an example of how an Oracle table is displayed. There could be more 13 or more prompts.

(For this example, we are only showing the first 5 examples.)

Islander's Letter Prompts

A ♦	Heartfelt Admirer's Letter: A secret admirer has been captivated by you.
2 ♦	Friendship Letter: True friendship knows no bounds in Solitaria.
3 ♦	Acts of Kindness Letter: Thanks for your kindness.
4 ♦	Encouragement Letter: Sometimes, all we need is a gentle nudge.
5 ♦	Generosity Letter: Spirit of generosity fills the air.
	... and more.

Action Example

Let's take a peek at what happens when we perform the action of Checking the Mailbox. Oh, look at that! We've got ourselves a letter, and it's from none other than Chris Yolen, a charming fictional character from Solitaria. How delightful!

Chris has taken the time to send us an encouraging letter. Isn't that just wonderful? It's always nice to receive some positive vibes, especially from the friendly islanders of Solitaria. So, let's open up that letter and bask in the warmth of Chris's kind words. Who knows what exciting adventures await us next?

Next, it's time to decide what to do with this delightful piece of correspondence. You have a couple of options. You can either jot down the details in your journal, preserving this special moment for future recollection. Or, if you're feeling extra creative, why not expand it into a full-fledged story?

Journal Entry Example

Today, I embarked on my daily ritual of checking the mailbox on Solitaria Island. Little did I know that this seemingly ordinary task would lead me down a path of surprise. As I opened the mailbox, a colorful envelope caught my eye, bearing the name of Chris Yolen—a name that sparked curiosity and excitement within me.

With trembling hands, I carefully unfolded the letter and began to read the heartfelt words by Chris Yolen, the master of Whimsy and Wit Inn, had sent me an encouragement letter. The pages danced with magic as I devoured every line, feeling a surge of inspiration coursing through my veins.

" I hope this letter finds you in good spirits and surrounded by the enchantment that permeates our beloved realm. I couldn't resist penning this missive to extend a warm embrace of friendship and encouragement.

I must confess, dear friend, that your presence on Solitaria has not gone unnoticed. The island whispers tales of your adventurous spirit and kind heart, weaving them into the very fabric of our community. It is an honor to share this magical place with someone as special as you.

Until our paths intertwine once more, I bid you farewell, and may the spirit of Solitaria forever guide and inspire you."

As I finished reading, a smile spread across my face, illuminated by the warmth of Chris's kindness. This letter, a precious gift, reminded me of the boundless imagination that dwells within us all. It urged me to capture the essence of Solitaria in my journal, to preserve the magic and share it with others.

Action with Time Token

Now, let's dive into an Action that is a bit more time-consuming. In this Action, you'll have the chance to discover a brand new landmark in the lush and mysterious woods of our beloved island.

This type of Actions will require you to allocate a chunk of your precious time by advancing the **Time Token** on your character sheet.

#3. Explore the Woods

New Landmark: Close your eyes and picture yourself venturing deeper into the woods, your senses heightened with anticipation. The rustling leaves and soft sunlight filtering through the canopy guide your way as you seek out the secrets of the forest. ***Proceed to Fate Step***. (*Once a day*).

On a Critical Success:
With a stroke of luck and a twinkle in your eye, you find yourself standing before a mesmerizing new landmark. Its beauty captivates your senses, leaving you in awe of the intricate details and the stories it holds. Advance 1 TS.

On a Plot Twist:
As you tread deeper into the woods, you stumble upon a landmark that seems oddly familiar. A sense of déjà vu washes over you, and you realize that you have indeed encountered this particular place before. While it may not be a brand new discovery, it still holds its own charm and secrets. Advance 2 TS.

On a Failure:
Alas, despite your best efforts, your search for a new landmark proves fruitless. The forest keeps its secrets tightly guarded, and this time, it eludes your grasp. But fret not, for even in the absence of a new discovery, the journey itself holds its own magic. Advance 1 TS.

On a Success:
Congratulations are in order, for you have successfully uncovered a new landmark! Your persistence and keen eye have paid off, revealing a hidden gem in the heart of the woods. Immerse yourself in its enchantment, explore its nooks and crannies. Advance 1 TS.

On a Critical Failure:
Oh, the fickle nature of fate! Despite your best intentions, your quest for a new landmark takes an unexpected turn. Whether you find yourself lost in the depths of the woods or stumble upon a familiar spot, the outcome leaves you feeling a sense of disappointment. Advance 2 TS.

If you've are **Successful** in finding a **New Landmark** add it to a new **Location Sheet**. Proceed to draw a card from the Main Deck and look at the result of the draw.

A. Found Nothing: Sometimes, the mystery lies in what is not there. But fear not, for even the absence of a landmark can spark your curiosity and lead you on unexpected paths.

2. Lake: A tranquil oasis nestled within the woods, offering shimmering waters and a serene ambiance.

3. Hill: A gentle slope that offers a panoramic view of the landscape.

4. Mountain: A majestic peak reaching for the sky, beckoning you to conquer its heights.

5. Giant Tree: Behold, a magnificent arboreal wonder that stands tall and proud.

6. Whisering Falls: Follow the sound of gentle cascades and discover a hidden waterfall tucked away in the heart of the woods.

7. Enchanted Clearing: Step into a magical space where sunlight dances through the leaves, illuminating a carpet of vibrant wildflowers.

8. Ancient Ruins: Uncover the remnants of a forgotten civilization, now covered in moss and mystery.

9. Fairy Circle: Stumble upon a circle of mushrooms, said to be a gathering spot for mischievous fairies.

10. Sacred Ruins: Uncover the remnants of a long-lost civilization hidden deep within the woods.

J. Talking Animals' Den: Enter a clearing where animals gather to hold their secret council.

Q. Treehouse: Stumble upon a whimsical treehouse nestled among the branches.

K. Waterfall: Listen to the melodious symphony of cascading water as you stumble upon a magical waterfall.

Explore the Woods > New Landmark > Success > Talking Animal's Den

Picture this: you've bravely chosen the action to Explore the Woods, and with bated breath, you draw a card from the deck to reveal your fate.

And what do we have here?
It's none other than a New Landmark!

Congratulations, my friend, your journey has led you to a remarkable discovery. But hold on tight, because our fate doesn't stop there. We must proceed with the thrilling Fate Steps to determine if we've successfully stumbled upon this new gem.

Drumroll, please!
And guess what?
Luck is on your side today! You've indeed found a New Landmark, marking a pivotal moment in your grand adventure. It's a Talking Animal's Den!

Can you believe your luck?
The woods are truly buzzing with enchantment and surprises. Now, let your imagination run wild as you envision this extraordinary den, where charming creatures engage in whimsical conversations.

Journal Entry Example

Today, my journey through the mystical woods of Solitaria led me to an extraordinary discovery. As I ventured deeper into the emerald-green foliage, a sense of anticipation filled the air. It was as if the very trees whispered of hidden wonders waiting to be unveiled.

With each step, my curiosity grew, and soon, my eyes fell upon a sight that made my heart leap with joy. Right before me stood a brand new landmark, like a secret waiting to be uncovered. I couldn't resist the urge to let out a triumphant drumroll, for in that moment, I knew something marvelous was about to unfold.

Behold, for I had stumbled upon none other than a Talking Animal's Den! Can you believe the sheer serendipity of it all? The woods, it seemed, were alive with enchantment, and I was about to become a part of it.

With bated breath, I approached the den, wondering what delightful creatures I might encounter within. Would it be a wise old owl, ready to impart ancient wisdom? Or perhaps a mischievous fox, full of playful riddles? The possibilities were as endless as the starry night sky.

As I drew closer, the den revealed its secrets, and to my astonishment, charming little creatures with sharp ears emerged to greet me. Their whimsical voices carried on the breeze, their words woven with the magic of the forest itself. Oh, the tales they had to share, the stories that danced in their eyes!

In this haven of conversation, I found myself immersed in a symphony of voices. Each creature had a tale to tell, a secret to whisper, and I listened with rapt attention. From tales of ancient legends to playful anecdotes of woodland mischief, the den brimmed with a kaleidoscope of stories waiting to be heard.

I shall forever cherish this moment, this connection with the enchanting inhabitants of the Talking Animal's Den. Who knows what other surprises await me in this magical realm?

Time is of the essence, my dear!
To keep the wheels turning in Solitaria, we must **Advance the Time Token**, represented by the oh-so-fancy **#TS** (that stands for Time Section, in case you were wondering).

In this delightful little tale we've spun, *our Success has cost us **1TS***.
But wait, there's more! You can now add a **New Landmark** to your **Location Sheet**.
Now, with the Action completed and immortalized in your journal and playkit sheets, it's time to journey onward to the next stage of our grand adventure.

In this example, you've learned about **Time** and **adding** new item to **Sheets**.

Bartering

Another important Action to understand in Solitaria is Trading. A dance of give and take, where treasures are exchanged. Trading in Solitaria, is done with the Bartering System and depends on an Item's Worth.

Bartering can be done in Friend's Action, Trading Box, or More.

Here's a step-by-step breakdown of how to embark on a barter:

1. **Seek a Trading Partner**: Find yourself a trading buddy. We're talking about a target person to trade with, and to determine this lucky individual, simply shuffle the deck of Islander Sheets and draw one at random.
2. **Set a Goal**: Before diving into the intricate world of barter, it's time to set your sights on a goal. Choose from three categories: Give Your Word, Make A Promise, or Take an Oath and create a new goal or add it into existing goals.
3. **Unveil the Trade Item**: If you're feeling adventurous, consult the Item Oraclopedia for inspiration, or go ahead and unleash your creativity by generating your very own unique item through the Item Generator. Remember, at least two items are available for trade. Draw a card and follow the instruction in the Item Oraclopedia or Item Generator, and that card shall determine the item that's up for grabs in this trade.
4. **The Bartering Begins**: Armed with your trade item, it's time to unleash your persuasive prowess! To perform the barter, proceed to Fate Draw.

Barter Action:

On a Critical Success: Oh, what a moment of glory! When the stars align, and the trade gods smile upon you, a Critical Success graces your bartering endeavor. With this splendid stroke of luck, you walk away with both items in hand.

On a Plot Twist: Ah, the whims of fate! In the midst of your barter, a Plot Twist emerges, adding a delightful twist to the tale. Fear not, for this twist is not of doom but of fortune! As you receive the item, its worth value grows by +1, sweetening the deal even further.

On a Failure: Alas, not every venture ends in triumph. Sometimes, despite your best efforts, the barter falters, and a Failure befalls you. But do not despair, for such is the nature of trade. Gather your wits and try again another day.

On a Success: Rejoice, for your skill in the art of bartering shines through! With a triumphant Success, the fruits of negotiation are yours to claim. You gain an item, proving your prowess in the trading game.

On a Critical Failure: Alas, a shadow falls upon your path. A Critical Failure befalls you, and in its wake, your item slips from your grasp. Not only that, but you've spent a lot of time on this trade. Advance Time Token with additional 1TS.

Envision your result and write the trade into your journal. Once your trade is completed Advance Time Token by 1TS.

Check for any relevant "Goal" and add +1 to the Goal's Track Box if your trade is succesfull. If not, add -1 to the Goal's Track Box.

Bartering Mechanics

Worth in Bartering

So, here's the deal: The **Worth** value of your traded item holds the key to your success when trading. If your item boasts a higher Worth Value, you're in for some good fortune! It positively impacts your success rate during the all-important Fate Draw.

The flip side. If your traded item carries a lower Worth Value, your fate might not be so kind. It's not all doom and gloom, but it does negatively affect your success rate during the Fate Draw.

Example of Bartering

Journal Entry Example

As I checked my mailbox this morning, a letter from an islander named Lily caught my eye. Little did I know that this letter would open the doors to a thrilling bartering opportunity!

Lily expressed her desire to trade some of her prized possessions for items that caught her fancy. Eager to embark on this adventure, I shuffled through my deck of Islander Sheets and drew Lily's sheet. She would be my trading partner for the day.

Before diving into the trading process, I set a goal for myself, opting to "Give My Word." I wanted to ensure that the trade would be mutually beneficial and bring joy to both Lily and myself.

With my goal in mind, I drew a card, as instructed by the Barter Action, to determine the item up for trade. The card revealed a magnificent ancient artifact—a relic from a forgotten era. Excitement coursed through me as I imagined the possibilities of what I could acquire in return.

Taking a glance at the Item Oraclopedia, I familiarized myself with the artifact's worth value—a whopping +7. It dawned on me that the difference in worth value would significantly impact the fate of this barter.

As Lily presented her array of enticing items, I carefully assessed their worth. We engaged in lively discussions, haggling over various possibilities. Moments of uncertainty and anticipation hung in the air as we weighed the value of each item against the cherished relic.

And then, Fate Draw. With a twist of fate, the outcome of our bartering revealed itself. As luck would have it, I achieved a Critical Success! To my delight, Lily graciously agreed to trade her coveted items for the artifact. It was a win-win situation, and I couldn't contain my excitement.

With the successful completion of the trade, I gained not only the items Lily offered but also kept the artifact as a token of our successful barter. This unexpected turn of events truly brightened my day.

Action Reminder

Actions Outcome

As you embark on various Actions, remember that an Action may cause the Time Token to advance. Within each action's instructions, you will find guidance on how it affects the progression of time.

For instance, a Critical Failure, resulting from an arduous trade, demands an additional Time Token advancement of 1TS. This represents the extra time consumed during the lengthy negotiation process.

Envision Meaning

When envisioning the results of your actions, let your imagination soar. Picture the unfolding events and document them in your journal. By capturing these moments, you immortalize your adventures in the vivid world of Solitaria.

Goal

Every action you undertake serves a purpose, aligning with a specific goal. As you accomplish smaller or grander objectives along your journey, mark your progress by adding the corresponding numbers to your Goal's Track Box.

Similar to an islander's Favor, the Goal's Track Box holds great significance, empowering you to leverage your achievements for strategic advantage.

Yet, there may be occasions when you yearn to undertake a specific action without pursuing a predefined goal. Fear not, for the realm of Solitaria embraces your autonomy and grants you the freedom to engage in actions of your choosing, unhindered by set objectives.

Know your Character

Player Sheet

Imagine a sheet that's all about you, like your own magical autobiography. This is your Player Sheet, and it's where you'll find all the important details about yourself.

Player Sheet

5

3-Section
Clock

· · · · · · · · · · · ·
Spend 1
Power
to Upgrade

4-Section
Clock

· · · · · · · · · · · ·
Requires
Blessing

5-Section
Clock

1

Name: Pronoun: Age:

Gender: Species: DOB: Refer to
Page.47

Dreams :

Passion:

2 Energy Power Ability Cap

♦   ♣   ♥   ♠   **4**

3 Name	Power	Ability

Follow the instructions from Pg.38 to Pg.43 on how to use the various playkit and game sheets.

Player Sheet

①　Player Information

1. **Name**: Your unique moniker that sets you apart from everyone else.
2. **Age**: How many times you've journeyed around the sun.
3. **Pronouns**: The words others use to refer to you (like "he," "she," or "they").
4. **Gender**: How you identify in terms of masculinity, femininity, or non-binary.
5. **Species**: Are you human, elf, gnome, or something entirely fantastical?
6. **Birthday**: In Solitaria, your character's birthdate is represented by a number and suit from a poker card, reflecting the unique influences of the available seasons during Session 0 on their journey.
7. **Dream**: Your deepest aspirations and hopes for the future.
8. **Passion**: The driving force that keeps you going, your personal inspiration.

②　Energy and Power

But wait, there's more! You're blessed with **3 Energy** and **2 Power**. (*Energy is like your stamina, used for performing actions throughout the game like foraging or crafting. Power, on the other hand, is what you need to activate your abilities or anything magical.* **You consume energy and power as you use them.**)

Energy: After a full day of adventuring, you automatically replenish your energy when you go to sleep. As you close your eyes and drift into dreamland, the magical energy within you renews itself.

Power: Unlike energy, power is a bit trickier to replenish. You won't naturally regain power by sleeping or resting. Instead, you can replenish power by performing specific actions, such as engaging in a powerful ritual with the help of Island Spirits or receiving a blessing from the Goddess herself.

③　Ability

In the beginning, your Ability section is empty, but don't worry! As you play, you'll access and learn new abilities. Just remember that the total number of abilities you can learn is limited by your Energy + Power. So, in this case, your Ability Cap is 5. You learn Abilities by requesting them from the Goddess or through Seasonal Events. Every ability typically consume 1 or 2 Power to perform.

④　Attributes ♥♦♠♣

Now, let's distribute your **4 sets of attributes** among the **4 suits**. These suits represent different aspects of your character. You are blessed with **-1, 0, +1, and +2 bonuses** to allocate. Simply write these bonuses in the provided boxes. These bonuses will come into play during the **Fate Draw**, *triggering bonus value when you draw cards.*

For example if you draw a ♥ during a Fate Step and your attribute for ♥ is +2.
You gain a +2 to your Fate Card during Fate Step.

Player Sheet Example

Name: Kohei Takahashi	**Pronoun:** He/Him		**Age:** 27
Gender: Male	**Species:** Human		**DOB:** 6♣-Lantern Season

Dreams : To cultivate harmony between humankind and nature through compassion and understanding. Life's ultimate purpose is to transcend desire and dwell in the beauty of things as they are.

Passion: An unlikely young man, Kohei spent most of his days gazing at clouds in his youth when other children were learning practical skills. Drawn to solitude and poetry, Kohei nourished a secret dream to one day have a small farm where he could live simply with the land.

Energy	Power	Ability Cap
3	2	5

♦	♣	♥	♠
+1	+1	+2	0

Example

Allow me to introduce you to Kohei Takahashi, a 27-year-old male who embodies the essence of simplicity and harmony. Born on the 6♣ Lantern Season, his birth date is uniquely tied to the ever-changing seasons of Solitaria, where each island boasts its own distinct climate.

In Solitaria, your character's dreams and passions play a vital role, inevitably shaping the path towards your objectives. Aligning your goals with your dreams or passion yields a significant advantage during the **Blessed Union** calculation phase, providing a +1 or even a +2 bonus.

For Kohei, his dream is to foster harmony between humankind and nature through compassion and understanding. He believes that life's ultimate purpose transcends desire, allowing one to appreciate the inherent beauty of things as they are. This vision guides his actions and fuels his passion.

Dream and Passion connection to the Blessed Union

To fully embrace the blessings of the Goddess upon completing his goals, Kohei's initial objective must be closely tied to his dreams and passion.

By intertwining his aspirations with his purpose, he unlocks the full potential of the Blessed Union.

For example, his initial goal could be to establish a thriving organic farm where he can cultivate a sustainable relationship with the land, spreading his message of harmony and compassion far and wide.

By pursuing this goal, he aligns his actions with his dreams, paving the way for a profound and fulfilling Blessed Union.

 Ability

Abilities in Solitaria possess unique names, power costs, and distinct effects. To acquire an ability, one must approach the divine presence of the Goddess. Pay her a visit when you've completed your "Why?" Goal and make a request for an Ability. If your Divine Favor aligns with the requirements, you might be granted one.

Examples

Let's explore a few examples of abilities and how they can be utilized within the game:

Stroke of Luck
Power: 2
Ability: With a mere stroke of luck, you can elevate the outcome of a Fate Draw. Move a result up a single tier, transforming a Failure into a Success, or a Success with Plot Twist into a Critical Success. Remember this sequence: Critical Failure > Failure > Success > Plot Twist > Critical Success.

Physical Enhancement
Power: 1
Ability: Engage in physical activities such as adventures, fishing, or field work with enhanced prowess. Gain an additional +1 to your attribute bonus during Fate Draw.

Joker's Blessing
Power: 1
Ability: The Joker's Blessing bestows upon you exceptional fortune. Double your attribute bonus during Fate Draw, amplifying your chances of success.

Angel's Touch
Power: 1
Ability: In times of need, the Angel's Touch grants rejuvenation. Recover 2 Energy, replenishing your vitality and allowing you to continue your endeavors.

Chrono Cross
Power: 1
Ability: Harness the manipulation of time itself through the Chrono Cross ability. Move your Time Token backward by 1 section, enabling you to gain more time.

Obtaining more abilites

Occasionally, you may come across opportunities to increase your Energy or Power, thereby raising your Ability Cap. When such opportunities arise, you gain the chance to acquire more abilities. Simply grab an extra ability sheet and add it to your character sheet, expanding your repertoire of skills and abilities.

Like this Token

At the top of your **Player Sheet**, you'll find **3 Clocks**. These charming clocks help you keep track of the game time. **Grab a token** or any small object that fits in the clock sections.

When you engage in actions that require time to complete, simply **Advance the Time Token by 1 section**. You'll see this action represented as "*Advance Time Token by #TS.*"
(*It's important to note that actions not associated with the Time Token can be taken without advancing it, they don't consume time.*)

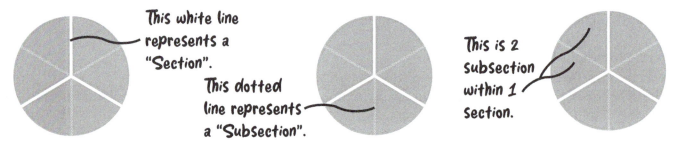

This white line represents a "Section".

This dotted line represents a "Subsection".

This is 2 Subsection within 1 Section.

Each **Time Section** has **2 Subsections**. You can use **1 Energy** to move the token **1 Subsection** instead of a whole **Time Section**. This allows you to stretch your time and perform more actions in a day.

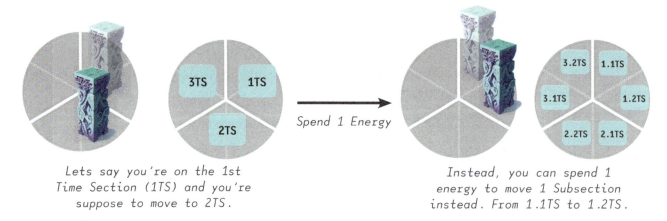

Lets say you're on the 1st Time Section (1TS) and you're suppose to move to 2TS.

Spend 1 Energy

Instead, you can spend 1 energy to move 1 Subsection instead. From 1.1TS to 1.2TS.

When you progress from **1.2TS** to **2.1TS**, there's an interesting twist. If you decide not to use any energy for your next action, you'll leap ahead from **2TS to 3TS**, completely skipping **2.2TS**.
Energy grants you the ability to do more within a given timeframe.

Without spending energy, time progresses as usual with **Time Section (TS)** instead of **Subsection (TSS)**.

Upgrading Clock

If you want to go from a 3-section clock to a 4-section clock, you can **unlock it for a day** with **1 Power**. But keep your eyes peeled for a rare **5-section clock**! It can only be unlocked through a Goddess Action, a special blessing from the Goddess, or in a unique event.

Typically cost 1 Power and last for a single day usage.

You can only upgrade to the 5-section clock through a special event or blessing.

Understanding The Clock

A day in the game is equivalent to **one complete cycle** of the Clock. Think of it this way: **1 Day = 1 Clock Cycle**. During this cycle, you have a total of **3 Time Sections (TS)** to spend.

Each Time Section represents an action or task you can perform. *(It's important to note that not all actions consume time or TS. Some actions can be completed without using up any Time Sections.)*

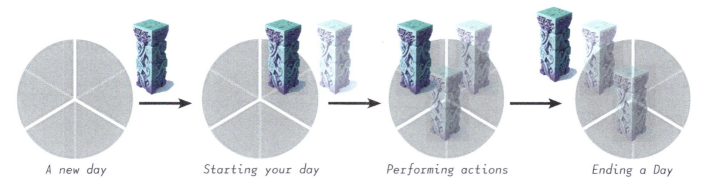

A new day   Starting your day   Performing actions   Ending a Day

Your day begins with your Time Token at **0TS outside of the Clock**. As you start your day and carry out your actions, you will move your Time Token to the **1TS** section on the Clock. Your day continues until your final action takes the Time Token from the **Final 3TS off the Clock**.

This means your Time Token is on the 3TS or 3.2TS section, and you must move the Time Token outside of the clock. That action will mark the end of your day, and you'll be magically compelled to return home and rest because you're too tired to continue.

Premature End

There's another way your day can end prematurely: when your **Energy reaches -1**. If you deplete all your Energy, envision the final action you're performing until completion, and as your energy runs out, you will automatically return home to rest.
(Note: **This applies whether you're on 2TS, 1TS, or any other Time Section.**)

Remember, managing your time and energy wisely is essential for a successful and fulfilling day of adventuring. Plan your actions strategically, considering the time they consume and the energy required.

For Journaling, learn how to use the date system on Pg.47 to keep track of your journal entries.

Passage of Season

What are Seasons?

In Solitaria, the seasons are anything but ordinary!
Forget about the usual spring, summer, fall, and winter.
Solitaria dances to its own rhythm, celebrating unique
seasons based on the island you find yourself in.

Now, you might be wondering, "Why are there more than
4 seasons or even fewer?"
Well, my friend, Solitaria doesn't conform to the rules of
the normal world. It likes to keep us on our toes!

*(So, embrace the unexpected and be prepared for a mix of
different unique seasons in every Island Map).*

Length of Seasons in Solitaria

Each season is determined by the **number of times you shuffle the Main Deck.**
*(A season can be as short as a single deck shuffle, extend to two shuffles, or even surpass three shuffles. As you
play Solitaria, you will be drawing card from the Main deck for prompts and generating information for the
world you're playing in. Once you've exhausted the 52 cards from the Main Deck, the season ends.)*

Shuffle the entire deck and start a new season with this newly shuffled deck of cards.

Here are some examples of seasons in Solitaria:
1. **Season of Floating Islands**: During this season, the landscape is adorned with floating islands
   suspended in the sky. Players can use special tools or abilities to navigate and explore these aerial
   realms, discovering hidden treasures and encountering extraordinary creatures.
2. **Season of Glowing Mushrooms**: The world becomes a mesmerizing forest filled with
   bioluminescent mushrooms. The soft glow illuminates the environment, creating a magical
   ambiance. Players can embark on quests to gather rare mushroom varieties or solve puzzles using the
   mushrooms' unique properties.
3. **Season of Enchanting Star Showers**: The night sky comes alive with dazzling meteor showers and
   shooting stars. This season offers players opportunities to make wishes upon falling stars, participate
   in celestial-themed events, or uncover ancient stargazing secrets.
4. **Season of Whirling Winds**: Powerful gusts of wind sweep through the land, creating swirling
   patterns and lifting objects into the air. Players can harness the wind's energy for activities like flying
   kites, gliding, or even solving wind-based puzzles.
5. **Season of Luminous Fireflies**: Fireflies blanket the world, casting a soft, warm glow. This season
   invites players to catch fireflies, create beautiful light displays, and embark on quests to restore
   balance to the Glow population.
6. **Season of Eternal Night**: Darkness blankets the land, but the world illuminates with glowing plants
   and mystical phenomena. Players can navigate the shadows, seek out nocturnal creatures, and unveil
   the secrets of this enigmatic season.

How does Season affects gameplay?

The seasons of Solitaria, those mischievous shapeshifters that bring a touch of magic to our gameplay!

Seasons are not merely cosmetic changes but impactful elements that shape the gameplay.

Weather: The seasons in Solitaria have a direct influence on the weather. Each season comes with its own weather patterns, which can range from sunny skies to gentle rain or even wild storms.

So, pack your umbrellas, bask in the sunshine, or brace yourself for the occasional downpour. Check the weather with Rize Spirit daily.

Activity: The seasons don't just dictate the weather; they also shape the quests, objectives, and activities you'll encounter. The inhabitants of Solitaria, with their mischievous spirits, design quests and challenges that align with the unique essence of each season.

So, get ready to embark on quests that may involve gathering seasonal ingredients, participating in festive celebrations, or helping the islanders cope with the quirks of the current season.

Keep an eye out for hidden surprises and secret activities that are exclusive to each season! Check special activity happening near you in each Season's Page.

Season-specific Events: Now, here's where the seasons truly shine with their whimsy! Brace yourself for special events that magically unfold during each season.

These events can grant you extraordinary abilities, forge new friendships, ignite rivalries, and even bestow unexpected gifts upon you. Check seasonal events happening near you in each Season's Page.

Resource Availability: The seasons also have a charming influence on the availability of resources in Solitaria. Certain items, creatures, or even access to specific locations may vary depending on the season.

For instance, during the vibrant blossoming season, you might stumble upon rare flowers that hold powerful properties.

In the snowy season, cozy up by the fireplace with hot cocoa and seek out elusive creatures who thrive in the frosty landscapes. Check the Item Oraclepedia.

Islander Interaction: Last but certainly not least, the seasons affect the interactions you have with the islanders. Just like the weather, the islanders' moods and activities are influenced by the seasons.

Engage in lively conversations, share stories, and deepen your connections as you partake in the season-specific events alongside the islanders. Learn their traditions, celebrate together, and witness the bonds grow stronger with each passing season.

Figure out your friend's favourite and least favourite seasons. Some of their favourite gifts might only be available during certain time of the year.

Weather System

Just like in the real world, the weather here is ever-changing and adds a touch of unpredictability to your adventure. Now, here's the twist: you can use the weather to tell your story.

For example, if the weather forecast indicates a stormy day, you might not be able to engage in certain outdoor activities or attend a scheduled Special Event.

But fear not!

If the weather interferes with your plans, consider it a temporary delay. The event or activity will be reschedule.

Importance of Weather Check

First things first, my friend. **As soon as you wake up, make it a habit to check the weather**. Just like you check the time or brush your teeth, this is an essential part of your morning routine in Solitaria. This is your **(0) Pre-day check**, indicated on your trusty **Island Map**.

To check the weather, seek guidance from ***Rize Spirit***. Consult with this enchanting spirit and **draw a card from Main Deck**. It will reveal the weather.

Will it be a sunny day with clear skies? Or perhaps a gentle rain shower to water the plants and bring forth a rainbow? The card holds the secret to the day's weather, and it's always exciting to see what it unveils.

Changing Weathers

But wait! The weather in Solitaria is not always set in stone. As you go about your day, you may stumble upon someone mentioning a change in the weather. When this happens, don't fret!

Simply draw a new prompt from your deck to determine the updated weather conditions. It's like a magical switch that can turn a sunny day into a thunderstorm or vice versa.

So, stay alert and be prepared for unexpected weather shifts that may influence your plans and activities.

Date System

Dates in Solitaria have a unique significance, influencing how days and seasons are recorded.

(Remember, seasons are determined by the number of times you shuffle the Main Deck. This can range from a single shuffle to two shuffles or more. The duration of a season can vary, encompassing both shorter and longer periods.)

Recording a Date

Within a single day, you may find yourself drawing from the Main Deck **multiple times, exceeding the three-card threshold**.

In Solitaria, **one day might be equivalent to more than three cards**. To record the date, follow the format: **Cards Number + Suits + Season.**

For example, let's say you draw four cards in a single day: 3♠, K♦, 7♠, and 2♣ during the Season of Glow.

The recorded date would appear as:

3K72-♠♦♠♣ Glow

On the following day, you draw only three cards: A♥, 2♦, and Q♠.

A2Q-♥♦♠ Glow

Now, let's consider a longer day, where you employ various abilities and expend additional energy to perform more actions.

As a result, you draw seven cards from the Main Deck, obtaining the following: 5♥, J♠, 4♠, K♠, K♣, A♦, and 9♣.

5J4KKA9-♥♠♠♠♣♦♣ Glow

A Season's Length

Once you have **exhausted these cards, consult the Season's Length**, which specifies the number of shuffles required (e.g: 2 or 3 shuffles).

To record a **second or third shuffle season**, include an **asterisk (*) in the date**.
(Note: that the first shuffle of the season does not require an asterisk.)

Initial Shuffle: 3K72-♠♦♠♣ Glow

Second Shuffle: 3K72-♠♦♠♣ Glow*

Third Shuffle: 3K72-♠♦♠♣ Glow**

Date Format

You can choose to write the dates in various formats, such as horizontaly as previously shown, vertical, or even a mix of both, example:

Vertical	Mixed
A2Q ♥♦♠♠ Glow	A2Q ♥♦♠ Glow

You're all set! Head to Pg.76 and play the tutorial as you travel to the Floating Islands.

Event System

In Solitaria, each season brings forth unique events that occur on specific dates. **Events can be found on the Season's page**, along weather, festival, and special event informations.

(When an Event takes place, it presents you with special actions or additional opportunities to engage with the game. You have the freedom to choose whether to participate in these actions or simply proceed with your day, allowing the event to pass by.)

Let's explore an example of how an Event is depicted on the Season of Glow's page. But before we delve into that, let's briefly touch upon the characteristics of the Season of Glow.

Season of Glow

The verdant islands of Solitaria see the coming of an enchanted season marked not by the change of weather or position of the sun, but by the awakening of magical light in the bellies of tiny winged creatures. As the amorous fireflies emerge from their arboreal slumber and take to the balmy night skies in search of mates, their bottoms radiate an otherworldly glow that illuminates the forests and fields below.

The Solitarians eagerly await the first sighting of these living lanterns, for it signifies the start of the Season of Glow, a time of natural wonder, blessings, and merriment. Each island competes to attract the most fireflies, hoping their shores and trees become the most dazzling, as it is believed the insects' presence will bring good fortune in the year to come.

At season's end, islanders gather for an annual celebration of togetherness and cheer on the isle deemed most aglow. There, they sip an age-old concoction of fermented berries and island citrus while watching the last lightshows of the year and toasting the beauty and mystery of their tiny winged visitors.

Events

Here's an example event that might occur during the Season of Glow.

Honey Spread

9♥ / 3♦ / 7♠ / J♦ / A♣

Once a year, the islanders of Solitaria gather to continue an age-old tradition meant to draw the dazzling fireflies to their shores. They assemble a special concoction, a honeyed draught rich with the nectar of flowers found only in their little corner of the world. Under cover of night, each islander ventures out and applies the sweet secret formula to a single tree on their isle.

As the Season of Glow begins and the fireflies emerge, they are irresistibly drawn to the islands saturated in this natural perfume. The little insects illuminate each tree, competing to outshine the stars themselves.

In the example provided, you'll notice the presence of an **event** called "Honey Spread." This event is **accompanied by a series of cards** (9♥ / 3♦ / 7♠ / J♦ / A♣) and a description that provides further details.

While most elements are self-explanatory, the card sequence may require some clarification.
The cards are **separated** by "/," which signifies "**or**." 9♥ or 3♦ or 7♠... and so on.

When you **Draw a card from the Main Deck**, if any of these cards **appear on a given day**, you have the **opportunity** to **activate** the **Honey Spread Event** during the **Season of Glow**. This event grants you the ability to perform an action. For instance, an example of an Event action could be:

Gather Nectar

As you explore the vibrant meadows of Solitaria during the Season of Glow, you stumble upon a swarm of industrious bees buzzing around a field of fragrant flowers. You decide to join in their quest for nectar. *Proceed to Fate Step:*

Critical Success: Your luck knows no bounds as you uncover more than enough honey to satisfy your needs. In a remarkably short amount of time, you amass a substantial quantity of honey, worth a whopping 7 units. Your efficiency allows you to avoid advancing your Time Token for this action.

Plot Twist: You stumble upon a vial of sweet honey, but to your surprise, someone else is already collecting it. The other party, recognizing your presence, proposes a barter. They offer to exchange the honey for something of similar worth. Negotiate with them and decide on a fair trade.

Success: Your determination and careful approach pay off. You successfully gather a vial of sweet, golden honey, which amounts to 5 units in total worth.

Failure: Despite your best efforts, the bees prove elusive, and you struggle to find any traces of honey. Your search ends in disappointment as you return empty-handed.

Critical Failure: Misfortune befalls you as you not only fail to find any honey but also waste a significant amount of time. In the case of a critical failure, *advance your Time Token by an additional 1TS*, acknowledging the extra time wasted during your unfortunate endeavor.

After completing the action, advance your **Time Token by 1TS**.

Lightshow Finale

A♦ & 5♦ / 9♠ & K♣

(req: must complete Honey Spread Event)

On the final night of the season, all islanders head to the winning isle for a grand celebration. They drink deeply of their traditional brew while watching the fireflies dance their last dance. At midnight, The Goddess graces everyone with her presence and grants her divine favor for the year to come.

Within the event description, you may encounter an additional symbol "**&**." In the example provided, the card combination reads as A♦ & 5♦ / 9♠ & K♣. This signifies an "**and**" condition.

If you draw either a set of A♦ and 5♦ or a set of 9♠ and K♣ from the Main Deck, you can activate this event and witness the Lightshow Finale.

However, please note that this event has an **additional requirement** indicated within brackets: (req: must complete Honey Spread Event). This means that regardless of whether you've drawn the required card combination mentioned above, you must first successfully complete the preceding Honey Spread Event in order to progress and partake in the Lightshow Finale.

The Honey Spread Event, as an example, may present completion requirements such as:

Successfully complete each of the actions under the Honey Spread Event, including the gathering, concocting, and spreading of the Thousand Year Old Spread Recipe.

These completion requirements act as milestones, ensuring that you have successfully accomplished specific tasks within the previous event before moving forward to the next.

Event Time Management

Passage of Time during an Event

Events can be triggered and activated at any time during the day. Typically, this poses no issue when events occur earlier in the day, allowing you to engage with them without any hindrances.

However, what happens if an event is activated during the final Time Slot (TS) of the day?
What if you find yourself lacking the necessary energy or power to perform the required actions?

Fear not, for Solitaria has a solution. The time within an event are extended **Overtime**, ensuring that you still have the opportunity to complete them. Although **you perform the actions today**, a**ny additional advancement of the Time Token is carried over to the next day.**

Example

To illustrate, let's say you engage in two more actions at the end of the day, during the 3rd TS. You decide to undergo the **Overtime** under an event, resulting in a Time Token advancement of **3TS**. **Keep this in mind as you end your day** with the Nite Spirit. **Perform your Nite Spirit action as usual** and go to sleep.

The next day, you immediately advance the Time Token by those 3TS.

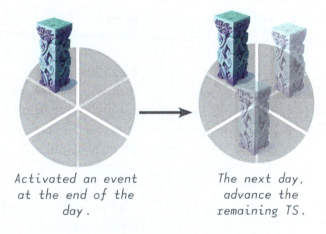

Activated an event
at the end of the
day.

The next day,
advance the
remaining TS.

In this scenario, envision your character feeling exhausted from their efforts the previous day. They may spend the day recuperating, sleeping through most of it, or perhaps only awakening towards the end of the day and mustering the energy to undertake minimal actions before retiring to bed once more.

The concept of time in Solitaria recognizes that events may occur at inconvenient moments, allowing for a realistic and immersive experience. So even if an event spans across multiple days, the flow of the game adapts to accommodate the effects of fatigue and the need for rest, ensuring that your character's actions align with their physical capabilities.

Islander Sheet

Feature of Islander Sheet

Lets talk about the Islander Sheet. This sheet is **used as a card, to be shuffled and drawn.** It's as if the islanders themselves are eager to be discovered through the twists of fate!

Certain actions such as Rize Spirit's "Someone's looking for you" means to perform the **Randomize Islander Ritual (***refer to Other Actions***)**, it utilizes the Islander card shape, making it easy to shuffle and draw randomly.

Who are the islanders?

Now, who exactly are these intriguing islanders, you may ask?

Well, they are the residents of Solitaria, ranging from the Divine Goddess herself to the mystical Island Spirits, the friendly residents, and even the creatures that inhabit this realm such as the livestock or animals.

Each one has their own unique story and role to play in your stay in Solitaria. Just like your own Player's Sheet, the Islander Sheet features several key elements that help you unravel the mysteries of each islander you encounter.

Here's what you will find in an Islander's Sheet:

1. **Name**: The islander's unique name, which gives them their distinct identity.
2. **Age**: The age of the islander, providing a glimpse into their life journey.
3. **Pronouns**: The preferred pronouns the islander wishes to be addressed with, respecting their individuality.
4. **Gender**: The islander's gender, allowing you to understand their personal identity.
5. **Species**: The fascinating species to which the islander belongs, be it human or a fantastical creature.
6. **Birthday**: A special day to celebrate the islander's birth, offering an opportunity for joyful surprises.
7. **Dream**: The islander's dreams and aspirations, giving you a glimpse into their desires and hopes.
8. **Hidden Gift**: A mysterious gift the islander possesses, waiting to be discovered through the unfolding of your journey.
9. **Favor**: A measure of the islander's fondness for you, indicating the depth of your relationship and potential support they may offer.
10. **Attributes**: A set of unique qualities and characteristics that define the islander's personality and abilities.
11. **Notes**: A space to jot down any personal observations, hints, or reminders about the islander as you delve deeper into their story.

Islander Examples

Name: Hikari	**Pronoun:** They/Them		**Age:** 87
Gender: Non-Binary	**Species:** Faerelk	**DOB:** 4♣ Glowing Mushroom	

Dreams : Create a tranquil sanctuary where nature and creatures harmonize.

Passion: Aspire to create a haven that captures the essence of Autumn's serene beauty.

Hidden Gift: **Favor:** +3

Description: Hikari, the enigmatic faerelk, exudes an ethereal grace as they navigate the world, their fur swaying gently in harmony with each step. With a calming presence and wise eyes that mirror a tranquil pond, Hikari interacts with others with a serene demeanor, carrying themselves as a bridge between the mystical and the mundane, inviting all to embrace the beauty of simplicity and find solace within the embrace of nature.

0 ♦	+1 ♣
+1 ♥	+2 ♠

Introducing an Islander

Allow me to introduce you to Hikari, a new Islander friend we have recently encountered in our journey. Hikari, a gentle and enigmatic being, is a Faerelk—a mythical creature gracefully blending the elegance of a deer with the cleverness of a fox.

Let's explore the unique qualities that define Hikari:

Name: Hikari
Age: 87 (equivalent to early adulthood in Hikari's species)
Pronoun: They/them
Gender: Non-binary

A short description of Hikari. She is born on 4♣ Glowing Mushroom, Hikari's spirit is deeply intertwined with the season of Autumn and all its captivating allure. Their dream encompasses the creation of a tranquil sanctuary—a haven where nature and creatures coexist in perfect harmony, offering solace and rejuvenation to weary souls. Inspired by the gentle dance of colorful leaves and the crisp fragrance of the bountiful harvest season, Hikari is driven by an unwavering motivation to bring this vision to life.

While Hikari's hidden gift remains a mystery to us for now, we have had the pleasure of interacting with them and embarking on an adventure through the Forest. Our shared experiences have garnered us three favor points, reflecting the budding friendship between us.

Hikari possesses unique attributes, denoted by symbols that guide our Fate Draws during crucial moments. Their attributes are as follows: 0♦, 1♣, 1♥, and 2♠. These attributes hold significance in determining the outcomes of our actions, much like the Fate Draws we encounter throughout Solitaria.

Islander: Favor

Key component: Favor

The **magical currency** that makes the world go 'round in Solitaria! Think of it as the **heart-shaped gemstone of your relationships with the islanders**. It's a key component in building connections with the islanders.

You see, favor is like a magical currency that flows between you and the islanders. It's all about the little acts of kindness, the heartfelt gestures, and the moments that make your connections shine.

When you do something nice for an islander, it's like sprinkling them with favor points, earning you their trust, admiration, perhaps a little twinkle in their eye.

Giving Favor

Now, let's talk about the two sides of the favor coin. On one side, we have the **Giving of favor**. *Picture yourself bestowing a favor upon an islander, like offering them a precious gift or lending a helping hand in their time of need.*

Each act of generosity adds up, and you get to jot down a +1 in the islander's sheet, marking your selfless deed.

Earning Favor

1. **Spend quality time with the islanders**: Be there for them, listen to their stories, and share unforgettable moments
2. **Bestow heartfelt gifts**: Surprise the islanders with tokens of your affection. Whether it's a shiny trinket, a handcrafted masterpiece, or a quirky knick-knack, the thought and effort behind it matters.
3. **Be a helpful hero**: When they are in need, lend a hand! Help them with their tasks, solve their problems.
4. **Trade treasures**: Discover what each islander finds valuable and engage in trades. By offering something they hold dear, you'll gain their favor.
5. **Cherish small moments**: Sometimes, it's the little things that matter most. Be present during those everyday joys and sorrows, offering comfort and support when needed.

Head to Page. 60

Learn more about earning Favor in Page.60 with Gifts and the importance of the Favor Economy.

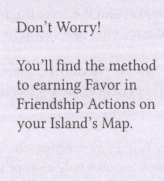

Don't Worry!

You'll find the method to earning Favor in Friendship Actions on your Island's Map.

Goal

Your journey begins with a purpose—a Goal. This foundational game mechanic sets the stage for your adventure, and it all starts during Session 0.

You are not limited to a single Goal throughout your stay in this wondrous realm. You have the freedom to add more goals as you stay longer in Solitaria.

Solitaria offers three distinct types of goals for you to pursue. Let's explore them together:

Give Your Word: (GYW)
By choosing this goal, you bind yourself to a personal commitment. It could be a promise you make to yourself or a vow to assist a particular character or faction within the game. Remember, your word holds weight in Solitaria, and fulfilling your promises may unlock unforeseen opportunities.

Make A Promise: (MAP)
Similar to giving your word, making a promise involves declaring your intent to undertake a specific task or fulfill an obligation. This could be an agreement with an important non-player character (NPC) or a solemn vow to safeguard a treasured artifact. As you immerse yourself in Solitaria, honoring your promises can yield remarkable consequences.

Take an Oath: (TAO)
Taking an oath signifies a profound commitment, often accompanied by a ceremonial ritual or solemn declaration. By swearing an oath, you pledge yourself to a cause, a code of conduct, or the protection of something valuable. Oaths in Solitaria carry great significance, shaping the path of your adventure in extraordinary ways.

Your "Why?"
Additionally, there exists another type of goal, one that is revealed through special events or triggered by specific actions. This category of goal is known as **your "Why" in life**. Upon entering Solitaria, you will establish your first "Why," a fundamental aspect of your character's **dream and passion**.

Throughout your journey, you will maintain at least **two goal sheets: the Misc Goal Sheet** and **Your First "Why?" Goal Sheet**.

(As you progress and uncover new objectives, additional goal sheets will be introduced. Whenever the need arises to create a new goal sheet, carefully follow the instructions provided, ensuring a seamless and engaging experience.)

Why?	*Escape the grind, unwind.*	
Detail:	*It's my chance to escape the pressures, deadlines, and stress of my everyday life and finally give myself the break I truly deserve.*	
GYW	Bellam wants to trade.	1
MAP	Request to explore forest.	2

Goal Sheet Components

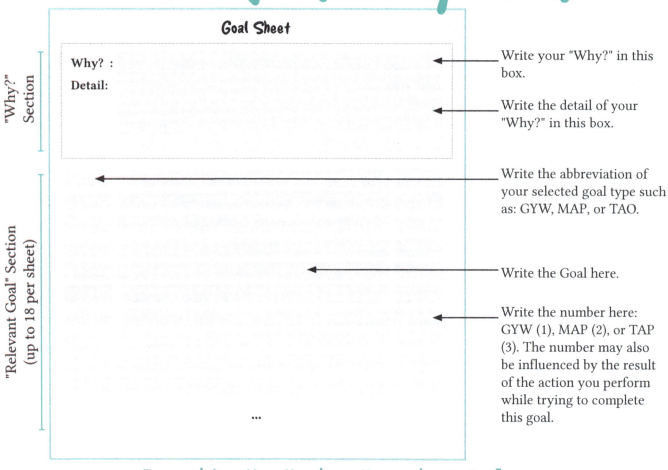

Goal Sheet

Why? : — Write your "Why?" in this box.

Detail: — Write the detail of your "Why?" in this box.

"Why?" Section

"Relevant Goal" Section (up to 18 per sheet)

Write the abbreviation of your selected goal type such as: GYW, MAP, or TAO.

Write the Goal here.

Write the number here: GYW (1), MAP (2), or TAP (3). The number may also be influenced by the result of the action you perform while trying to complete this goal.

...

Everything You Need to Know about Goals

Sections

Each goal sheet consists of two sections: **"Why?" section** and **"Relevant Goals" section**.

Starting with the "Why?" section, it captures the essence of your motivations within Solitaria.

When you first embark on your journey during Session 0, you'll create your first Goal Sheet. In the "Why?" section, express the reasons why you chose to enter Solitaria.

It could be a desire to escape the bustling city life, seek new experiences, immerse yourself in a fantasy world, or embark on a journey of self-discovery.

Pen down your initial "Why?" and **provide details** that elaborate on it.

Now, let's explore the second section of the Goal Sheet, which is the "**Relevant Goals**" section.

- *This section is reserved for goals that align with your chosen "Why?" section.*

Within the "**Relevant Goals**" section, you'll find three empty spaces:

1. The first space is dedicated to writing the **abbreviations** for the **three types of goals**: Give Your Word (GYW), Make a Promise (MAP), and Take an Oath (TAO).
2. In the second space, **jot down the goal itself,** and in the adjacent "**Track**" space, **write a number. (***The number you choose depends on the type of goal you've selected: 1 for GYW, 2 for MAP, and 3 for TAO.***)*

As you progress through the game, the instructions you encounter will guide you on how to fill in the details of your Goal Sheet based on your actions and choices.

Other Goal Sheets: 2nd Sheet

Moving on to the **second Goal Sheet**, we have the "**Misc Goal**" sheet. In the "Why?" section of this sheet, simply write "**Anything goes here**" or something similar.

This section is where miscellaneous goals find their place, those that didn't quite fit into the other parts of your goal sheets.

Blessed Union: Completing a Goal

Once you believe you've **completed a goal** or **filled the Goal Sheet** to the best of your ability, it's time to **Seek** the presence of the Goddess and **Present** her with your Goal Sheet. This action is known as the "**Blessed Union**."

During the "**Blessed Union**," the Goddess invites all the Spirit Island to assemble and **Judge** the **Fulfillment of your goal**. The judge, **Examines** your **Goal's Track**, **Calculates** its overall **Value** and its connection to your **Dream** and **Passion**.

Calcultating Blessed Union

A positive total value indicates a higher likelihood of success, while **negative total value** increases the chance of failure.

There are two possible outcomes from the Blessed Union: **Completion or Incomplete goals.**

If you've **completed the goal**, you'll be presented with a choice. You can either **conclude your journey and return to your life outside Solitaria** or **opt to continue your stay and receive a new Goal Sheet to fill once again**.

In the case of an **Incomplete goals**, you'll also receive a **new Goal Sheet. Fill it with a similar goal to the previous unfinished one, or begin anew.**

Completing a goal triggers a "Blessing."

If the Goal is connected to your Dream and Passion, you get +1 for each connection.

The more positive values you have, the higher the success rate of the Blessing, and vice versa.

A Blessing may **bestow additional** Divine Favor, increase your Favor with another Islander, boost your Energy or Power, and possibly reward you with valuable or perhaps even worthless items.

Inventory Sheet

Your Inventory

This is where you keep **record** of all the treasures and trinkets you gather on your journey. Think of it as your very own pocket, stash, box, or a treasure trove, neatly organized in a delightful table format.

> You can use different names for your inventory sheet, such as stash, recipe, food recipe, backpack, and so on. These sheets can help you keep track of the items you have by filling out the Inventory's Title Section. You can make your inventory sheet as detailed as you want by adding more information about your items.

Inventory Page 1: On Person

Name	Worth	Description
Phoenix Feather Quill	16	Crafted from the radiant plume of a phoenix, this enchanted quill brings words to life on parchment
Crystal Ball	4	Its iridescent glow and energy make it a valuable tool for those seeking guidance and foresight.

Now, let's delve into the details of this sheet.

The Inventory Sheet is **divided** into **columns** that will help you keep a record of your belongings.

Here's what you'll find in each column:

1. **Location**: You can leave this empty or write a location to keep your items.
2. **Name**: This is where you jot down the name of the item you've acquired. Is it a shimmering crystal, a mystical potion, or perhaps a quirky gadget? Give it a name that captures its essence and uniqueness.
3. **Description**: Ah, the description! This is your chance to provide a vivid portrayal of the item. Paint a picture with your words, my dear. Is it glowing with a mesmerizing aura? Does it emit a faint tinkling sound? Let your imagination run wild as you describe its appearance, properties, and any intriguing quirks it may possess.
4. **Worth**: Here, my friend, you'll assign a value to the item with a number. Think of it as its relative importance or rarity. Is it a common item found everywhere, or a rare artifact that is very valuable to someone? Or does it have a high monetary value? Assign a worth to each item to keep track of their significance as it will come in handy during your next Barter Trade.

(Note: Items serve a limited function in terms of game mechanics. Their primary purpose lies in trading, crafting, gifting, and utilizing them to enhance the narrative aspects of the game. While items may not directly impact gameplay mechanics, they play a significant role in shaping interactions and adding depth to your journey.)

Worth System

A quirky way to measure the value of items and establish fair trades. You see, when you engage in trading, it's all about finding items of similar worth or making up the difference with a little extra favor. *It's like saying, "Hey, I'll trade you this enchanted amulet worth 3 for that magical potion worth 2, but you owe me a favor!" And voila, you've got yourself a deal!*

Now, don't confuse **Worth** with **Favor**. While an item's worth determines the trade, it's the Friend's Actions that determine the amount of **favor gained or lost** during the **Fate Draw**. So, it's not just about the difference in worth; it's about the impact of your actions through Fate Draw.

Item's Worth Reference Table

Feel free to refer to this table when determining the worth of the marvelous items you come across in Solitaria. Assigning a worth to each item will help you gauge their rarity, importance, monetary value, quality, and volume.

Worth	Rarity	Importance	Monetary	Volume
1	Common	Low	Minimal	Small
2	Uncommon	Moderate	Affordable	Medium
3	Rare	Significant	Valuable	Large
4	Very Rare	High	Priceless	Huge
5	Extraordinary	Historical	Stupendous	Enormous
6	Fabled	Unparalleled	Immaculate	Storied
7	Exquisite	Monumental	Astronomical	Massive
8	Legendary	Majestic	Inestimable	Gigantic
9	Mythical	Transcendent	Incalculable	Colossal
10	Divine	Supreme	Infinite	Titanic
11	Eternal	Cosmic	Unfathomable	Vast
12	Celestial	Phenomenal	Immeasurable	Immense
13	Enigmatic	Mythic	Priceless	Epic

Examples

Here's an example using the table for a Rare item of moderate importance, valuable, and in small quantities:

Item: Crystal Shard
Worth: 9 (Rare+Moderate+Valuable+Small)
Description: A shimmering fragment of a mystical crystal, said to hold ancient powers. It is highly sought after by collectors and alchemists alike.

Item: Golden Feather
Worth: 8 (Uncommon+Low+Minimal+Huge)
Description: A feather plucked from the wings of a legendary phoenix, radiating a brilliant golden hue.

Item: Starlight Elixir
Worth: 22 (Divine+Exquisite+Infinite+Small)
Description: A vial containing a shimmering liquid that sparkles like the night sky. It is believed to possess the power to heal any ailment.

Item: Songbird's Feather
Worth: 5 (Common+Low+Affordable+Small)
Description: A delicate feather plucked from a vibrant songbird, renowned for its enchanting melodies. Though common and of low importance, it holds sentimental value to those who appreciate the beauty of nature. Its affordability and tiny size make it a charming keepsake or a component in crafting intricate accessories.

Gifts and Favors

Items in Solitaria offer various possible actions, including the options to perform **Favor** and **Gifts**. When it comes to your **inventory**, you don't always have to rely on **bartering**. You can also perform a simple act of giving which can make a significant impact in an Islander's life.

> You may only perform "*Gift*" with a crafted item.

Gifting

By presenting an item to someone who truly needs it, you not only provide them with assistance but also have the potential to **enhance your favor** with them. This, in turn, influences how they perceive you, painting you in a brighter light as your **Favour Points increases**.

It's important to note that every Islander in Solitaria adores receiving gifts. However, their **favorite gifts** remain a **mystery**. To **uncover** an **Islander's favorite gift**, you'll often need to **engage in bartering** or **gift-giving activities. Then** seek the guidance of the **Island's Spirit**.

This is accomplished through **Nite Spirit** or **Island Spirit actions**, which encompasses a range of interactions with the islanders, including "Appreciate", "Discern", "Island Spirit's Wisdom" Actions.
Example:

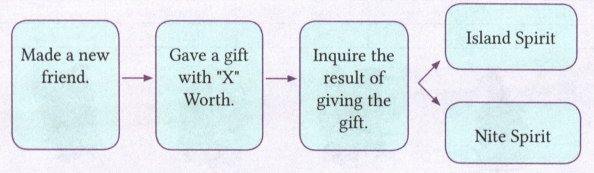

The Island Spirit and Nite Spirit play a crucial role in offering their insights regarding the Islander's response to the gifts you have given. This insightful process is facilitated through the **Fate Step**.

Imagine this scenario: You have presented a gift to your friend, and you're eager to know if they truly appreciate it. Fear not! Leave it to me, the Nite Spirit, who aids in resolving your uncertainties and ensuring peaceful nights. Let's discover the outcome together.

During the Fate Step, add +1 to your Fate Draw for every 10 Worth Value of the item you're giving.

Critical Success: Ah, they absolutely loved it! Their eyes sparkle with delight and gratitude. You've struck a chord with your thoughtful gesture, earning a substantial +2 Favor in their eyes.

Plot Twist: Their reaction seems a bit enigmatic, making it difficult to gauge their true sentiments. However, I caught a glimmer of intrigue in their eyes. Should we take it a step further and discern if this gift is their favorite? If you wish to uncover this mystery, proceed to the "*Discern*" Action.

Success: Excellent! They genuinely liked the gift you presented. Their appreciation is evident, resulting in a +1 Favor. Your efforts have made a positive impact on your relationship with the Islander.

Failure: Unfortunately, the gift didn't resonate with them as much as you had hoped. Their response indicates a lukewarm reception, resulting in a slight dip of -1 Favor. Do not be disheartened, as sometimes personal preferences can vary.

Critical Failure: Oh dear! It appears they were less than thrilled with the gift you offered. Their disappointment is palpable, leading to a substantial drop of -2 Favor. It seems this particular gift missed the mark.

Remember, your day concludes after this action. Take a moment to reset the Time Token, symbolizing the passing of another day. It's also a good opportunity to reflect upon your experiences and emotions. Consider recording your daily events in a journal, capturing your thoughts, hopes for tomorrow, and contemplating the day that lies ahead.

Delightful surprises often await those who draw the lucky card. When fortune smiles upon you and grants you this opportunity, you are bestowed with an additional chance to perform connecting actions that propel the story forward.

One such action is the "*Discern*" action, which allows you to uncover whether the gift you presented to an individual holds enough significance to become their favorite. To discover this, we must once again utilize the Fate Step:

Critical Success: The stars align in your favor, revealing the truth you seek. The recipient of your gift indeed cherishes it as their favorite. Their eyes light up, their smile widens, and you sense a genuine connection forming. The bond between you strengthens, granting you a deepened understanding of one another. When you present a favorite gift, proceed to *Friend's "Appreciate"* action. If successful, you gain +3 Favor when gifting their favorite item.

Plot Twist: Although the recipient's reaction was not an outright declaration of their gift preference, subtle hints and glimpses of excitement suggest that you may be on the right track. The Goddess grant you +1 Divine Favour for your effort.

Success: The mists of uncertainty begin to clear as you discern that the gift you presented holds a special place in the recipient's heart. They express their appreciation and gratitude, indicating that it holds significance to them. When you present a favorite gift, proceed to *Friend's "Appreciate"* action. +2 Favor.

Failure: Alas, the gift you bestowed does not claim the coveted title of their favorite. While they may appreciate the gesture, it does not hold the same level of significance.

Critical Failure: The cards reveal a disappointing truth. The recipient does not consider the gift you offered as their favorite. Their reaction is one of indifference or even disappointment. -1 Favour.

Updating the Islander's Sheet

After successfully discerning an Islander's favorite gift through the "Islander's Secret" action and the subsequent Fate Step, it's time to **update** the Islander's sheet with this newfound knowledge. This update ensures that you have a clear record of their preferred item, allowing you to deepen your connection with them through thoughtful gift-giving:

Hidden Gift: A rare autumn blue flower with 3 petals. (+3)

For instance, if the Islander's favorite gift is a rare autumn blue flower with three petals, you would add the following entry to their sheet: Gift: A rare autumn blue flower with 3 petals. (+3). This notation signifies that gifting this specific item to the Islander will garner a significant +3 Favor, cementing your bond with them and demonstrating your attentiveness to their preferences.

In cases where an Islander's favorite gift results in a +2 Favor, simply include a small bracketed notation: (+2). This indicates that presenting their favorite item yields a respectable increase in favor, strengthening your relationship. For a more general situation where a hidden favorite gift is discovered, use the universal (+2) notation, recognizing the positive impact of gift-giving even without specific knowledge of their preference.

By updating the Islander's sheet with these details, you create a comprehensive reference that aids in planning future interactions. Armed with the knowledge of their favorite gift, you can engage in meaningful exchanges that enhance your favor and foster a sense of closeness with the islanders.

Favourite Gift Restriction

The favor bonus associated with a **Favorite Gift** holds special significance and can only be obtained through successfully completing a Friend's "Appreciate" action.

This deliberate design choice ensures the uniqueness and importance of discovering and presenting someone's favorite gift.

By tying the favor bonus exclusively to this action, the game mechanics prevent any potential abuse or exploitation.

How to get items

There are several ways to acquire more items in the game, allowing you to **expand** your inventory and resources. You can **engage** in **collecting**, **crafting**, **foraging**, or **trading** with other islanders.

Collect

Collecting actions such as fishing and foraging go hand in hand, providing opportunities to acquire items while exploring the forest or embarking on adventures.

Whether it's a leisurely stroll or a thrilling quest, keep an eye out for hidden treasures.

Your Island Map holds various locations to explore, such as the Woods or the Lake. Within these locations, you'll find actions like Forage or Fishing, offering opportunities to obtain items.

While there are **other actions** that can also reward you with items, let's focus on the concept of obtaining an item through exploration, whether it be from the wild or through farming.

The underlying process remains the same. To obtain an item, you select the appropriate action, such as Foraging, and proceed through the sequence outlined for that specific action.

Similar to any other action in Solitaria, once you have decided the necessary actions, you will move on to the Fate Step.

This crucial step determines the outcome of your Foraging action and whether or not you successfully gather anything during your exploration of the wilderness.

Venturing into the forest in search of valuable resources? Take heed, for the woods hold mysterious and potentially frightening beings. Let's proceed to the Fate Step to determine the outcome of your exploration:

Critical Success: Remarkable! You stumble upon something truly extraordinary amidst the dense foliage. (Oracle: Valuble Item from the Woods).
Plot Twist: Curiosity piques, and you find yourself unsure of the nature of your discovery. The enigmatic forces of the Discovery Oracle leave you questioning the true essence and purpose of the newfound object. Further investigation may be required. (Discovery Action)
Success: Your efforts bear fruit as you uncover a common item from the Woods Oracle. Although not rare or extraordinary, this discovery still proves useful. (Oracle: Common Item from the Woods).
Failure: Alas, your search yields no valuable findings. The woods withhold their secrets, leaving you empty-handed.
Critical Failure: Misfortune befalls you, and in an unfortunate turn of events, you lose an item from your inventory. Envision the item that slips through your grasp, leaving you to reflect upon how it slipped away.

To proceed, draw a card from the Main Deck and consult the respective Oracle indicated within the parentheses "()" above to uncover your discovery. Envision your discovery and your adventure in the Woods. Advance your Time Token by 1TS.

Acquiring Items

After completing the action, proceed to **Draw a card** from the **Main Deck**, which will determine the item you've discovered, as indicated by the corresponding **Oracle**:

Valuble Item from the Woods			
A♠	Moonstone Pendant	8	A shimmering pendant adorned with a moonstone, said to possess mystical properties that bring clarity.
2♠	Ancient Rune Tablet	6	A weathered tablet inscribed with ancient runes, holding secrets of forgotten wisdom and arcane knowledge.
3♠	Silvershade Cloak	9	A cloak woven with threads of silver, granting the wearer an enhanced stealth in moonlit environments.
... and more.			

Common Item from the Woods			
A♣	Evergreen Charm	2	A small charm shaped like an evergreen tree, said to bring good fortune and prosperity to its bearer.
2♣	Forestberry Potion	3	A potion crafted from the sweet and tangy forestberries.
3♣	Mossy Trail Map	1	A weathered map revealing hidden paths and shortcuts within the forest, making navigation easier.
... and more.			

Remember: Items play a limited role in terms of game mechanics. Their primary functions revolve around trading, gifting, and adding depth to your narrative experience.

Once you have **drawn the card** and **determined the item**, it's time to let your imagination take flight. **Add the item into your inventory** and **envision** the scene of how you stumbled upon this newfound treasure and bring it to life within your journey.

For instance, you might have come across a Moonstone Pendant (Worth: 8), left behind by the Elves.

Journal Entry Example

You won't believe what happened today. I was wandering through the deep woods, just minding my own business, when something caught my eye. Nestled amidst a bed of vibrant moss, I discovered a Moonstone Pendant, shimmering with an otherworldly glow. Can you believe it? It's one of those rare treasures left behind by the elusive Elves.

The pendant itself is something out of a dream. It's a delicate piece, hanging from a dainty silver chain. The moonstone at its center is mesmerizing, casting an ethereal light that seems to dance with every movement. I could swear I heard whispers of ancient secrets as I held it in my hand.

I can't help but wonder about the stories and legends behind this pendant. What kind of magical properties does it possess? Does it bring clarity and tranquility, as the rumors say? Or perhaps it holds a deeper connection to the moon and its mystical powers. Regardless, it's undeniably valuable, with a Worth of 8. Just imagine the adventures and possibilities this pendant could unlock.

I'll cherish this Moonstone Pendant as a reminder of this extraordinary day in the woods.

Island Estate Sheet

The Island Estate Sheet serves as a **record for all the assets present on your island**. It ensures proper **organization** and **management of your farms, livestock, and other action assets**.

Each type of asset, such as farm crops or livestock. There exist other type of assets in different islands such as beekeeping, bird nests, or fish farms, will have its own dedicated sheet to maintain clarity.

The name of the estate sheet such as Farm, Livestock, Bee, Fish, or others.

Island Estate Sheet

Name: **Produce Worth:**

  Produce:

  Notes :

Fill in the information of the Livestock, Crop, or Species that produce products.

Name: **Produce Worth:**

  Produce:

  Notes :

When you perform actions like planting a crop or obtaining a livestock, you will update the corresponding sheet. For example, when planting a crop, fill in the relevant information such as the crop's name and its type. Cross out the entry once you've harvested the produce from the crop.

Name: Moon Flower Seed   **Produce Worth:** 5

  Produce: Moon Nectar.

  Notes : Planted on 2♣ and 2♦. A delicious sweet nectar known as Moon Nectar.

For livestock, simply note down the type of produce they provide and add it to your inventory. The livestock remains on your island until you decide to trade or release them.

The Island Estate Sheet helps you keep track of your assets, making it easier to manage your resources and plan your actions accordingly. As you venture through Solitaria, the sheet will gradually fill with the fruits of your labor, showcasing the thriving life on your secluded island.

Remember to update the sheet whenever you perform relevant actions or make changes to your estate. *This way, you can maintain a comprehensive overview of your assets and ensure the smooth functioning of your island community.*

Farming and Livestock

Now, the game wouldn't be complete without the fulfilling activities of **farming** and tending to your **animals**. These tasks allow you to cultivate vegetables, nurture your livestock, and even feed the fish in the lake. Let's delve into these actions and their mechanics:

Farming: Engage in the Farming action to gain fresh vegetables. Once you've harvested the vegetables, make sure to jot them down in your Inventory. As you savor the bounty of your harvest, you can remove the entry from your notes, relishing in the satisfaction of reaping what you've sown. Steps for Farming:

1. To begin farming, select a seed to plany and write it in the Island Estate Sheet.
2. Then, Draw cards from your Fate Deck according to the Seed Oraclopedia and write them as the **"Time to Harvest"** in the Island Estate Sheet.
3. Consult the Plant Oraclopedia to determine the number of cards required for your seeds to mature and be ready for harvest. Proceed to Fate Step. If successful, you simply plant the seeds and prepare for the upcoming harvest by drawing a cards for **"Time to Harvest"**.
4. Those seeking to enhance the quality of their produce, utilize the **"Tend the Farm"** action to increase the Worth of your crops before they reach maturity.
5. Once the vegetables have matured, perform the **"Harvest"** action to automatically collect them. Record the harvested produce's information in your Inventory
6. Advance Time Token by 1TS.

Livestock: Tending to your animals offers its own rewards. When you engage in the **"Livestock"** action, not only do you feed and provide sustenance to your livestock, but you also gain an additional advantage:

By providing nourishment, you unlock an extra +1 bonus to your next Fate Draw when engaging in activities such as fishing or harvesting your farm's produce, livestock's milk and meat. Capture these bonuses in your Bonus Sheet, crossing them out as you utilize them to signify their use. Advance TT by 1TS.

When it comes to farming and tending to your livestock in Solitaria, the culmination of your efforts lies in the act of harvesting. This is the moment when you gather the bounties you have nurtured, be it the vegetables grown on your farm or the produce yielded by your beloved animals.

Livestock

Livestock are special creatures on your island that serve as a valuable resource for **producing** milk, meat, and other products. They are **recorded** as a single species in your **Island Estate Sheet,** with each individual holding a specific **Worth** value. There is **no breeding** involved in keeping livestock. They are treated as **abstract items**, which means they **can be traded or bartered**.

Name: Sheep	**Produce Worth:** 3
Produce: Wool and Milk.	
Notes : Received from Monai during the Island's Glow Festival. Great source of Wool and Milk.	

Converting a Livestock to Islander

If you find a particular livestock too adorable to be used solely for its resources and wish to give it a more **prominent role on your island,** you can **transform it into an Islander.**

By **removing** it from the **Island Estate Sheet** and transferring it to an **Islander Sheet,** you can **grant it a distinct personality** and turn it into a **beloved member of your community.**

Once a livestock **becomes an Islander,** it **can no longer be included** in the **Island Estate Sheet**:

Name: Fluffington	**Pronoun:** He/Him	**Age:** 3
Gender: 3 y/o	**Species:** Sheep	**DOB:** Q♣ Season of Glow

Dreams : To roam freely through lush meadows and bring joy to everyone he encounters.

Passion: Spreading warmth and comfort through his luxuriously soft wool.

Hidden Gift: **Favor:** +1

Description: Fluffington is a magnificent enchanted woolly sheep with a dazzling coat of pure white wool that shimmers under the sunlight. His large, expressive eyes hold a spark of curiosity and playfulness. He possesses an air of elegance as he gracefully trots around the island, his wool flowing like a fluffy cloud. Fluffington's presence radiates a calming aura, making him a beloved companion to all who meet him.

0 ♦   +2 ♦

+1 ♥   +1 ♠

Ensure that you update the relevant information when transitioning a livestock into an Islander. Fill in the new entry on the Islander Sheet, providing the livestock's name, species, and any notable details or personality traits. This way, you can keep track of their individuality and contributions to your island's vibrant community.

Remember, your livestock are more than just sources of items and materials—they can become cherished companions and important characters in the narrative of your solo adventure in Solitaria. Embrace the whimsical nature of your island and the unique stories that unfold with each interaction.

Creatures

You will find a collection of creatures that inhabit the world of Solitaria. These creatures are elusive and often hidden from the sight of the islanders, as they are protected by the Goddess herself.

While you cannot interact directly with these creatures, you can **record** your **observations** and **encounters** with them in your **journal**.

The Creature Oraclopedia

The Creature Oraclopedia provides brief descriptions, images, and general details about each creature. While not exhaustive, it serves as a helpful reference to understand the characteristics and nature of the creatures you may come across during your adventures.

2♠	Worth: 10	Stardust Fox
Ethereal glow, ability to create shooting stars		
A mystical creature with shimmering silver fur that glows with a soft, celestial light. It has the unique ability to conjure shooting stars at will, leaving a trail of stardust in its wake. Known to be elusive and enchanting, the Stardust Fox is often associated with wishes and dreams, bringing a touch of magic to the night sky.		

Custom Creatures

In some cases, you may encounter a unique creature that is **not documented** in the **Oraclopedia**. This could be a **new species** that you have discovered or wish to **customize**.
(In such instances, you have the freedom to fill in the details yourself, using your imagination and creativity. Feel free to give it a name, describe its appearance and behavior, and create a unique entry in your journal for this newfound creature.)

If you're looking for inspiration to create a new species, you can use the **Oracle** to **generate ideas**. The Oracle prompts you with various elements and characteristics that you can combine to form a new creature.

A♠	Agile: Quick and nimble in movement.
2♠	Nocturnal: Active during the night.
3♠	Playful: Enjoys engaging in games and activities.
4♠	Sociable: Thrives in group settings and enjoys social interactions.
5♠	Territorial: Defends and marks its territory.
... and more.	

Journal Entry Example

Today, I embarked on an adventure into the depths of the Forest that lies just beyond my backyard. Armed with curiosity and a sense of wonder, my goal was to observe and discover the wonders hidden within its ancient trees.

As I stepped into the Forest, the air was crisp and filled with the sweet fragrance of blooming flowers and earthy moss. The sunlight filtered through the canopy, creating a dappled pattern on the forest floor.

The first creatures I encountered were the common inhabitants of the Forest. Playful squirrels scampered along the branches, their fluffy tails swishing in the air. Colorful birds flitted from tree to tree, their melodious songs filling the air with a symphony of nature's music. Delicate butterflies danced gracefully, their vibrant wings carrying them from one wildflower to another.

As I ventured further into the heart of the Forest, I was filled with anticipation, wondering if I would catch a glimpse of something truly extraordinary. And then, it happened. A creature unlike any I had ever seen emerged from the shadows. It was the rare Stardust Fox, with its silver fur shimmering with ethereal glow. It moved with an elegant grace, leaving a trail of stardust in its wake. I could hardly believe my eyes! In awe, I observed the Stardust Fox as it weaved through the trees, seemingly dancing with the moonlight.

Throughout my adventure, I took meticulous notes and sketched the various creatures I encountered. As the sun began to set, casting a warm golden hue upon the Forest, I reluctantly bid farewell to the magical realm I had explored.

Harvest

Farming

As you plant your seeds and **record** the details in the **Island's Estate Sheet**, you set a "**Time to Harvest**" by **Drawing cards from the Main Deck**. Each card **represent** a day for your seeds to mature.

Once you've **exhausted all the cards** from the **Fate Deck** that **marks** the appointed "**Time to Harvest**", it means **it is time** for you to begin **harvesting** your crops.

Keep a close eye on this **timeline** when **Drawing Cards** from the **Main Deck during other actions**, and be sure to revisit your farm regularly to reap the benefits of your labor. The harvest is automatic, and you'll find the matured vegetables ready for collection.

Remember record the items you've harvested into your inventory.

Livestock

When you decide to perform the Livestock action, you embark on a **direct interaction** with your animals. As you engage in the act of harvesting, you receive **instant rewards** for your care and attention. Whether it's milk, meat, eggs, or other precious resources, the outcome is instantly bestowed upon you. Record in inventory. Below you will see the difference in the Harvesting action:

Harvest: Farm	Harvest: Livestock
Ah, the joys of farming! The humble path to satiating one's hunger.	Ah, the companionship of livestock, a partnership as old as humanity's quest for independence.
Critical Success: A stroke of fortune smiles upon you, enhancing the worth of your produce by +1. Your harvest shines with a touch of extraordinary.	**Critical Success**: A stroke of luck befalls you, enriching the worth of your produce by +1. Your livestock has truly outdone itself.
Plot Twist: Oops! Looks like you planted the wrong seed. Fear not, for randomness brings forth a new seed. Draw a card from the Main Deck and consult the Plant Oraclopedia to discover the produce that sprouts from this unexpected twist of fate.	**Plot Twist**: The livestock has developed a peculiar taste for an unexpected delicacy. Draw a random Food Item card and feed it. +1 Worth to your produce.
Success: Your efforts have paid off! You gather the exact produce that you intended to harvest, savoring the fruits of your labor.	**Success**: Your livestock has been fruitful today! You gather the produce you set out to acquire, relishing in the satisfaction of their contributions.
Failure: Though your plant didn't thrive as expected, you still manage to salvage something from the remnants. You collect a Plant Leftover, a humble addition to your collection with a worth of 1.	**Failure**: Unfortunately, your livestock didn't produce anything on this particular day. Sometimes, even the most industrious creatures need a break.
Critical Failure: Alas, the plant met an untimely demise, leaving you with naught but disappointment.	**Critical Failure**: Oh dear, it seems your livestock has fallen ill. Any produce harvested today must be discarded, as your attention turns to caring for the well-being of your beloved animals. Proceed to the "Livestock Care" action.
Remember to advance the Time Token by 1TS, marking the passage of time dedicated to farming.	Be sure to advance the Time Token by 1TS, acknowledging the passage of time.

Craft

Crafting in Solitaria is the backbone of self-sufficiency in this isolated floating island. When you reside far away from civilization, it's up to you to create the items you need.
Forget about same-day delivery—here, you're the maker of your own destiny.

Crafting encompasses a wide range of skills and activities, **from cooking and blacksmithing to transforming raw materials into useful items**. Surprisingly, even seemingly unrelated tasks like baking a cake or constructing the Death Star reveal a shared underlying **working concept** when you take a closer look.

Crafting

Gather the necessary ingredients and combine them in a harmonious blend. Crafting has its own **unique set of actions**, distinct from other activities, yet following the **same concept of collecting items**. By the **end** of the process, you'll be **rewarded** with **new item** resulting from the **fusion** of various components.

Crafting revolves around the **transformation** of raw materials into a **finished products**. The **Worth** of the crafted item is determined by a simple formula:

Item 1's Worth + Item 2's Worth + Item 3's Worth = The Worth of your crafted item.

Craft Oraclopedia

Solitaria provides an invaluable resource—The Craft Oraclopedia—an extensive reference guide for crafting. It offers a plethora of ideas and recipes for items you can create. Here's an example of a craft you can perform.

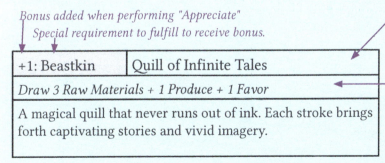

Bonus added when performing "Appreciate"
Special requirement to fulfill to receive bonus.

Name of the Crafted Item

Materials Required: *Draw the number of cards shown and refer to relevant Oracle mentioned. In this case:*

+1: Beastkin	Quill of Infinite Tales
Draw 3 Raw Materials + 1 Produce + 1 Favor	
A magical quill that never runs out of ink. Each stroke brings forth captivating stories and vivid imagery.	

1. *Draw 4 Cards and refer to the Raw Material and Produce Oracle.*
2. *Perform the Islander Randomize Ritual and imagine asking an islander for one Favor to help you with the recipe.*

Use the cards and the Favor to create a dish that matches the Oracle's guidance. Don't be afraid to unleash your creativity and customize your own crafts. Just ensure that your crafting process follows a logical sequence and remains grounded in realism.

Crafting Steps

Now, let's dive into the **Crafting action** itself:

1. **Start by setting a new Goal**—a goal to craft something new. **Consult** the **Craft Oraclopedia** to find the item you wish to create and note down its requirements.
2. Once you have identified the necessary ingredients, **list** them in your **new Goal**.
3. **Gather** all the **required** ingredients and prepare for the Craft Action which involves the **Fate Step**.

Oh! So, you're eager to embark on a crafting endeavor, are you? Well, my friend, you've come to the right place. Welcome to the enchanting Workshop, where the spirits of creativity and ingenuity are ever present. Proceed to Fate Step:

Critical Success: Your craftsmanship shines, resulting in an improved version of the intended product. Its Worth increases by +1, reflecting your exceptional skill and attention to detail.
Plot Twist: In a surprising turn of events, you create a unique variation of the intended product. Refer to the "*Plot Twist*" Table for exciting possibilities and unexpected outcomes. (*If it is a customized product, envision a product variation, maybe a different colour, shape, or function.*)
Success: Congratulations! You successfully craft the desired product exactly as intended, meeting all the requirements and specifications.
Failure: Despite your best efforts, you fail to bring the product to life. Unfortunately, all the ingredients used in the crafting process are lost. Take note of the valuable lesson learned and persevere in your future crafting endeavors.
Critical Failure: Oh no! Your attempt at crafting goes awry, resulting in a significant setback. You not only fail to create the product but also waste valuable time and resources. As a consequence, advance the Time Token by an additional 1TS. Let this be a reminder that even the most skilled crafters can face challenges.

Upon completing the Craft Action, remember to advance the Time Token by 1TS, signifying the passage of time required for your crafting journey.

Envision your progress from the start of the action until its completion, whether successful or unsuccessful. Don't forget to record the newly crafted item in your Inventory Sheet.

Journal Entry Example

With the sun shining brightly overhead, I set my sights on creating something new, something magical. I set out on my Goal to craft a Celestial Amulet, a mystical talisman said to hold the power of the stars themselves.

Consulting the Craft Oraclopedia, I noted down the requirements for this enchanting amulet. Moonstone shards, captured stardust, and a dash of moonlight essence were the key ingredients that would bring this celestial creation to life. With a sense of anticipation, I gathered these precious materials, eager to begin.

As I held the moonstone shards in my hands, I marveled at their ethereal beauty. The captured stardust shimmered and danced, yearning to be part of something extraordinary. And the vial of moonlight essence seemed to emit a soft, enchanting glow, hinting at the magic it contained within.

Now came the moment of truth—I performed the Craft Action, immersing myself in the rhythmic dance of creation. With each careful step, I blended the moonstone shards, sprinkling in the captured stardust, and finally adding a few drops of the precious moonlight essence. As the ingredients intertwined, a sense of wonder filled the air, as if the very essence of the celestial realms was being harnessed in my hands.

To my delight and relief, the Fate Step revealed a Success! My hands had skillfully woven together the moonstone shards, the captured stardust, and the moonlight essence, giving birth to the Celestial Amulet I had envisioned. Its intricate design gleamed with the light of a thousand stars, radiating an otherworldly glow. Filled with a sense of accomplishment, I recorded the details of this wondrous creation in my journal.

Premade Characters

In Solitaria, we understand that sometimes you may want to jump right into the game without spending too much time creating characters from scratch. That's why we provide a collection of **pre-made characters**, also known as **non-player characters (NPCs)**, for your convenience.

These NPCs are **ready-made** and can be easily incorporated into your adventures. However, if you prefer, you can always **create your own unique islander** using the **islander sheet** and **oracles** provided.

To access the pre-made characters, simply **download** them from our **official website** or **game resources**. These characters come with their own backgrounds, personalities, and sometimes even special abilities or items.

They can **serve** as companions, allies, or even adversaries in your journey through Solitaria.

*It's important to note that while these pre-made characters are **fully developed**, these pre-made characters encompass a variety of roles and personalities, including essential in-game characters such as Spirits and the Goddess herself.*

Name: Seraphina, The Goddess of Solitaria   **Pronoun:** She/Her

Gender: Female   **Species:** Divine Being   **Divine Favor:** 0

Description:
+2   +2
+2   +2

A divine presence embodying the essence of nature, magic, and the interconnectedness of all living beings. With radiant emerald eyes and a gentle smile, she watches over the realm, guiding adventurers on their quests and bestowing blessings upon those who seek her wisdom.

While they may not have traditional character stats, they may also bring additional actions and interactions to the game.

Some of these actions may require **Favor**, which represents the islanders' goodwill towards you, or **Divine Favors**.

Whether you choose to utilize the pre-made characters or create your own islanders, the choice is yours. Solitaria offers flexibility and encourages your own creativity and imagination. Feel free to mix and match, customizing your gaming experience to suit your preferences and the story you want to tell.

Oraclopedia

We understand that **creativity** and **inspiration** are vital to your journey. That's why we've created the **Oraclopedia**, a collection of oracles designed to spark your imagination and guide your storytelling.

What is an Oracle?

Solitaria is a game that lets you use an Oracle to enhance your creativity. An Oracle is a simple but powerful tool that helps you generate any element you need for your game. You just need to draw a card from the Main Deck and consult the Oracles to find what you are looking for. When you finish the generation session, put all the cards you used in the Oracles back into the Main Deck. Do not put them in the discard deck. Instead, shuffle them with the Main Deck.

Important Note: Only cards that you draw during an action are discarded. This means that if an action asks you to draw a card and refer to an Oracle, those cards are put in the Fate Deck.

What is in the Oracles?

Whether it's a character name, a story prompt, or an item to discover, the Oraclopedia has it all. If you draw a card for a story prompt, unleash your imagination and craft a captivating story based on the prompt. Let the card inspire your narrative, leading you to surprising and exciting events that will keep you hooked.

For character creation, the Oraclopedia fills the sections in the islander's sheet, providing you with unique traits, backgrounds, and motivations for your characters. Let the oracle inspire you as you bring your islanders to life, weaving their stories into the fabric of Solitaria.

When it comes to **items**, the Oraclopedia is a treasure trove of possibilities. As you discover new items during your adventures, add them to your inventory or create exciting stories around finding those items. You might even encounter other islanders who desire a particular item and are willing to barter with you. Remember to note the Worth of the item, set a goal, and engage in a lively trade.

But the Oraclopedia isn't limited to just names, prompts, and items. It can also **assist** you when you find yourself **stuck or facing a creative block**. When you need fresh ideas or topics of conversation, turn to the Oraclopedia to inspire and unstick your imagination. Let the oracle guide you through moments of uncertainty, providing the nudge you need to continue your journey.

Use Actions Instead

However, if you're uncertain about the next action to take or the direction to tell your story, please seek guidance from the Island Spirit, Rize Spirit, Nite Spirit, or even the powerful Goddess herself.

They can offer insights, blessings, or help you set new goals.

Welcome aboard the magical train that will take you to
a world of cozy adventures and heartwarming stories

If you are ready to play, begin here. If you need to learn the game mechanics, go back to Pg. 4 or Pg.10.

Invitation to Solitaria

The time has come for a remarkable journey to the enchanting realm of Solitaria. As you stand at the precipice of this grand adventure, I invite you to reflect on the life you are leaving behind and the yearning that drives you to embark on this extraordinary quest.

Close your eyes and **transport yourself back to the realm of ordinary days,** **before** the allure of Solitaria captured your imagination.
- What did your life look like?
- How did you spend your days?
- Were you nestled in a bustling city, surrounded by towering buildings and honking cars?
- Or perhaps you resided in a peaceful countryside, where the gentle rustling of leaves and the soft babbling of streams filled the air.

Picture yourself in your familiar surroundings.
- What were your routines and responsibilities?
- Did you wake up early to greet the sunrise, or did you revel in the tranquility of night?
- How did you interact with others—friends, family, colleagues?
- What dreams did you harbor, and what passions stirred within your heart?

Now, my adventurous soul, **consider the yearning that tugs at you,** **drawing you** towards the mystical allure of Solitaria.
- What sparked your desire to leave behind the comfort and familiarity of your previous life?
- Was it a yearning for discovery, a longing for freedom, or an insatiable thirst for adventure?
- Perhaps you sought solace amidst nature's embrace or sought to unravel the secrets of a realm untouched by mundane realities.

Take a moment to pen down these memories and aspirations.
Capture the essence of your former life and the driving force that propels you towards Solitaria. Let your words paint a vivid portrait of your desires, aspirations, and the unique spirit that sets you on this journey.

As we prepare to depart, remember that the allure of Solitaria lies not only in its captivating landscapes and creatures but also in the transformative power it holds for those who dare to venture within. Open your heart and mind to the possibilities that await you, for Solitaria has a way of awakening the dormant magic within each of us.

With your belongings securely packed and your spirit alight with anticipation, let us **step forward** into the unknown. **Safe travels**, my dear. May Solitaria unveil its secrets, guide your steps, and **grant** you the extraordinary experiences you seek. **Embrace** the magic that awaits, and let your spirit soar amidst the enchantment of Solitaria.

Session 0

I hope the journey to reach this station was not too arduous. Whether you trekked through treacherous mountains, sailed across stormy seas, or simply stepped out of your own front door, you have made it to this extraordinary point of departure.

Your method of transportation is assigned in the introduction letter at *Pg.7*.

As you settle into your seats, let me introduce myself. I am your trusty Conductor, here to guide you through Session 0. Before we embark on this journey, let us ensure that you have all the essentials in your possession.

Please check your luggage and ensure that you have the following items:

1. **Journal**: A blank canvas to record your thoughts and experiences.
2. **Pen**: Your trusty companion to fill the pages of your journal with your tales.
3. **Deck of 52 Poker Cards** (*without the Jokers*): A versatile tool that will aid you in your Fate Draws and generating prompts and oracles.
4. **Player Sheet**: Your character sheet, where you will record your abilities, strengths, and growth throughout your journey.
5. **Island Estate Sheet**: A record of your farm, livestock, and other assets.
6. **Islander Sheet**: Your personal sheet to create and develop unique islanders.
7. **Goal Sheet**: A canvas for you to set and track your goals.
8. **Ability Sheet**: A repository of your character's special abilities and skills.

Before we start, take your **Poker Cards**, *Shuffle* it. *Draw* 5 cards and *Discard* these 5 cards to form your **Initial Fate Deck**. *Place* the rest of the 47 Cards in the middle as the **Main Deck**.

Follow the Sequence of Conversation below:

Now that you have all the necessary tools and items, let's delve into the creation of your unique character. Let's begin with the basics. What shall we call you, dear? What *[Name]* resonates with your spirit and will be spoken across the realms? And how shall we address you? Share with us your preferred *[Pronouns]*, so that we may honor and respect your identity.

Ah, *[Age]* is just a number in the realm of Solitaria. But for the sake of our records, how many times have you encircled the sun?

And now, let us determine your *[Gender]*. Are you a fearless warrior, a wise sage, or perhaps a mischievous trickster? Let your true essence guide you as you choose the gender that best represents your spirit.

As you arrived here, did you feel a tinge of magic, a change within your being? Look into the mirror and tell us, what *[Species]* do you see staring back at you? Are you a noble elf, a cunning fox, or a are you still human? Embrace the creature reflected and let it shape your destiny.

Now, let's move on to your *[Date of Birth]*. Remember, time flows differently in Solitaria, and we have our own unique way of recording it. Record your DOB manually. To keep things simple, choose a card from the deck or draw one randomly to determine your birthdate. The number and suit on the card will be your new birthdate, with the suit functioning as a randomizer for the season. If it's a ♦, ♣, ♥, or ♠, it corresponds to the 1st, 2nd, 3rd, or 4th season.

Important Notes: Cards drawn from an action go to the discard deck. This means that cards you draw and use whether for an Action, Plot Twist, an Oracle, or any other reason because of an Action ends in the Fate Deck.

I will pass you a pamphlet in the next page. It provides an overview of the Enigma Aerie, our floating island destination. Refer to the four unique seasons, each with its own charm and wonders, and pick a season for your Date of Birth.

Enigma Aerie

We begin with the **Season of Floating Island**, where the island's magical properties are at their peak. Next, we venture into the **Season of Whirling Winds**, a time of swirling breezes and adventurous spirit. The **Season of Whispering Mists** follows, casting an air of mystery and intrigue. And finally, we conclude the year with the **Season of Glow**, a time of radiant beauty and enchantment.

About Enigma Aerie

Nestled high in the sky, the Enigma Aerie is a breathtaking floating island within Solitaria. Its ethereal beauty is accentuated by a serene lake, its surface shimmering under the warm sunlight. A sacred shrine dedicated to the revered Island Spirit stands as a beacon of spiritual guidance. A grand temple offers adventurers a chance to pay homage to the Goddess, seeking her blessings and divine favor. A cozy cabin provides respite and a place to gather with fellow travelers. And beyond that, a verdant forest beckons with its mysteries, leading to a majestic mountain range that holds thrilling adventures and untold treasures.

Floating Island

Follow the Sequence of Conversation below:

Now, let's delve into your *[Passion]* and *[Dreams]*. What truly ignites your spirit and fills you with purpose? Take a moment to ponder and choose a path that resonates with your character.

Now, let's distribute your *[Attributes]* among the suits. Assign the values of *[0, +1, +1, and +2]* to each of the suits sections for your attributes.

Lastly, fill in the sections for energy, power, and ability cap. Start with the initial numbers of 3, 2, and 5, respectively. These will be your starting points as you embark on your grand adventure.

Follow the Sequence of Conversation below:

I can't believe it's already time for your stop. My how time flies, doesn't it? We've had quite the journey together, you and I. Chugging along, clickety-clack, through all kinds of weather and landscapes. I do hope you've enjoyed the sights out your window. I've always wondered what it might be like, having a whole island to oneself.

Soon, we will drop you off at your designated island. But worry not, dear, for you won't be alone. Someone special will be awaiting your arrival, ready to greet you and guide you through the wonders of your personal floating island.

They will be there to assist you, offer advice, and help you settle into your new home.

Follow the Sequence of Conversation below:

It's your first day on the island, and I'm thrilled to be here to greet you. I'm the Rize Spirit, your personal guide and planner. If you ever need assistance or are looking for something to do, just come find me. I'm known for my top-notch planning skills!

Oh, before we dive into the day, let's check the weather. You can count on me to provide accurate forecasts every day. Why don't you draw a card to determine the weather for today? It'll be a fun way to start your day.

♦	Sunny	♥	Rainy
♣	Cloudy	♠	Foggy

Excellent! Now, let's update your journal with the weather information. It's always handy to keep track of the weather patterns here in Solitaria. You'll find me listed under 0. Rize Spirit in the Island Map.

As a special welcome gift, here's a Sunmelted Choco. It's a delightful treat, sweet enough to make your taste buds dance with joy. Be sure to write it down in your Inventory Sheet so you can keep track of all the wonderful items you collect during your time here.

Sunmelted Choco	Worth: 4	The smooth and velvety texture melts on the tongue, releasing a burst of rich, creamy cocoa flavors.

Wonderful! Remember, it's important to update your sheets whenever you engage in an action or acquire new items. This will help you stay organized and keep a record of your adventures. And speaking of time, let's advance your Time Token by +1TS to signify your journey from the real world to Solitaria.

Oh, and before I forget, the Goddess of Solitaria would love to have a chat with you. I'll send you there with a touch of magic. You can also visit her at any time using the Divine Orb located in the Floating Temple on your Island Map. She's quite a remarkable person to get to know, so make sure to pay her a visit. Have a wonderful day, and I'll see you around!

Follow the Sequence of Conversation below:

Hello. I am Seraphine, the Goddess of Solitaria. It is my divine duty to oversee the realm of Solitaria and guide its inhabitants. I hope the Rize Spirit didn't startle you too much with her energetic presence.

How was your journey to Solitaria? You are among the select few who have chosen to escape the confines of their real life and find solace on their own personal floating island. It takes courage and a deep desire to realign oneself with their inner self. So, I'm curious, what is your "Why"? What passion and dreams have brought you to this mystical realm?

Take a moment to open your Goal Sheet and write down your "Why" in the designated section. This will serve as a reminder of your purpose and motivations during your time here in Solitaria.

Goal Sheet

Why? :

Detail:

Thank you for sharing your aspirations with me. Once you feel that you have completed your goal and are ready for the next step in your journey, feel free to visit me again. I am here to provide guidance and support whenever you seek it. Oh, and don't forget to advance your Time Token by +1TS to mark the passage of time.

Now, it's time for me to send you back to your island. Embrace the wonders that await you and continue your adventure with renewed vigor. May the blessings of Solitaria be with you on your journey.

Follow the Sequence of Conversation below:

Hey!

Nice to meet you! I'm the Chief of Solitaria. Think of me as someone who helps the Islanders get settled into their new floating island. Just like you, but with a few extra responsibilities. Don't worry, I enjoy every bit of it, especially meeting new people like yourself.

Oh, before we continue, how about taking a guess at my name? We have an Islander's Name Generator that can help you come up with a fitting name for me. Give it a try! If you have a name ready for me, give it a shot!

While you're at it, let's generate the rest of my information using the various Oracles. They're fantastic tools to help add depth to our characters. Take a fresh Islander Sheet, carefully cut along the dotted line, and fill in the details of my identity. I'm a male human and identify as he/him.

> **Name:** Chief of Solitaria   **Pronoun:** He/Him
>
> **Gender:** Male   **Species:** Human   **Favor :** 0
>
> **Description:**
>
>   The Chief of Solitaria.

By the way, here's a helpful tip for you. You can keep the Islanders as cards and shuffle them for any random encounters you might have, whether it's finding a mailbox, engaging in a bartering session, or encountering intriguing characters in the enchanting woods.

It's been delightful chatting with you, but it looks like the day is drawing to a close. Oh! Before I forget, remember to advance your Time Token by +1TS to mark the passing of time. See you around friend!
Enjoy your time in Solitaria!

Follow the Sequence of Conversation below:

Welcome back to your cozy room! It's such a pleasure to have a roommate. Don't worry, I'll be out of sight most of the time, but if you ever need me, just give a little call. I'm the Nite Spirit, here to help you unwind and bring your day to a peaceful close.

If you have any questions or want to know more about your encounters with fellow islanders, I'm here to provide insights. You can ask me simple yes or no questions like, "Did I make a good first impression today?" or "What did the train conductor think of me?". I'm here to offer guidance:

Whenever you find yourself in need of inspiration or guidance, I'm here to provide you with moves that can spark your imagination and shed light on the path ahead. This book is brimming with random tables designed to answer your burning questions. So, whenever you're seeking inspiration, simply peruse the oracles and see if any of them can assist you on your journey.

To utilize the oracles effectively, format your query as a yes/no question. Then, proceed to the Fate Step where your answer will be revealed:

Critical Success: Yes and yes! The answer is a resounding affirmative, and it brings about favorable circumstances or exciting possibilities.
Plot Twist: Draw a card and consult relevant oracles to generate new details or intriguing prompts that add twists to the answer.
Success: The answer is a straightforward yes.
Failure: The answer is no.
Critical Failure: The answer is a definitive no, and it further complicates matters. The negative response brings about adverse consequences or unforeseen complications. Draw a card and consult any relevant oracles.

For more detailed and specific questions, the Island Map will come in handy. But remember, the Goddess is a wonderful resource for answering those challenging questions that may require a bit more wisdom. She has a way of shedding light on the deeper mysteries. But for now, let's focus on wrapping up your first day.

Take all the cards you've drawn from the Main Deck and use them to determine today's date. Since we're currently in the Season of Floating Island, be sure to note that in your journal as well.

Now, you can reflect on your day, update your journal, and call it a night. Feel free to peruse the Island Map that I've left on the table. If there's nothing else you need, I bid you a restful night. Good night!

Enigma Airie Island Map on the next page.

Enigma Aerie

Other Actions

Island Map

Welcome to Enigma Aerie, your new floating home in Solitaria.
Familiarize yourself with the island map, imagine the sights, sounds, and scents that surround you.

Important Notes: Cards drawn from an action go to the discard deck. This means that cards you draw and use whether for an Action, Plot Twist, an Oracle, or any other reason because of an Action ends in the Fate Deck.

0	RIZE SPIRIT	Page.88

Discover the weather patterns that will shape your day and seek guidance on your planned activities by engaging with the ever-helpful Rize Spirit:

Check the Weather, Planning the Day

9	Nite SPIRIT	Page.135

Remember, the Nite Spirit is always there to offer guidance and assist you in unwinding at the end of the day with actions like Appreciate and Discernments:

Ask Question, Checklist Ritual

1	HOME	Page.91

Your home is a haven where you can relax, tend to your needs, and engage in various activities. Here are the actions available to you within your humble abode:

**Rest, Check Mailbox, Craft,
Personalize House**

2	HANGOUT	Page.96

A vibrant hub where you can connect with others, engage in meaningful interactions, and partake in various social activities. Here's a glimpse into the exciting actions that await you in this lively space:

**Friendship, Pen Letters,
Social Gatherings**

3	ISLAND SPIRIT	Page.102

A sanctuary where you can commune with the spirits of the island. Here are the enchanting encounters that await you in the presence of the Island Spirits:

**Island Wisdom, Foster Relationship,
Replenishing Energy,
Unearth Curious Findings**

4	Field	Page.108

Cultivate your land, nurture your animals, and reap the rewards of your labor. Here are the tasks that await you in your bountiful farmstead:

Farming, Tend the Farm, Livestock, Harvest

6	Lake	Page.119

An oasis where you can cast your line, ponder life, and enjoy a delightful feast. Here's a glimpse into the activities that await you by the lakeside:

Fishing, Reflections, Picnic.

5	Floating Sanctuary	Page.114

A place where you can seek the presence of the Goddess, immerse yourself in divine energy, and meet the Goddess. Step into the Floating Sanctuary and explore the following actions that await you:

**Power Recovery, Guidance, Ritual,
Nurture Divine Favor, Blessed Union**

8	Adventure	Page.129

A lively tapestry of experiences awaits you on this floating paradise. Here are the activities that will ignite your sense of adventure and curiosity:

**Creature Sighting, Islander Encounter, Rustling
Sounds, Foraging,
Discover New Landmarks**

7	Island Activity	Page.123

A lively tapestry of experiences awaits you on this floating paradise. Here are the activities that will ignite your sense of adventure and curiosity:

Take a Stroll, Investigate, Recreational

Other Actions (Pg.139):
Randomize Islander, Rumors, Goal Actions, and Friendship Favor Event

0: Rize Spirit

Another day dawns upon Enigma Aerie, and it's time to embrace the wonders that await you. I hope you had a restful sleep and feel ready to embark on new adventures today. If not, don't worry, you can stay home and daydream too.

Before we begin our day, there are two things we need to do: **Check the Weather** and, optionally, **Planning the Day**. If you need a refresher on how the game flows, head to *Page 18 and 19 for the Gameplay Instruction*.

Action: Check the Weather

First, let's determine the current season on Enigma Aerie. Take a moment to recall or consult your *Island Map* to confirm the season we find ourselves in.

Season of Floating Island	Season of Whirling Winds	Season of Whispering Mists	Season of Glow

Now, ***Draw a card from the Main Deck***, and consult the ***Weather Oracle***. This will unveil the weather conditions that will shape your day. Will it be a sunny and bright day, or will rainclouds loom overhead? Check both suits and number. *(Remember to record the weather in your journal, as it may influence your day.)*

Note: If you see an *(asterick) on a calendar date/ weather, it means there is a special event that day. Look at the season's festival section to find out if you have celebrated the season yet. If not, you may consider to celebrate it.

Season of Floating Island

♦	Sunny	*Step into a world of warmth and radiance with a sunny day.*

A	2*	3	4*	5*	6	7	8	9*	10	J*	K*	Q
Sunny with fluffy clouds			Golden Sun's Glow*		Dramatic bursts of Solar Flares			Playful Sunshower		Glowing Sunbeams		

♣	Windy	*A breezy day with gusts of wind that playfully tousle your hair.*

A	2*	3	4*	5*	6*	7*	8*	9	10	J*	K	Q
Cloud river flowing between islands			Calm winds around 5 mph			Whistling Wind			Gentle mini tornado		Roaring Gale	

♥	Drizzle	*Light raindrops fall from the sky, creating a gentle mist around you.*

A*	2	3*	4	5	6	7*	8	9*	10	J	K	Q*
It's a sunny day instead.			Rainbows arching between Islands			Gentle rain showers		Glistening mist covering islands				Torrential Downpour

♠	Rain	*Steady rain showers soak the ground, creating a soothing ambiance.*

A*	2	3*	4*	5	6*	7*	8*	9*	10*	J	K*	Q*
Misty Waterfalls			Raindrop Symphony		Roaring Thunderstorm		It's a sunny day instead.			Soothing Rainfall		

Season of Whirling Winds

♦	Cloudy	Overcast skies create a mysterious atmosphere, casting a soft light.

A*	2*	3	4*	5*	6*	7	8	9*	10*	J	K	Q*
Misty Veil			Dancing Stormclouds			Hints of Sunlight		Moody Atmosphere			Gray Blanket	

♣	Windy	Powerful gusts of wind sweep through the floating island.

A*	2	3*	4	5*	6	7*	8*	9*	10	J*	K	Q
Spiraling Cyclones*			Gentle Breezes		It's a cloudy day instead.			Wind Chimes		Roaring Wind		

♥	Gale	Fierce winds howl, making it a challenge to move around.

A	2*	3	4*	5*	6	7*	8*	9	10*	J*	K*	Q*
Powerful Gusts			Thrashing Waves of Clouds			Rolling Clouds			Chilled Air		Spiraling Cyclones	

♠	Sleet	Icy pellets mix with rain, creating a unique blend of precipitation.

A	2*	3*	4	5	6*	7*	8	9*	10*	J*	K*	Q
Icy Pellets			Freezing Rain		Frosty Haze		Crystal Icicles			Giant Snowflakes the size of a palm		

Season of Whispering Mists

♦	Windy	Gentle breezes carry the enchanting whispers of the misty forest.

A*	2	3	4*	5*	6	7*	8*	9	10	J*	K*	Q
Eerie Howling			Swirling Leaves		Gentle breeze carrying whispers*			Whistling Tunes		Loud Cyclone		

♣	Misty	A mystical fog blankets the landscape, adding an air of intrigue.

A	2*	3	4	5*	6*	7	8	9*	10*	J	K	Q*
Dancing Wisps of Fog			Enveloping Fog		Muffled Sounds*			Dancing Shadows in the Mists		Luminous Glow within the Mists		

♥	Rain	The heavens open up, and a steady rainfall drenches the landscape.

A*	2*	3*	4*	5*	6	7*	8	9*	10*	J*	K	Q*
Misty Showers			Cascading Veils and Soft Footsteps			Melodic Rain			Whispering Rainfall*		Luminous Droplets	

♠	Snow	Flurries of delicate snowflakes blanket the landscape

A	2	3*	4	5	6*	7	8*	9	10	J*	K*	Q
Silent White Blanket of Snow			Icy Storm			Soft crackling sounds			Snowstorm		Frosty Trails	

Season of Glow

♦	Clear			Crisp blue skies provide a perfect backdrop for your island adventures.								
A	2	3*	4	5	6*	7*	8	9	10	J	K	Q*
Glittering Dewdrops*			Playful Sunshower		Crystal-Clear Skies			Hints of Sunlight		Sparkling Raindrops		

♣	Drizzle			Light raindrops create a shimmering effect, adding a touch of magic.								
A*	2	3	4*	5*	6	7*	8	9	10	J	K	Q
Glowing Droplet of Water			Glistening mist covering islands		Rainbows arching between Islands			Misty Veil		Gentle rain showers		

♥	Foggy			A thick blanket of fog descends upon the floating island.								
A*	2*	3	4*	5	6*	7*	8	9*	10*	J	K*	Q*
Dancing Lights in the Fog			Thick Mist Blanket		Flickering Lights		It's a clear sunny day instead			Luminous Glow within the Fog		

♠	Storm			Thunder booms and lightning crackles across the sky.								
A	2	3	4	5*	6	7*	8*	9*	10*	J*	K*	Q
Luminous Rain Curtain*			Gusty Winds		It's a cloudy day instead			Radiant Lightning		Icy Storm		

Action: Planning the Day

If you already have a plan in mind for today, feel free to proceed. But if you're seeking guidance, move to the next step: **Draw a Card from the Main Deck**. You may choose to either **Daydream** (*check the suits*) or have a **Productive Day** (*check the number*).

Daydreaming		For a Productive Day	
♦	Create a new Islander and their floating Island.	A	Someone's looking for You: **Look for Someone.**
♣	Craft a new item by brainstorming from scratch.	2	The Spirits are acting strange: **Visit the Spirit**
♥	Envision another Islander's day and journal it.	3	There's light coming from the Orb: **Visit the Temple**
♠	Envision what is happening throughout Solitaria.	4	The Lake looks lively today: **Perform a Lake Action**
		5	A letter has just arrived. **Check Your Mailbox**
		6	Feeling a creative itch? **Express Yourself**
		7	Today is a beautiful day. **Perform a Leisure Activity**
Once you've determined the weather and, if desired, planned your day, you're all set to embark on new day in Solitaria.		8	The outdoor is calling. **Go on an Adventure**
		9	I heard some noises on the Island. **Investigate**
		10	There's a new gossip in town. **Perform Rumor Action**
		J	A "**Random Scenario**" is triggered.
		Q	Care to tend the field? **Perform Field Actions**
Return Home Page.86		K	A "**Seasonal Scenario**" is starting. (*Flip to the Seasonal Scenario Page for the current season to get started.*)

1: Home

Your humble abode is more than just a place to rest your weary feet. It's a canvas for self-expression, a refuge for relaxation, and a hub of creativity. Take a moment to explore the wonderful actions that await you within the cozy confines of your humble home.

Check Mailbox: Anticipation awaits as you open your mailbox to discover letters, messages, and surprises from fellow islanders. Stay connected, exchange heartfelt words, and uncover secrets hidden within each correspondence.

Rest: Take a moment to relax and rejuvenate. Sink into a cozy chair, curl up on the couch, or retreat to your peaceful bedroom for a restful break. Recharge your energy and prepare for the day that lie ahead.

Craft: Unleash your inner artisan and indulge in the joy of creation. Transform raw materials into extraordinary items that hold both practical and aesthetic value. Whether it's crafting exquisite jewelry, fashioning tools, or concocting potions, let your imagination guide your hands.

Personalize House: Unleash your creativity and infuse your living space with your unique style. Decorate, rearrange, and make your home truly reflect your personality and taste.

Action: Check Mailbox

Take a moment to check your mailbox and see if any letters or messages have arrived for you. Here's what can happen when you check your mailbox:

Fate Step.		
Critical Success	As you open the mailbox, you discover a letter specifically addressed to you. It seems like an exciting and important message awaits you.	If there are any letter addressed to you from an Islander, check if it is a reply from any of your past letter. If not , proceed to "**Randomize Islander**" to generate a random Islander.
Plot Twist	Unexpectedly, your mailbox reveals something out of the ordinary. **Check the drawn Fate Card** and **consult the Plot Twist table** to uncover the twist that accompanies the contents of your mailbox.	
Success	Good news! Among the mail, you find a letter addressed to you. It's always nice to receive some mail. **Check the drawn Fate Card's Suit**: ♦♥:It's an Ad Flyer|♣♠:Letter from an Islander	

Plot Twist	
You find ... in your mailbox.	
♦	A creature.
♣	A little note.
♥	An item.
♠	An Ad Flyer

Failure	Your mailbox contains **no letters or surprises**. It seems that this time there's no correspondence waiting for you.
Critical Failure	Oh no! The letter you find in the mailbox appears **damaged and unreadable**. It seems to have endured some mishap during its journey. What do you do?

If you are expecting a reply from a letter you've sent to arrive to day, but you've not received it, check again another day. ***It might've been delayed.***

Envision the emotions that come with checking your mailbox—anticipation, joy, disappointment, or intrigue. Take a moment to immerse yourself in the scenario and visualize the impact of each outcome. feel free to consult any relevant ***Oracle*** for inspiration on any relevant ideas that may come your way.

7. Island Activity

Immerse yourself in the vibrant tapestry of activities that the island has to offer. Let your curiosity guide you as you embark on thrilling adventures and delightful pastimes.

Take a Stroll: Set out on a leisurely walk to explore the island's picturesque landscapes and hidden gems. Discover new sights, sounds, and secrets that await around every corner.

Investigate: Uncover the mysteries and enigmas that lie beneath the surface of the island. Engage in investigative quests, search for clues, and solve puzzles to reveal hidden truths and unlock thrilling discoveries.

Recreational: Indulge in recreational pursuits that bring joy and entertainment to your island life. Engage in various leisurely activities such as games, sports, crafting, or creative endeavors to relax, unwind, and nurture your spirit.

Action: Take A Stroll

Go on a leisurely stroll through the enchanting landscapes of the island, where the wonders of nature unfold before your eyes. Take in the sights, soak in the atmosphere, and let your imagination roam free.

Fate Step.			
Critical Success	Luck smiles upon you, and you stumble upon an unexpected item during your stroll. ***Draw a card from the Fate Deck*** and consult the ***Item Oraclepedia*** to uncover the nature and significance of your find. ♦ ♥:***Common Item*** ♣ ♠:***Rare Item***	**Plot Twist**	
		You find ...	
		♦	A Spirit appears. Perform any Island Spirit Action without Advancing Time Token.
Plot Twist	The island surprises you with a twist. ***Draw a card from the Fate Deck*** and consult the ***Plot Twist Table*** to unveil the discovery.	♣	You stumbled unto a scene: Go to the ***General Scenario Oracle***.
Success	You leisurely explore your surroundings, immersing yourself in the beauty of the island. This pleasant walk leaves you refreshed and uplifted, granting you a ***+1 bonus*** to your next ***Fate Step***. ***Record*** this bonus on your ***Bonus Sheet***, ready to enhance your future endeavors.	♥	A Creature appears before you. Draw another Fate Card: ♦: Tiny ♥: Small ♣: Medium ♠: Big
Failure	Although you enjoy your walk, no remarkable discoveries or encounters unfold before you.		
Critical Failure	Misfortune befalls you as you sustain an injury during your walk. Perform a ***Randomize Islander Action*** and ***visualize*** the arrival of an islander who comes to your aid. However, their assistance comes at a cost, resulting in a loss of ***-1 Favor.***	♠	You found yourself walking before an unfamiliar path and ended up in the wilderness. Perform an Adventure Action.

Envision the scenic surroundings, the gentle breeze, and the captivating sights as you immerse yourself in this rejuvenating experience. ***Advance your Time Token by +1TS*** to mark the passing of time dedicated to your stroll, and savor the memories and reflections it brings.

Action: Investigate (Search)

Step into the role of a skilled tracker as you embark on a thrilling search for a specific item, Islander, creature, or spirits.

Begin by determining the object you're on the hunt for. Write down the specific target you aim to find in your notes. With your target in mind, carefully navigate the island and pay close attention to your surroundings, seeking any signs or clues that may lead you. Use any relevant oracle to guide you.

Fate Step.		
		Encounter Table
Critical Success	Your keen tracking skills prove fruitful, and you successfully locate the object you were searching for. Celebrate the triumph of your hunt. **Draw a Card from the Fate Deck**: ◆ ♥: A critical success is not possible with this result, only a regular success. Refer to **Success** below. ♣ ♠: *Gain +1 when you perform a Fate Draw for Floating Sanctuary: Nurture Divine Favor. Write* this blessing into your **Bonus/ Note Sheet.**	◆ Inclement Weather: a sudden rainstorm drenches the trail.
Plot Twist	As you follow the trail, you stumble upon something entirely different and unexpected. *Draw a card from the Main Deck* and refer to the "*Encounter Table*" to reveal this discovery.	♣ Mischievous Wildlife: Group of animals playfully scatters the tracks.
Success	Your tracking expertise pays off, and you *successfully* locate the object of your search. Rejoice in the your discovery.	♥ Distorted Tracks: You encounter a rocky terrain that distorts the footprints.
Failure	Your search turns out to be *fruitless*, you do not find trace or clue related to your target.	
Critical Failure	A challenging obstacle impedes your tracking progress, leaving you at a loss. *Draw a card from the Fate Deck* and refer to the "*Encounter Table*" to determine this setback.	♠ Fading Clues: The tracks you've been following gradually fade away.

Envision the details of your tracking journey, the terrain you traverse, and the clues that lead you closer to your target. As you immerse yourself in this action, *Advance your Time Token by +1TS to* mark the passage of time dedicated to your tracking adventure.

Action: Investigate (Tracking)

Engage your keen senses to uncover any unusual signs or tracks on the island.

Begin by keenly observing your surroundings to detect any signs of something amiss on the island. What do you see? Look closely for any peculiar tracks or unusual occurrences.

Fate Step.

Critical Success	A stroke of extraordinary luck befalls you, and you discover a strange and mysterious sight that demands your attention. Consult the **Strange Scenario Oracle**.	**Examples:** -Mysterious footprints - Peculiar rock formations arranged in a pattern - Abandoned tools or equipment in an unexpected location - Unsettling whispers or faint voices in the distance
Plot Twist	The island surprises you with an unexpected turn of events. Draw a Card from the Fate Deck.	
Success	Your observations confirm the presence of creature tracks, pointing to a creature. **Draw a Card from the Fate Deck**: ♦: Tiny ♥: Small ♣: Medium ♠: Big	

	Plot Twist
♦	General Scenario
♣	Strange Scenario
♥	Refer to **Success**
♠	A glimpse of Real World Scenario

Failure	Despite your best efforts, your investigation yields no unusual traces or signs.
Critical Failure	Misfortune strikes as you encounter something unexpected and potentially dangerous but you didn't stay to find out. You **spend -1 Energy** to run home as fast as you can. (if you do not have any energy, Discard 3 cards from the Main Deck and skip the next day)

Envision the outcome of your inquiry, whether the Goddess bestows divine favor upon you or if your good intentions didn't meet her criteria at this time. **Advance the Time Token by +1TS** to acknowledge the passage of time, recognizing the significance of your benevolent actions in nurturing divine favor.

Action: Recreational 1

Determine which game you'd like to play and *Shuffle your Fate Deck.*

	Skipping Stone	
1	Skipping Base	*Draw the first card.* The drawn card becomes your skipping base. Now, it's time to put your stone-skipping talents to the test.
2	Gameplay	*Draw more cards from the fate deck*, one at a time. *Compare* each card to your skipping base.
3.1	Sink	If the card is *lower than your skipping base*, your stone *sinks* right away
3.2	Skip!	If the card is *equal to or higher than your skipping base*, your *stone skips* once or more, depending on the difference between the cards. For example, if your skipping base is 5 and you draw a 7, your stone skips 3 times (once for matching the base, and twice for the extra 2 points).
4	Game Over	*Keep drawing cards until your stone sinks* or you *skip 13 times*. If you skip 13 times, you hear a doink sound and you find a fish or an item in the water. *Draw a Card from the Main Deck*: ♦: Common Item ♥: Rare Item ♣♠: Fish

	Screaming Echo	
1	Choose a Word	*Choose a word to shout* to the void. This is the word you will shout outside of your island.
2	Determine the response	Shout the word as loud as you can and wait for a response. *Draw a Card.* You will hear either: *Same Suit or Number*: An echo reflected from your own. *Different Suit and Number*: A word shouted back by someone else.
3.1	If it was an echo	If you hear an echo, the fun doesn't end there! *Draw another card from the Fate Deck*, which represents your "Echo Score." This score indicates how loud and clear your echo was.
3.2	Another voice	If the response is from someone else's shout, not an echo. Restart by choosing another word and start from step (2).
4	Calculate Score	Add the Echo Score to your *total score*. Remember, the goal is to achieve a high score through successful echoes.

Envision the excitement of the Screaming Game, shouting your heart out and Skipping Stone, gracefully gliding over the water's surface.
After the game concludes, *Advance your Time Token by +1TS*.

Action: Recreational 2

Determine which game you'd like to play and **Shuffle your Fate Deck.**

Before beginning the game, ensure that there are **more than 10 cards in the Fate Deck**. You can only play this game if the deck meets this condition.

Thoroughly **shuffle** the Fate Deck.

Hide and Seek with Spirits

1	Draw Spirit Cards	**Draw 4 cards from the Fate Deck.** These cards represent the spirits you must find during the game. Make sure to remember or write down their identities.
2	Draw Cards	Continuously **Draw Card** reveal the cards.
3	As you hunt for the spirits, you have **3 chances** to manipulate the Fate Deck. You can either:	
3.1	Return a Spirit Card to the End of the Deck	By returning a spirit card, you extend the game and **gain a glimpse of the top 2 cards**. Afterward, you choose 1 card to return to the bottom of the deck.
3.2	Draw 2 Cards from the Bottom	This option also extends the game, allowing you to v**iew the bottom 2 cards of the Fate Deck**. You then select 1 card to return to the bottom of the deck.

Game Rules

Your goal is to **locate all the specified spirits** within the deck size limits mentioned in the Game Rules.

If you **successfully find all the spirits** before reaching the designated number of final cards, you emerge **victorious**. However, if the Fate Deck dwindles to only # cards before you find all the spirits, you lose the game.

1. **10 to 24 Cards**: Find all **4 spirits** before you reach the **last 3 cards** in the Fate Deck to win the game.
2. **25 to 34 Cards**: Search for **8 spirits** before the **last 5 cards** in the deck for a victorious outcome.
3. **35 or More Cards**: Seek **12 spirits** and conclude the game before the **final 8 cards** are drawn from the Fate Deck.

Envision the thrill of Hide and Seek with the Spirits, employing your strategic wit to locate the elusive entities. After the game concludes, **Advance your Time Token by +1TS**, reminiscing on the excitement of your spirit-hunting adventure.

**Return Home
Page.86**

8. Adventure

Venturing into the wilderness may seem enticing, but be wary of the perils that lurk after nightfall. The Spirit and Goddess, in their wisdom, will intervene and prompt you to return home for your own safety. The wilderness at night poses significant dangers that are best avoided. Listen to their guidance and seek refuge within the safety of your home until daylight returns.

Action: Wilderness Adventure

If you want to explore the wilderness and have an adventure, you have two options. You can either **do the action below right away**, or **draw a card and let the wilderness surprise you**. This action will randomly pick one of these Actions: Creature Sighting, Islander Encounter, Rustling Sounds, and Discover New Landmarks.

♦ ***Creature Sighting:*** Keep your eyes peeled for extraordinary creatures that might reveal themselves during your journey.

♥ ***Islander Encounter:*** In this vast wilderness, you might stumble upon fellow islanders.

♣ ***Rustling Sounds:*** Listen carefully to the sounds of the wilderness as they might lead you to hidden surprises.

♠ ***Discover New Landmarks:*** Venture into uncharted territories and unearth new landmarks hidden within the wilderness.

Foraging: Embrace your survival instincts and forage for resources to sustain your journey.

Action: Creature Sighting

Keep your eyes peeled for fascinating creatures that inhabit the wilderness.

Fate Step.		
Critical Success	Oh, what a fortunate sight! You spot a rare creature. ***Draw a card from Fate Deck and consult the Rare Creature Oraclepedia.***	
Plot Twist	Nature surprises you with an unexpected twist. ***Draw a card from the Fate Deck*** and consult the ***Plot Twist Table*** to reveal a curious encounter, whether it be an islander, another creature, an item, or a new revelation.	
Success	Your keen observation pays off as you spot a creature of interest. ***Draw a card from Fate Deck*** and consult the ***Common Creature Oraclepedia*** for insights of the creature.	
Failure	Despite your best efforts, no notable creatures cross your path during this adventure.	
Critical Failure	Unfortunately, you encounter a rather strange situation during your creature sighting. ***Draw a Card from the Fate Deck*** and consult the ***Strange Scenario Oracle.***	

Plot Twist	
♦	Islander
♣	Creature
♥	Item
♠	***Quick Scenario:***

-A mischievous creature flits through the trees, leaving a trail of sparkling dust.
-A pack of playful creature dances in a sunlit meadow, their laughter echoing through the air.
-You encounter a friendly islander playing a soothing melody on a handmade flute

Immerse yourself in the wonders of the wilderness as you keep a keen eye out for fascinating creatures. ***Envision*** each encounter and its consequences, embracing the spirit of adventure. After completing the creature sighting, ***Advance your Time Token by +1TS***, reflecting the passage of time during your sightings.

Wrap up your day with the '***Appreciate***' Action, seeking the ***Nite Spirit***'s counsel. Discover the effects of your actions on your friendship and the shifts in your '***Favor***' as the day unfolded.

Action: Islander Encounter

As you explore the wilderness, keep an eye out for fellow islanders.

Fate Step.		

		Plot Twist	
Critical Success	An extraordinary meeting unfolds, enriching your relationship with the islander. Perform the *Randomize Islander Action* to determine whom you encounter. *Add +1 to your Fate Step* when you perform the *Nite Spirit's* "*Appreciate*" action. Add this bonus to your *Bonus Sheet*.	♦	*Quick Scenario:*
		♣ ♥	Islander
		♠	Creature
Plot Twist	The encounter takes an unexpected turn. *Draw a card from the Fate Deck* and consult the *Plot Twist Table* to reveal the twist of fate.	-The encounter takes place near a stunning new landmark neither of you knew existed.	
Success	You engage in a pleasant conversation with a fellow islander, fostering your bond with them. *Perform the Randomize Islander* Action to determine whom you meet.	-The islander mistakes you for someone else, leading to an amusing case of mistaken identity.	
Failure	No islanders cross your path during this venture, leaving you to savor the solitude of the wilderness.	-The islander challenges you to a friendly game or competition.	
Critical Failure	Unfortunately, your encounter leads to a *misunderstanding* with the islander. *Perform the Randomize Islander* Action to determine whom you meet and envision the situation.	-The islander is accompanied by a mysterious animal companion.	

Immerse yourself in the wonders of the wilderness as you search for fellow islanders. *Envision* each encounter and its consequences, fostering connections and deepening relationships. After completing the islander encounter, *Advance your Time Token by 1TS*, reflecting the passage of time during your exploration.

Reflect on your day and seek wisdom from the *Nite Spirit* by performing the '*Appreciate*' Action. Uncover the consequences of your actions on your friendship and the alterations in your '*Favor*' during your daily endeavors.

Action: Rustling Sound

Listen closely to the rustling sounds in the wilderness.

Fate Step.

Critical Success	Your keen ears catch the distinct sound of something extraordinary. ***Draw a card from the Fate Deck*** and consult the ***Quick Scenario*** to unveil the mystery behind the rustling.	**Encounter Table**

Encounter Table	
♦	Common Item
♣	***Quick Scenario:***
♥	Islander
♠	Creature

Plot Twist	Luck is on your side as you stumble upon an item, either: ♦ ♥: Common Item ♣ ♠: Rare Item
Success	You stumbled upon a pleasant surprise. ***Draw a card from the Fate Deck*** and consult the ***Encounter Table***.
Failure	The sighting turns out to be nothing more than a mere gust of wind, leaving you without any significant encounters.
Critical Failure	A sudden attack by a: ♦ ♥: An Islander ♣ ♠: Creature It catches you off guard. To escape, you must spend *-1 Energy*. If you have **no Energy** remaining, **an Islander comes to your rescue**, but it comes at a cost of *-1 Favor*. In the unfortunate event that you have no Favor, ***Discard 3 cards*** from the ***Main Deck***. You wake up the next day injured and unable to engage in further activities, ***skipping*** it.

Quick Scenario side column:

-A playful critter scurries through the bushes, enticing you to follow its mischievous trail.
-Startled by your approach, an Islander emerges, explaining they were simply foraging for herbs for their cooking.
-As you investigate the source, you stumble upon a hidden stash of valuable items left behind by a traveler.
-A playful family of birds frolics in the foliage, creating a rustling sound as they move.

Immerse yourself in the wonders of the wilderness as you listen closely to the mysterious rustling sounds. ***Envision*** each sound and its consequences, heightening your sense of adventure. After exploring the rustling sounds, ***Advance your Time Token by +1TS***, reflecting the passage of time.

At the end of your day's adventures, don't forget to connect with the **Nite Spirit** using the '**Appreciate**' Action. This will shed light on the impact your actions had on your friendship and the fluctuations in your '**Favor**' today.

Action: Discover New Landmark

Venture into uncharted territory to uncover new and intriguing landmarks.

	Fate Step.	
Critical Success	Luck favors you as you stumble upon a big and unmistakable landmark. ***Gain +2 Favor*** with any islander you've met during this adventure session as a gesture of appreciation for your remarkable find.	If you spotted a creature: Draw a random Fate Card and consult the result to determine whether it was a tiny, small, medium, or big creature sighting.
Plot Twist	Surprisingly, the landmark seems to move, revealing itself to be a **Creature** instead. ***Draw a Card from the Fate Deck*** and head to the ***Creature Oraclepedia***.	
Success	You've come across a ***medium-sized landmark***, which still proves valuable. ***Gain +1 Favor*** with any islander you've met during this adventure, acknowledging your resourcefulness.	If it's a large landmark and tiny or small creature, envision the large landmark to be made up for a large amount of these tiny and small creatures.

If you spotted a creature: Draw a random Fate Card and consult the result to determine whether it was a tiny, small, medium, or big creature sighting.

If it's a large landmark and tiny or small creature, envision the large landmark to be made up for a large amount of these tiny and small creatures.

		Size	
Failure	The landmark may be small and seemingly insignificant, but you diligently note it down, hoping it might prove useful in the future.	♦	Tiny
		♣	Small
Critical Failure	The unfortunate twist of fate results in the landmark's collapse due to strong winds. It turns out to be a temporary object, and you can no longer rely on it for guidance.	♥	Medium
		♠	Big

Immerse yourself in the wonders of the wilderness as you venture into uncharted territory. Envision new discovery and its consequences, uncovering remarkable landmarks along your path. After discovering any landmarks, ***Advance your Time Token by +1TS***, reflecting the passage of time during your exploration.

Take a moment before bedtime to seek the ***Nite Spirit***'s guidance through the '***Appreciate***' Action. Discover how your actions have affected your friendship and the changes in your '***Favor***' for the day.

Action: Foraging

Foraging provides an opportunity to collect items from the wilderness. Utilize the **Raw Material Oraclepedia** to determine your findings.

Fate Step.		

Critical Success	Your keen eye and intuition lead you to discover a rare and precious **Raw Material**, enhancing the Raw Material's **Worth by +3**.	Plot Twist	
		♦	Islander
		♣	Creature
Plot Twist	An unexpected twist adds intrigue to your foraging expedition. **Draw a card from the Fate Deck** and consult the **Plot Twist Table** to reveal a curious encounter.	♥	Raw Material
		♠	Quick Scenario:
Success	Your efforts are rewarded as you stumble upon a common, yet useful **Raw Material**. It may not be rare, but it still adds to your inventory.	-You stumble upon a patch of wild berries ready for pickin. -While foraging near a stream, you notice a glimmering object in the water. -You encounter a fallen tree trunk, and upon investigation, you find a hollow space. -While traversing rocky terrain, you spot a vein of precious ores glinting in the sunlight. -In the shade of tall trees, you find bountiful nuts falling to the ground. -You catch sight of a rare and exquisite insect species fluttering by.	
Failure	Despite your search, you only manage to find a regular, everyday item. It may not be particularly remarkable, but it serves its purpose. **Draw a card from the Fate Deck** and consult the **Common Item Oracle.**		
Critical Failure	Unfortunately, your foraging journey ends with **empty hands** as you return without any valuable items. It seems luck was not on your side.		

Immerse yourself in the wonders of the wilderness as you embark on a search for valuable resources. **Envision** each foraging endeavor and its consequences, gathering valuable items for your journey. After completing the foraging expedition, advance your **Time Token by +1TS**, reflecting the passage of time during your wilderness exploration.

Before retiring for the night, make sure to consult the **Nite Spirit** using the '**Appreciate**' Action. This will reveal how your actions have impacted your friendship and influenced your '**Favor**' today.

Return Home Page.86

9. Nite Spirit

The Nite Spirit is a constant presence, ready to provide guidance and support as you wind down at the end of each day. Remember, the Nite Spirit is a valuable resource that can help you navigate your journey and make the most of your time on the island. Take advantage of these actions to connect with the Nite Spirit and enhance your understanding and appreciation of your experiences here in Solitaria.

Ask Questions: Oh, I love a good chat! Feel free to hit me up with the "Appreciate" and "Discern" actions. Whether you wanna express gratitude, seek answers, or just ponder life's mysteries, I'm all ears! Ask away, and I'll sprinkle some sparkly wisdom your way.

Checklist Ritual: Time to do a little reflection dance! Let's go through your day's adventures together. What were the highlights, the hurdles, and the dreams you're chasing? We'll celebrate your wins, identify areas for growth, and set intentions for tomorrow's journey.

So, whenever you need a friendly chat or some mystical checklist action, I'm just a thought away. Embrace the magic of the Nite Spirit, and let's make your island adventure even more enchanting! See you in the twilight glow! ✨🌙

Ask Questions: Appreciate

I, the Nite Spirit, am here to guide you through the process of unraveling the true impact of your actions and nurturing those meaningful relationships. Let's dive into the steps to find out how your thoughtful gestures and interactions with the Islanders have left an impact in their life:

1	Remember the *Islander* you wish to assess. *Recall* the interaction you had.
2	Craft your query in the form of a *Yes/No question*. Use these questions: *"Did they appreciate the gift I gave them?"* or *"Did they enjoy our chat?"*
3	This appreciation check is linked to *actions involving Islanders*, such as *A Helping Hand, Chit-Chat, Barter, Pen Letters, Social Gatherings*, or any other interactions you've had today.
4	Depending on the outcome of your interaction with the Islander, the Nite Spirit grants you *bonus* when you perform the *Aprreciate's Fate Step*.

Critical Success	+3	Plot Twist	+2	Success	+1	Failure	-2	Critical Failure	-3

5	If your question relates to a *gift* you presented, for every *10 Worth* value of the item, *add +1* to your *Appreciate's Fate Step* result.

Fate Step.

Critical Success	Oh, I see a glimmer of magic here! Their eyes sparkle with delight, and gratitude fills the air. They absolutely loved it, my friend! You've struck a chord with your thoughtfulness, earning a substantial *+2 Favor* in their eyes. How delightful!
Plot Twist	Hm, this one is intriguing! Their reaction seems a bit enigmatic, leaving us to wonder about their true sentiments. However, I sense a glimmer of intrigue in their eyes. Shall we take it a step further and discern if this gift holds a special place in their heart? If you wish to uncover this mystery, venture forth to the *"Discern" Action*.
Success	Ah, excellent! Your gift has truly resonated. Their appreciation is evident, resulting in a *+1 Favor*. Your earnest efforts have left an positive impression on your relationship with them.
Failure	Alas, it appears that the gift did not strike the chord you had anticipated. Their response indicates a lukewarm reception, resulting in a slight *dip of -1 Favor*. Individual tastes and preferences can vary. Sometimes, it's the intention that truly matters.
Critical Failure	Oh dear, it seems that the gift missed the mark entirely. Their disappointment is evident, leading to a substantial drop of *-2 Favor*. Take this as a chance to learn and understand, for even the most well-intentioned gestures may not always resonate as intended.

Remember, my friend, that this action marks the conclusion of your day's adventures. As you *reset the Time Token*, take a moment to reflect upon your experiences. Consider capturing your thoughts, hopes for tomorrow, and the lessons learned in a journal, for self-reflection is a path to growth.

Ask Questions: Discernment

In your journey on this mystical island, you have the opportunity to uncover the hidden treasures of a deepening friendship. The "Discern" action is your key to unlocking the mystery of whether the gift you presented holds a special place in an Islander's heart, making it their favorite.

Every gift you make has a "**+number:species type**". This means that you get a **bonus** of +number when you perform this Discernment action for the gift you've given to the Islander.

*For example, if you give a **+2:Aviankin** gift to an Aviankin: Bird Islander, you can **add +2 to your Discernment Action during the Fate Step**.*

Recall the name of the Islander and the *thoughtful gift* you bestowed upon them.

Fate Step.	
Critical Success	The celestial alignment favors you, revealing the cherished secret you seek. The gift you presented is indeed their favorite! Your bond strengthens, and the "Appreciate" action becomes your next destination when gifting their favorite item. A successful presentation rewards you with a generous *+2 Favor*, a testament to the depth of your understanding.
Plot Twist	Hmmm, the recipient's reaction isn't crystal clear, but subtle hints and glimmers of intrigue suggest something intriguing. Could it be that you've struck the right chord? The Goddess grants you *+1 Divine Favor* for your perseverance in deciphering this enigmatic response.
Success	The fog of uncertainty starts to clear, revealing a glimmer of understanding. Your gift holds significance for them, even if it isn't their ultimate favorite. Their appreciation shines through, and a *+1 Favor* is a wonderful acknowledgment of your effort.
Failure	Oh dear, it appears that while they appreciate your gesture, the gift didn't claim the coveted title of their favorite. It happens; personal tastes can differ, and that's perfectly okay.
Critical Failure	Alas, the cards hold a less favorable truth. The gift you offered didn't resonate as their favorite. Their reaction might indicate indifference or even disappointment. Fear not, for learning from such experiences is a valuable part of the journey. A *-1 Favor* reminds us that not every gift can touch the depths of one's heart.

Update the *Islander's sheet* with this newfound knowledge, keeping a clear record of their preferred item. This wisdom will guide you in future encounters, allowing you to strengthen your friendship through thoughtful gift-giving.

Checklist

As the day comes to a close, it's essential to wrap up your adventures and ensure everything is in order for a peaceful night's rest. Let's go through the checklist together:

1	*Journal*	Take a moment to reflect on your day's journey and record your experiences, thoughts, and emotions in your journal.
2	*Islander Interactions*	Reflect on your interactions with the islanders. Have you encountered any moments that call for the "Appreciate" or "Discernment" action?
3	*Season Check*	Stay in sync with the ever-changing seasons of this mystical realm. Verify the current season to guide your journey.
4	*Reset Time Token*	Move the Time Token to mark the end of the current day, symbolizing the passage of time and the start of a new day of exploration.
5	*Update Energy and Power*	Adjust your Energy and Power levels based on the actions you've taken during the day. Remember, each adventure consumes energy, and power may fluctuate depending on your interactions.
6	*Remove Used Bonus/Note*	Clear any Bonus or Note Sheets you used during the day. This ensures a fresh start and helps you stay organized.
7	*Delayed Actions*	Review any pending tasks like letter writing, crafting, farming and harvesting, seasonal events, scenarios, and goals.
8	*Add New Records*	Add new friends encountered during your journey to your records. Add new friends encountered during your journey to your records.
9	*Update Used Items*	If you used any items during your adventures, make sure to update your Inventory Sheet accordingly. This helps keep track of your resources and ensures you're well-prepared for future encounters.
10	*Update Your Goals*	Check your Goal Sheet and mark the progress you've made toward achieving your objectives.
11	*Update Playkits*	**Player Sheet:** Your main character's sheet, keeping track of your vital statistics and abilities. **Island Estate Sheet:** Details about your floating paradise and the resources it offers. **Islander Sheet:** Information about the unique characters you encounter on the island. **Goal Sheet:** Your personal goals and aspirations for the journey. Bonus/Note Sheet: Used for various temporary bonuses or notes. **Inventory Sheet:** A record of the items you possess. **Ability Sheet:** Details of special abilities and skills you acquire during your adventures.

Return Home
Page.86

Other Actions

In addition to the highlighted actions on the Island Map, you have the freedom to engage in various other actions. These actions can be performed at any time or when specific requirements are met.

Randomize Islander: Interact with new or existing islanders to discover exciting surprises, potential friendships, and deepen your connection with the inhabitants of the island.

Rumors: At any moment when you're in the company of an islander, engage in conversations and gather intriguing rumors and information about the island, its mysteries, and its inhabitants.

Pursuing Goals: Chart your course and set personal objectives to guide your adventures. Define your aspirations and keep track of your progress towards achieving them.

Favor Scenario: You've been working hard on your relationship with your favorite Islander, and now you have a chance to show them how much you care. A favor scenario is a special event where you can spend some quality time with them and make them happy.

Randomize Islander

The Randomize Islander action allows you to encounter a random islander and add an element of surprise to your interactions. Follow these simple steps to use this action effectively:

1	**Cut Islander Sheets**	Start by *cutting* all the *Islander Sheets* into *individual card formats*, making each islander easily accessible.
2	**Shuffle or Mix**	When you wish to perform the Randomize Islander action, *shuffle or mix the Islander Sheets* together. This ensures a random selection.
3	**Introduce New Islanders**	As part of the mix, *add an empty Islander Sheet* to create opportunities to meet new islanders and expand your social connections.
4	**Optional Inclusions or Exclusions**	For specific scenarios or scenes, you have the option to *include or exclude certain islanders* from the mix. This way, you can tailor the encounters to suit the narrative.
5	**Direct Interactions**	If you already have an islander in mind for an interaction, you can *bypass* the Randomize Islander action and directly engage with that individual.
6	**Draw and Engage**	Finally, *draw an Islander Sheet* from the top of the pile. Repeat this process as many times as required for your story or scene. The islanders you draw will make an appearance in your adventure, bringing their unique personalities and stories to life.

The Randomize Islander action adds an element of unpredictability to your journey, introducing you to new characters and fostering a dynamic and ever-evolving island community.

Action: Rumors

Rumors are an intriguing addition to your interactions with other islanders and spirits. They can only be *activated* when you are with another *Islander* who shares the rumor with you, often arising during a *friendly Chit-Chat or a talkative Spirit*. To embark on this action, follow these steps:

1	**Target Selection**	You have two options to *start* the Rumors action: *1.* **Perform the Randomize Islander action** to select the person who will share the rumor with you. *2.* Alternatively, **head straight to the Rumor Oracle** to generate an interesting tidbit.
2	**Drawing Cards**	*Draw a card from the Main Deck* to begin the rumor. *Continue drawing cards*, but *stop* immediately if you encounter a *duplicate suit*. This marks the end of the rumors you've heard.
3	**Piece Together the Rumor**	Jot down the information you've gathered in your *journal* and *craft a cohesive story* from the bits and pieces. Immerse yourself in the whispers and secrets hushes.
4	**Sharing the Rumor**	If you decide to *share the rumor* with *another Islander*, proceed to the Fate Step.

Fate Step.	
Critical Success	The *rumor spreads like wildfire*, captivating everyone involved, yet nobody suspects you as the source. It becomes the talk of the town, influencing various interactions.
Plot Twist	Oh no! *Draw a card from the Fate Deck* to determine the twist: ♦ ♥: *Perform Randomize Islander.* Someone involved in the rumor confronts you, you lose *-1 Favor* with that individual. ♣ ♠: The rumor proves to be true, you receive *+1 Bonus* to your n*ext Fate Step* when performing the *Nurturing Divine Favor Action* from The Goddess, who enjoys a bit of gossip.
Success	The *rumor spreads* and becomes a topic of conversation among the islanders.
Failure	Unfortunately, the *rumor fails to gain traction* and doesn't catch on.
Critical Failure	The rumor spreads, but it proof to be *fake* and the consequences have a negative impact on the community and everyone involved. You lose *-1 Favor* from all individuals affected.

Envision the Rumor's effects and consequences as it takes root in the community, and *Advance the time token by +1TS* to mark the passage of time. Let the whispers and tales weave the rich tapestry of your island adventures.

Goal (Why?)

In Solitaria, setting and achieving goals are crucial to your progress and gameplay. Choose a Goal Type: Give your Word (GYW), Make a Promise (MAP), or Take an Oath (TAO).
Goals are divided into *two main sections*:

Overarching "Why" Goals:	Everyday Goals:
Initial Creation: At the beginning of the game, the Goddess will introduce you to the concept of "Why" goals. You must fill in this section on your *Goal Sheet*, *defining your primary objective* or the core purpose driving your actions on the island.	***Setting a Goal Action***: Beyond the overarching "Why," you can also *set everyday goals* through the "*Setting a Goal*" Action. These objectives may involve crafting a superior knife, helping your neighbor with a leaking roof, or any other personal ambitions you wish to pursue.
Completion and New "Why": As you progress through the game, you may complete your overarching goal by performing the "Blessed Union" Action. Once achieved, *create a new sheet* and *develop a fresh "Why" goal* to continue playing.	***Flexibility***: These everyday goals can be *tailored according to your preferences and interests*. They offer opportunities for exploration, creativity, and deeper connections with the islanders and spirits.

Goal Setting & Completion

When you wish to set a goal, you have *three* options: ♦♥:*Give Your Word (GYW)*, ♣:*Make a Promise (MAP), or* ♠:*Take an Oath (TAO)*.

1	Determine the broader category to which your new goal aligns. If none fit, you can park it under the "*Misc Why*" category.
2	*Assign an abbreviation to the chosen goal type (GYW, MAP, or TAO) and provide a **descriptive name** for your goal.*
3	The *score section* will be filled later during the *Goal Completion Fate Step*.
4	*Check* the last Fate Step from the Action *leading up* to the completion of the goal. This will determine the *bonus* you receive *when performing Fate Step*:

Critical Success	+3	Plot Twist	+2	Success	+1	Failure	-2	Critical Failure	-3

Fate Step.

Critical Success	The goal was a resounding success, and you *gain +1* on top of the goal score.	If you completed the goal, add the Goal Score for the type of commitment you've chosen in the Goal Sheet.		
Plot Twist	The completed goal leads to another request or scenario. *Set another goal* and consult relevant oracles to *generate new scenario or request.*			
Success	You've successfully completed the goal you committed to.	**Goal**	**Goal Score**	
Failure	Unfortunately, you were unable to complete the goal as intended.		*Success*	*Failure*
		GYW	1	0
Critical Failure	Not only did you fail to accomplish the goal, but the score also suffers an *additional -1*.	MAP	2	-1
		TAO	3	-2

Let your goals guide you through your island adventure, as they provide purpose and direction to your journey. Embrace the challenges, celebrate the triumphs, and witness the unfolding narrative as you set and complete your aspirations within the floating paradise.

Favor Scenario

Favor Scenarios are special events that allow you to share a heartfelt moment with any Islander of your choice. To access these special events, you need to meet certain requirements depending on the progress you made:

Friendship	Drama	Romance
To perform a Friendship Scneario you need to pay 20 Favor from the intended Islander.	To perform a Drama Scneario you need to pay 25 Favor from the intended Islander.	To perform a Drama Scneario you need to pay 40 Favor and 10 Divine Favor. You also need to complete 1 Goal.
Have at least 10 entries in your Journal that involve the Islander.	Have completed at least 6 Friendship scenarios with the Islander.	Completed at least 4 drama scenarios related the Islander.

Entries can be from Scenario, Interaction, Friendship Action, Journal or Story.

Favor Scenarios are transformative moments where you deepen your bond with an Islander, learning more about them, yourself, and opening your heart. By fulfilling the requirements, you create cherished moments with the Islanders.

However, that's not all. Favor Scenarios are also rewarding mechanically:

Friendship	+1	Drama	+2	Romance	+3

Your favor with an Islander increases faster when you are at a higher Scenario Rank with them. Each rank of Favor Scenario gives you a permanent boost, +# (refer to the bonus above) to all favor gained with them when gifting a gift and other actions which will reward you with a Favor with them.

To start a Favor Scenario, you need to draw a card from the Main Deck and then go to the Oracle Section to choose a Favor Scenario for Friendship, Drama, or Romance.

Building strong connections with Islanders leads to them appreciating your gifts even more and enjoying your company to a greater extent. It's a testament to the power of genuine relationships on the floating islands.

**Return Home
Page.86**

Seasons

Four seasons mark the year in Enigma Aerie

The first is the Season of Floating Island	The second is the Season of Whirling Winds	The third is the Season of Whispering Mist	The fourth is the Season of Glow
When the sky is clear and the air is mild	*When the wind brings clouds of different shapes and tints*	*When the cold and fog envelop the islands in a twist*	*When magical fireflies put on a show*
You can gaze at the islands that soar above	*And seeds and berries and plants from afar*	*You need to dress warmly and listen closely*	*They light up the sky and chase away the mist*
And marvel at their beauty and wonder.	*That enrich the land and expand the repertoire*	*To the whispers and noises that fill the air softly*	*They warm up the air and bring blessings with a twist*
	Of recipes and ingredients you can explore	*What secrets and mysteries do they hide?*	*To the islands they visit before they go*

Season of Floating Island

Unveiling the Skies' Mysteries

The Season of Floating Island is a unique and enchanting time when the skies reveal their hidden island to all islanders, including those residing on the floating islands. It is a magical period that lasts for two decks. This extraordinary season is marked by the clearing of the mystical mist, unveiling the grandeur of the floating islands in all their splendor.

> **Length of Season: 2 Deck**

The Legend
Legend has it that the Season of Floating Island commences when the stars align perfectly, gifting the Goddess with the most potent magic at the dawn of the year. As the celestial bodies dance in harmony, their cosmic energy channels through the floating islands, awakening their hidden allure It is a time when the Goddess bestows her blessings upon the land, infusing it with life, hope, and rejuvenation.

A Gradual Unveiling
At the inception of this enchanting season, a celestial spectacle takes center stage—the unveiling of the Goddess Island. The skies part asunder, revealing a floating paradise where the Goddess herself resides.   With each passing day, the veil of mist lifts further, gradually revealing other hidden floating islands scattered across the heavens. The sight of landscapes, gardens, and creatures amidst the clouds leaves islanders in awe. Every morning brings newfound anticipation as they await the next island to make its appearance.

Season of Floating Island													
♦ Sunny			*Step into a world of warmth and radiance with a sunny day.*										
A	2	3	4	5	6	7	8	9	10	J	K	Q
Sunny with fluffy clouds			Golden Sun's Glow*		Dramatic bursts of Solar Flares			Playful Sunshower		Glowing Sunbeams		
♣ Windy			*A breezy day with gusts of wind that playfully tousle your hair.*										
A	2	3	4	5	6	7	8	9	10	J	K	Q
Cloud river flowing between islands			Calm winds around 5 mph			Whistling Wind			Gentle mini tornado		Roaring Gale	
♥ Drizzle			*Light raindrops fall from the sky, creating a gentle mist around you.*										
A	2	3	4	5	6	7	8	9	10	J	K	Q
It's a sunny day instead.			Rainbows arching between Islands			Gentle rain showers		Glistening mist covering islands				Torrential Downpour
♠ Rain			*Steady rain showers soak the ground, creating a soothing ambiance.*										
A	2	3	4	5	6	7	8	9	10	J	K	Q
Misty Waterfalls			Raindrop Symphony		Roaring Thunderstorm		It's a sunny day instead.			Soothing Rainfall		

////////////////////

Sunny with fluffy clouds: The golden sun graces the skies, painting it with fluffy clouds that drift like cotton candy.

Golden Sun's Glow: The sun exudes a radiant golden glow, casting an enchanting aura over the floating islands.

Dramatic bursts of Solar Flares: Intense solar flares add a touch of drama to the celestial canvas, igniting the heavens with bursts of cosmic energy.

Playful Sunshower: The playful dance of rain and sunshine brings joy to the floating islands, gifting them with brief and refreshing showers.

Glowing Sunbeams: Sunbeams shimmer and illuminate the skies, creating an ethereal spectacle for all to behold.

Cloud River Flowing between Islands: A river of clouds meanders between the islands, lending an otherworldly charm to the floating realm.

Calm winds around 5 mph: Gentle zephyrs caress the floating lands with a calm and soothing touch, adding serenity to the atmosphere.

Whistling Wind: The wind sings a melodious tune as it weaves its way through the sky, enchanting all who hear its soothing melody.

Gentle Mini Tornado: A miniature tornado playfully swirls amidst the clouds, adding a touch of whimsy to the floating islands.

Roaring Gale: The winds intensify into a roaring gale, unleashing their majestic power across the celestial expanse.

It's a Sunny Day Instead: On some days, the sun shines bright with no clouds in sight, illuminating the floating islands with unobstructed brilliance.

Rainbows Arching Between Islands: Vivid rainbows form graceful arches between the islands, showcasing nature's breathtaking artistry.

Gentle Rain Showers: Soft and gentle rain showers descend, blessing the floating lands with nourishing droplets.

Glistening Mist Covering Islands: The islands are veiled in a glistening mist, lending an air of mystique to their enchanting beauty.

Torrential Downpour: The heavens open up, unleashing a torrential downpour that cascades upon the floating islands.

Misty Waterfalls: Misty waterfalls cascade from the sky, adorning the floating lands with their ethereal allure.

Raindrop Symphony: The rhythmic pitter-patter of raindrops creates a harmonious symphony that fills the atmosphere with melody.

Roaring Thunderstorm: Thunderous claps echo through the skies as a mighty thunderstorm rumbles with electrifying power.

Soothing Rainfall: The gentle and soothing rainfall washes away the worries of the world, leaving a sense of calm and tranquility.

Special Feature

Golden Sun Blessing

		Result
The Golden Sun Glow's Blessing is a radiant gift from the heavens, infusing all it touches with warmth, hope, and divine energy. Those fortunate enough to witness this celestial phenomenon receive a divine gift.	♦	Recover +1 Energy
	♣	Recover +1 Power
	♥	Gain +1 Divine Favor
Draw a Card from the Fate Deck when the Weather falls on a *Golden Sun's Glow.*	♠	Trigger a Seasonal Scenario

Divine Island Unveiling

		Blessing
At the **start of the Season**, Draw a Card from the Main Deck. Whenever, you draw this card from the Card this Season will be the day the Goddess's Island is fully revealed. At this day every floating island will receive a blessing.	♦	If you have any plants you are waiting for Harvest can be immediately Harvested today.
	♣	Perform a Livestock Action today and gain +1 Bonus for Success or Critical Success.
	♥	Perform a Tend the Farm today and gain +1 Worth for Success or Critical Success.
Draw a Card from the Main Deck and return it.	♠	+1 Bonus to your Fate Card when performing a Fate Step today.

Festivals

Note: Each season has a Date for its seasonal festivals. You will see four options for each Date. When you draw a card from the Main Deck that matches the Date of the current season, you can choose to celebrate the festival or skip it. If you skip it, you can celebrate it later if you draw the same Date again. But you can only celebrate each festival once per season.

Lantern Festival

As the dawn of a new season approaches, islanders pay homage to the Fireflies that illuminated the previous Season of Glow. They believe that the gentle flapping of their wings dispersed the magical mist that shrouded the floating islands. To honor these benevolent creatures, islanders craft lanterns of various shapes and sizes. At nightfall, they release the lanterns, creating a dazzling spectacle of light.

Date
2♦
4♣
7♣
9♥

1. *Have you crafted your own lantern yet to join in the festivities?*
2. *What shape and color would it be?*
3. *Does watching the lanterns float by bring any special memories to mind?*
4. *What might you discover on this blessed isle this time around? New friendships? New skills? New adventures just waiting to unfold?*

Twilight Bazaar

An enchanting market that materializes right after sunset, set up within the edge of every island. Vendors from each island showcase their extraordinary wares. Islanders can indulge in delectable treats and elixirs, their flavors infused with rare herbs and secret recipes passed down through generations. They can also enjoy various forms of entertainment, such as puppet shows, fortune telling, and fire dancing.

Date
5♦
5♥
6♠
10♠

1. *What flavors and aromas flood your senses from the samples vendors offer you to try?*
2. *What visual details stand out about the puppets and their miniature stage? The act lifts your spirits - how does it make you feel inside?*
3. *What does the fortune teller say about your future when she lays out the pattern of tealeaves/tarot cards?*
4. *What details do you notice about the costumes of the performers?*

Songbird Serenade

A concert held in the Great Canopy Amphitheater in the Goddess's Island, where musicians from all corners of Solitaria come together. The melodies of various instruments resonate through the air, accompanied by the voices of singers. The Songbird Serenade is a celebration to unite and uplift Spirits. Islanders believe that by singing, they can express their gratitude and receive the Spirits protection.

Date
J♦
3♥
7♥
Q♥

1. *What plants and trees grow unusually tall? What sights, smells and sounds of nature fill the air?*
2. *What natural elements make up the open-air structure: wood, leaves, vines? Take in all the details you notice.*
3. *What instrument do they play? As the notes fill the air, how do they make you feel inside? What emotions do they stir up in your heart?*
4. *As they sing, what memories or images come to your mind?*

Starsong Ritual

	Date
A sacred ceremony conducted on the eve of the equinox, when the stars align in perfect harmony. Islanders gather at the Celestial Observatory, an ancient structure perched atop the highest peak of the Goddess Island. Guided by the celestial elders, they engage in mesmerizing chants and dances, invoking the blessings of the stars for harmony and prosperity in the coming year.	2♣
	6♣
	3♠
	9♠

1. As you climb the steps, what details stand out about the architecture?
2. Take in the smells and sounds of the ancient structure.
3. Describe what you see: what are the Islanders wearing, how are they arranged, what expressions do they have on their faces as they gaze at the night sky?
4. What images or memories does the songs it evoke in your mind?

Gossamer Gardens

	Date
Hidden within the heart of the floating islands lies a secret garden that blossoms only during the Season of Floating Island. Delicate and otherworldly flowers, glowing with radiant hues, carpet the landscape. Islanders are invited to wander through this sanctuary, breathing in the scent of the blossoms. The Gossamer Gardens are a celebration of the magic of nature, as well as a reminder of the preciousness of life.	4♦
	9♦
	J♣
	7♠

1. As you enter, describe the landscape that surrounds you.
2. As you lean in to breathe in its scent, how does it make you feel inside? What memories or thoughts does the fragrance evoke?
3. You sit and listen to the sounds of the garden. How does the music of nature in this sanctuary make you feel at peace within yourself?

Feast of Dream

	Date
Island families gather for a sumptuous feast, sharing dishes prepared with ingredients sourced from the floating islands. The aromas of spices and flavors of fruits tantalize the taste buds, creating a feast that not only satiates hunger but also nourishes the soul. The Feast of Dreams is a celebration of the bounty and generosity of the floating islands, as well as a time to bond with loved ones and share stories.	A♠
	4♠
	8♠
	Q♠

1. Describe the array of colors, textures and shapes of the foods. What tantalizing aromas waft up and cause your mouth to water?
2. As you take your first bites of the different dishes, how do the flavors transport you to the islands where these ingredients originate?

Starlight Storytelling

	Date
Gathered around campfires, islanders share mythical tales and legends passed down through generations. These captivating stories transport listeners to realms filled with magical creatures, epic quests, and eternal love, sparking the imaginations of young and old alike. The Starlight Storytelling is a celebration of the wisdom and creativity of islanders, as well as a way to preserve their culture and identity.	K♦
	8♣
	A♥
	K♠

1. Describe what you observe about the storyteller as they begin to weave their magical tale. What details - their gestures, expressions and tone of voice - bring the story to life?
2. Does the tale inspire you or give you hope?

Seasons Scenario

These are just some examples of the stories you can create, the possibilities are endless. Craft your own adventures with these story hooks for the season:

♦♣♥♠	Scenarios
A	You witness a rare phenomenon where the floating islands align perfectly, creating a bridge between them.
2	You befriend a lonely ghost who haunts one of the floating islands, and help them find peace and closure.
3	You enter a contest to design and decorate your own floating island, and compete with other contestants for the best prize.
4	You stumble upon a hidden garden on one of the floating islands, where you find a variety of exotic plants and animals.
5	You learn that one of the floating islands is actually a giant airship.
6	You find out that one of your neighbors has a secret hobby of collecting floating island memorabilia, and they invite you to see their collection.
7	You volunteer to help out at an animal shelter on one of the floating islands, where you bond with the adorable creature.
8	You get lost on one of the floating islands, and have to find your way back home with the help of some friendly locals.
9	You spot a shooting star falling from the sky, and make a wish that comes true in an unexpected way.
10	You find a hidden cave on one of the floating islands, where you discover a mysterious painting.
J	A mysterious floating island appears in the sky next to yours, and you receive an invitation to visit it from an unknown sender.
Q	A musician visits your floating island, and offers to teach you how to play an instrument.
K	A floating island passes by your window, and you see someone waving at you from it.

Last day of the Season

The final days of the Season of Floating Island were serene and beautiful. The floating islands soared in the azure sky, bathed in the warm sunlight. The people cherished the calm and harmony, admiring the endless horizon and the glittering stars. But then, a subtle shift occurred. T

he wind began to stir the mist, obscuring the sky with a gauzy curtain. The people sensed a drop in the temperature, and looked up. They beheld groups of weird looking clouds looming in the distance. The wind increased its force, bringing a gentle breeze that whisked away the dead leaves from the floating islands.

Return Home Page.86

Season of Whirling Winds
A Lively Ballet of Gusts

This season brings a dance of winds that swirls and shapes the islands, creating new landscapes and patterns. The winds also carry seeds, spores, and fragments of other islands, enriching the biodiversity and resources of each island. The Season of Whirling Winds is a source of inspiration and creativity for the islanders, who celebrate it with festivals, rituals, and art.

> **Length of Season: 2 Deck**

The Legend

It is said that the winds are guided by a mystical being called the Wind Dancer, who whirls and leaps across the skies, directing the winds in an elaborate dance. Some claim to have glimpsed this elusive spirit, describing a lithe figure in flowing robes that glows with an unearthly aura. The Wind Dancer is revered for bringing the change of seasons, but also feared for their capricious nature.

Changing Island Geography

The winds often drastically alter the geography of the floating islands, depositing new materials, carving cliffs and caves, splitting or merging landmasses. The islanders have learned to embrace this transformation, adapting to the ever-changing nature of their world. Sudden mountains and new lakes bring wonder and opportunity.

Weather

Season of Whirling Winds

♦	Cloudy	Overcast skies create a mysterious atmosphere, casting a soft light.

A*	2*	3	4*	5*	6*	7	8	9*	10*	J	K	Q*
Misty Veil			Dancing Stormclouds			Hints of Sunlight			Moody Atmosphere		Gray Blanket	

♣	Windy	Powerful gusts of wind sweep through the floating island.

A*	2	3*	4	5*	6	7*	8*	9*	10	J*	K	Q
Spiraling Cyclones*			Gentle Breezes		It's a cloudy day instead.		Wind Chimes			Roaring Wind		

♥	Gale	Fierce winds howl, making it a challenge to move around.

A	2*	3	4*	5*	6	7*	8*	9	10*	J*	K*	Q*
Powerful Gusts			Thrashing Waves of Clouds			Rolling Clouds			Chilled Air		Spiraling Cyclones	

♠	Sleet	Icy pellets mix with rain, creating a unique blend of precipitation.

A	2*	3*	4	5	6*	7*	8	9*	10*	J*	K*	Q
Icy Pellets			Freezing Rain		Frosty Haze		Crystal Icicles			Giant Snowflakes the size of a palm		

Misty Veil: A thin layer of fog that covers the islands, creating a mysterious and dreamy atmosphere.

Rolling Clouds: Large masses of clouds that move across the sky, changing shapes and colors as they go.

Hints of Sunlight: Small rays of sunlight that peek through the clouds, brightening up the islands and creating rainbows.

Moody Atmosphere: A dark and gloomy mood that pervades the islands, reflecting the uncertainty and tension of the season.

Gray Blanket: A thick layer of clouds that blocks out the sun, casting a dull and somber shade over the islands.

Gentle Breezes: Soft winds that caress and soothe the islands, bringing freshness and calmness to the air.

It's a cloudy day instead: A disappointing weather that contradicts the expectations of the season, showing no signs of wind or sun.

Wind Chimes: Musical sounds that are produced by the winds, as they blow through various objects and instruments on the islands.

Roaring Wind: Loud and powerful wind that howls and rages across the islands, shaking and tearing everything in its path.

Powerful Gusts: Intense winds that blast and push the islands, creating waves and currents in the air.

Thrashing Waves of Clouds: Violent movements of clouds that crash and collide with each other, creating thunder and lightning in the sky.

Dancing Stormclouds: Lively and playful movements of clouds that swirl and spin around each other, creating sparks and flashes in the sky.

Chilled Air: Cold and crisp air that freezes and bites the islands, making them shiver and frosty.

Spiraling Cyclones: Huge and dangerous winds that form circular shapes in the sky, sucking and spinning everything in their center.

Icy Pellets: Small and hard pieces of ice that fall from the sky, hitting and hurting the islands.

Freezing Rain: Cold and wet rain that freezes on contact with the islands, coating them with ice and snow.

Frosty Haze: A dense layer of fog that freezes in the air, creating a white and blurry vision of the islands.

Crystal Icicles: Long and sharp pieces of ice that hang from the islands, reflecting light and creating prisms in the air.

Giant Snowflakes the size of a palm: Large and beautiful snowflakes that fall from the sky, covering the islands with a soft and fluffy layer of snow.

Special Feature

Draw a Card from the Main Deck to determine what happened during a **Spiraling Cyclones**.
Result: ♦ ♥:Gift from Gusts   ♣ ♠:Mischevious Winds

Gift from Gusts		
With each gust, a sense of anticipation fills the air, for no one know what surprise or curious arrival the winds will bestow upon their land. An exotic plant might appear in a garden, or a creature native to another island could find itself in a new terrain.		**Result**
	♦	Common Item
	♣	Rare Item
	♥	Tiny Creature
	♠	Small Creature

Draw a Card from the Fate Deck to determine what the gust of wind had brought on your floating island.

Mischevious Winds		
		Blessing
While islanders delight in the whimsical gifts of the wind, there is a hint of trepidation, for something might be taken away as well. Unbeknownst to some, an item, creature, or piece of their island's geography might've been taken.	♦	An Item with a Worth of (1-3) from your Inventory has been taken.
	♣	An Item with a Worth of (4-7) from your Inventory has been taken.
	♥	An Item with a Worth of (8-11) from your Inventory has been taken.
	♠	It seems like nothing has been taken.

Draw a Card from the Fate Deck to determine what the wind had taken from you.

Festivals

Note: Each season has a Date for its seasonal festivals. You will see four options for each Date. When you draw a card from the Main Deck that matches the Date of the current season, you can choose to celebrate the festival or skip it. If you skip it, you can celebrate it later if you draw the same Date again. But you can only celebrate each festival once per season.

Wind Dancer's Festival

	Date
A grand celebration of the winds and their whimsical nature. Skilled dancers adorned in flowing garments twirl and spin, their movements mirroring the graceful dance of the breezes. The festival features performances, workshops, and competitions, where islanders can learn the art of wind dancing and showcase their skills.	6♦
	3♣
	4♥
	8♥

1. What music reaches your ears - what instruments and rhythms set the mood?
2. What scents are carried on the breeze?
3. As you watch the dancers, how do their colorful garments make you feel?

Kite Carnival

	Date
Colorful kites of various sizes and shapes take to the skies in a vibrant display of creativity and skill. Islanders gather in open fields, flying their meticulously crafted kites high above the wind-swept landscape. It's a festival of aerial beauty, as the skies become adorned with a multitude of colorful designs and patterns.	2♦
	Q♦
	5♣
	9♠

1. What shapes and designs catch your attention first?
2. What colors stand out against the clear blue sky?

Wind Chime Symphony

	Date
In the heart of the Goddess's Island Gardens, musicians comes together. Elaborate wind chimes of varying sizes and materials fill the gardens, their melodious tones harmonizing with the wind's gentle caress. Musicians play enchanting compositions, their melodies blending seamlessly with the natural music of the chimes. It is a serene and immersive experience, where the winds and melodies intertwine.	4♦
	8♣
	3♠
	6♠

1. As the winds stir the chimes, what variety of tones and notes fill the air?
2. How might the blending of aromas and melodies evoke feelings of within you?
3. What does the artisan tell you of the philosophy behind their work, and how chimes help celebrate the natural music that surrounds us?

Gust Gauntlet Race

	Date
Adventurous islanders participate in a thrilling race that tests their agility and skill in navigating treacherous wind currents. The racecourse winds through narrow canyons and across perilous bridges, challenging competitors to adapt to the unpredictable gusts. Spectators gather along the race route, cheering on the brave participants as they defy the whims of the wind.	7♣
	7♥
	10♥
	K♠

1. What do you see that warns of the unpredictable gusts that challenges the racers?
2. The first racers come into view - what about their clothing and equipment reveals their strategies for dealing with the wind?

Breath of Serenity Retreat

	Date
A serene retreat is held on a secluded island, offering a sanctuary of calm amidst the whirlwind season. Islanders seeking respite from the gusts can partake in meditation sessions, gentle yoga classes, and therapeutic massages. The soothing sounds of wind chimes and the rhythmic rustling of leaves create a serene ambiance that promotes inner peace and relaxation.	5 ♦
	9 ♣
	J ♥
	2 ♠

1. As you arrive at the tranquil retreat, what sights and sounds begin to put you into a more relaxed state of mind?
2. What visual cues - the sound of the instructor's voice, or the movement of sunlight through palm fronds - help keep you present and focused?

Whirlwind Artistry

	Date
Artists and craftsmen come together to exhibit their wind-inspired creations during the Whirlwind Artistry event. Intricate wind sculptures, kinetic installations, and wind-powered contraptions adorn the streets and plazas, turning the cityscape into an open-air gallery. The ever-changing winds breathe life into these enchanting artworks, evoking a sense of wonder and whimsy.	9 ♦
	J ♣
	Q ♥
	J ♠

1. What wind sculptures catch your eye first?
2. What sounds fill the air - the whistling of wind through metal grates, the rhythmic flap of fabric banners, or the chime of wind chimes set in motion?
3. How might they stimulate your own imagination?

Zephyr's Aerial Showcase

	Date
A prestigious event, Zephyr's Aerial Showcase brings together the most skilled aerial performers from across Solitaria. Suspended high above the ground, these daredevils and acrobats captivate audiences with their gravity-defying feats, gracefully maneuvering through the swirling winds. From mesmerizing aerial dances to breathtaking stunts, this spectacle showcases the boundless possibilities of the wind's embrace.	A ♣
	5 ♥
	7 ♠
	10 ♠

1. As you take your seat high above the performance arena, what do you see?
2. What sounds fill the air? The twirling of ropes, gasps from the crowd, the whoosh of air as the aerialists maneuver and flip through space?
3. What details about her garments reveal the care and artistry integrated into even the smallest elements of the performance?

Gusty Gastronomy

	Date
Culinary enthusiasts embrace the season by showcasing gusty gastronomic delights during this festival. Savor cloud-like pastries and fluffy soufflés, as chefs incorporate seeds, plants, and creatures brought by the wind, creating gusty gastronomic delights. The gustatory journey takes islanders on a culinary adventure inspired by the swirling winds.	A ♦
	10 ♦
	2 ♥
	K ♥

1. What sounds drift from the bustling outdoor kitchens
2. Close your eyes and take a slow breath - what fragrances fill your lungs?
3. You approach a chef, what food is she cooking and how does she prepare it?

Seasons Scenario

These are just some examples of the stories you can create, the possibilities are endless. Craft your own adventures with these story hooks for the season:

♦ ♣ ♥ ♠	Scenarios
A	A peculiar plant suddenly sprouts on your rooftop, its vibrant leaves shimmering with an otherworldly glow
2	As the sun sets, a mesmerizing display of colorful lights illuminates the skies. Islanders gather to witness the Aurora Aetheralis, a rare phenomenon.
3	A mysterious aerial acrobat enthralls islanders with breathtaking performances.
4	A clock tower, believed to be dormant for centuries, springs to life, chiming in a symphony that reverberates across Solitaria.
5	An unprecedented storm unleashes its fury upon the floating islands, causing debris and fragments of land to fall from the sky.
6	A haunting melody drifts through the air, captivating islanders as they follow the sound to an ethereal harp, seemingly played by unseen hands.
7	A flock of migrating birds, their feathers shimmering like precious gems, descends upon the town, guided by a mysterious figure cloaked in starlight.
8	Mysterious sculptures appear throughout the floating islands, each one a breathtaking work of art.
9	An eccentric collector seeks rare winds from each floating island.
10	The revered Goddess's Temple reveals a mysterious chamber that shifts and sways with the winds.
J	A figure is seen parachuting down from one of the floating islands.
Q	A large floating ship appears in the sky above, sailing between the islands.
K	Multiple smaller floating pieces of land merge together, creating a larger island.

Last day of the Season

The last day of the Whirling Winds arrived with a stillness that seemed unnatural after months of blustery gusto. Islanders awoke to find the sky veiled in a thick fog that muffled sound and limited vision, casting an ethereal haze over the landscape.

The usual breeze was conspicuously absent, leaving leaves and flags unfurled and banners limp. Wind chimes hung motionless and silent and even the clouds seemed hesitant, drifting slowly across the muffled sun. A hush had descended with the mist, as if the winds themselves were holding their breath in anticipation.

As night deepened, a chill descended with the mist. Without the wind to stir the air, the island's normal tropical climate gave way to colder temperatures. Fires were lit in hearths and gardens to ward off the unexpected cool, sending their flickering light and warmth into the fog.

Return Home Page.86

Season of Whispering Mists

An Enigmatic Embrace

The Season of Whispering Mists begins on the last day of the Seasons of Whirling Winds, when a strong unearthly wind blows across the land, bringing with it a dense mist that covers the sky and the ground. The mist is so thick that it blocks out the sun and the stars, creating a perpetual twilight. The mist also muffles all sounds, making it hard to hear anything beyond a few feet.

> **Length of Season: 1 or 2 Deck**

The Legend

As the previous season of Whirling Winds concludes its whimsical dance, the Season of Whispering Mists emerges like a hushed whisper, signaling a time of quiet contemplation and wonder. It is said that during this ethereal time, within this veil, one can hear the whispers of the hidden realms.

Long ago, when the floating islands were still young, the Goddess of the Skies and the Spirit of the Islands wove the seasons into the very fabric of the realm. Each season was blessed with unique wonders, but it was the Season of Whispering Mists that held a truly magical secrets.

The Silent Whispers

In this hushed and mysterious time, the whispers began. Islanders would gather on the edge of their island, their senses attuned to the mystic currents that flowed through the air. They would listen with rapt attention, as the whispers of the reached their ears. It was as if the very mists themselves held the wisdom and memories of the ages, and they chose this season to share their stories.

Season of Whispering Mists												

♦ Windy — *Gentle breezes carry the enchanting whispers of the misty forest.*

A*	2	3	4*	5*	6	7*	8*	9	10	J*	K*	Q
Eerie Howling			Swirling Leaves		Gentle breeze carrying whispers*			Whistling Tunes		Loud Cyclone		

♣ Misty — *A mystical fog blankets the landscape, adding an air of intrigue.*

A	2*	3	4	5*	6*	7	8	9*	10*	J	K	Q*
Dancing Wisps of Fog			Enveloping Fog		Muffled Sounds*		Dancing Shadows in the Mists			Luminous Glow within the Mists		

♥ Rain — *The heavens open up, and a steady rainfall drenches the landscape.*

A*	2*	3*	4*	5*	6	7*	8	9*	10*	J*	K	Q*
Misty Showers			Cascading Veils and Soft Footsteps		Melodic Rain			Whispering Rainfall*			Luminous Droplets	

♠ Snow — *Flurries of delicate snowflakes blanket the landscape*

A	2	3*	4	5	6*	7	8*	9	10	J*	K*	Q
Silent White Blanket of Snow		Icy Storm			Soft crackling sounds			Snowstorm			Frosty Trails	

Eerie Howling: A haunting wail fills the air, as if unseen spirits whisper through the winds.

Swirling Leaves: Leaves dance and twirl in a graceful ballet, carried by the gentle currents of the season.

Gentle Breeze Carrying Whispers: A soft breeze carries faint whispers, hinting at secrets hidden within the mist.

Whistling Tunes: Melodic tunes seem to emanate from the winds themselves, weaving a symphony of mystery.

Loud Cyclone: A mighty cyclone roars with intensity, disrupting the tranquility of the season.

Dancing Wisps of Fog: Wisps of fog twist and sway, creating an ethereal dance upon the floating lands.

Enveloping Fog: The mist envelops everything in its embrace, veiling the landscape in a shroud of enchantment.

Muffled Sounds: Sounds become hushed and muted, as if the mist absorbs the noise of the world.

Dancing Shadows in the Mists: Shadows play a mystical dance amidst the mist, captivating the imagination.

Luminous Glow Within the Mists: A soft and radiant glow emanates from within the mist, casting an otherworldly aura.

Misty Showers: Gentle showers fall from the heavens, as if the mists themselves shed tears of enchantment.

Cascading Veils and Soft Footsteps: The mist cascades like veils, accompanied by the soft sound of footsteps treading gently.

Melodic Rain: Raindrops fall in a melodic rhythm, adding a musical touch to the misty atmosphere.

Whispering Rainfall: Raindrops seem to whisper secrets as they gently patter against the ground.

Luminous Droplets: Each raindrop glistens with a luminous quality, reflecting the mysterious glow of the season.

Silent White Blanket of Snow: Snow descends in silence, blanketing the world in a hushed and magical serenity.

Icy Storm: An icy storm rages, creating an awe-inspiring display of frosty power.

Soft Crackling Sounds: The mist carries the soft crackling of embers, igniting the sense of coziness amidst the enchantment.

Snowstorm: A whirlwind of snow swirls through the air, transforming the floating lands into a winter wonderland.

Frosty Trails: Trails of frost form intricate patterns, leaving a magical trace of the season's touch.

Special Feature

You hear a whisper from the Mists during these weather: *Gentle breeze carrying whispers, Muffled Sounds, and Whispering Rainfall.*
Draw a Card from the Main Deck and refer to the "Whispers" Table below.

A♦: I know who killed him.	**A♣:** She is not your sister.	**A♥:** He has a hidden tattoo.	**A♠:** They are planning to escape.
2♦: I saw her with him.	**2♣:** He is a spy.	**2♥:** She is married to two men.	**2♠:** He has a hidden basement room.
3♦: She has a rare blood type.	**3♣:** She is allergic to water.	**3♥:** They are from the future.	**3♠:** I have a twin brother.
4♦: I found a golden turnip.	**4♣:** She is the chief's daughter.	**4♥:** He has a crush on you.	**4♠:** They are secretly married.
5♦: He is a legendary fisherman.	**5♣:** She has a hidden talent.	**5♥:** He is a ghost.	**5♠:** He/She is your long-lost sibling.
6♦: They are the best friends ever.	**6♣:** I have a secret diary.	**6♥:** She is a fairy princess.	**6♠:** I have a rare seed.
7♦: He has a secret lover.	**7♣:** He is the heir.	**7♥:** She stole the necklace.	**7♠:** They are planning to escape.
8♦: She is a runaway princess.	**8♣:** I have a mysterious curse.	**8♥:** He is a secret admirer.	**8♠:** She is a master chef.
9♦: They are the founders of the town.	**9♣:** He is a former spy.	**9♥:** They are the heirs of a fortune.	**9♠:** Glowseeds bloom under moonlight.
10♦: Wishing star grants desires.	**10♣:** Magic crystals heal broken hearts.	**10♥:** Follow river to hidden treasure.	**10♠:** A secret portal within the well.
J♦: Warm hearth attracts lost souls.	**J♣:** Gentle touch brings back lifes.	**J♥:** Wandering cat brings luck home.	**J♠:** Wooden sign reveals wisdom.
Q♦: Lost key unlocks enchanted door.	**Q♣:** Hidden diary under floorboards.	**Q♥:** Honeybees share secret paths.	**Q♠:** Worn-out book holds ancient spells.
K♦: Tea brews heart connections.	**K♣:** Mysterious letter under doormat.	**K♥:** Totem protects village spirits.	**K♠:** Lost song awaken forgotten memories.

Festivals

Note: Each season has a Date for its seasonal festivals. You will see four options for each Date. When you draw a card from the Main Deck that matches the Date of the current season, you can choose to celebrate the festival or skip it. If you skip it, you can celebrate it later if you draw the same Date again. But you can only celebrate each festival once per season.

Mystical Masked Ball

As the mist descends, islanders gather for an enchanting masquerade ball. Elaborate masks, adorned with intricate designs and shimmering accents, conceal identities and create an air of intrigue. The ballroom shimmers with soft candlelight, and the echoes of waltzing melodies fill the mist-laden air, evoking an ambiance of mystery and romance.

Date
5♥
9♥
3♠
6♠

1. *As you enter the ballroom, what sights capture your gaze first?*
2. *What touching words or unexpected gesture would you whisper to someone else?*

Whispers of Wisdom

Seers, oracles, and mystics come together in a grand gathering to share their visions and prophecies. Islanders seek their counsel, eager to gain insights into their personal journeys and unravel the hidden meanings behind the whispers carried by the mists. It is a time of deep introspection and the exploration of the mystical realms that intertwine with their own.

Date
2♣
6♣
A♥
Q♥

1. *What flickering shadows and images appear when you stare into the crystal mists?*
2. *Who among the islanders seeking guidance catches your eye, and you feel drawn to?*

Luminous Lantern Procession

Island streets come alive with the gentle glow of luminescent lanterns. Islanders gather for a procession, each carrying a lantern adorned with symbols and wishes. The soft light pierces through the mist, illuminating paths and hearts, creating a magical tapestry of hopes and dreams.

Date
4♦
7♦
10♣
4♥

1. *As you line up with your own lantern, what sights around illuminate first from the glow of the other lantern lights?*
2. *What tastes linger on your tongue as you bite into the fresh-baked foods?*
3. *What wish or message would you whisper to this islander before releasing your lantern to float into the night?*

Mistweaver's Market

A bustling marketplace emerges amidst the mist, showcasing exquisite handcrafted treasures and artifacts. Talented artisans and enchanters offer unique items imbued with the essence of the season. From enchanted crystals to ethereal artwork, the market becomes a haven for those seeking mystical trinkets and one-of-a-kind keepsakes.

Date
8♦
7♥
J♥
K♠

1. *As you wander the market stalls, what sights first catch your eye?*
2. *Who draws your attention among the artisans?*
3. *What wish or hope do you have for the artisan who created these magic items?*

Mistborn Fireworks

	Date
The mist is a canvas for the most spectacular show of the season. These fireworks are not ordinary ones, they are made with a special blend of alchemical ingredients that react with the mist, creating unique patterns and effects. Some fireworks create shapes of animals, flowers, or stars, while others explode into rainbows, glitter, or smoke.	A♦
	5♦
	J♦
	8♠

1. *As the first firework shoots into the misty sky, what incredible sights greet your eyes?*
2. *What aromas from food stands and street merchants fill the air as islanders gather in anticipation for the wondrous display of magical fireworks?*
3. *Who do you sit with and where did you pick to celebrate the occasion?*

Enchanted Labyrinth

	Date
A labyrinth weaves its way through a serene grove, its paths obscured by the mystical mist. Island dwellers venture into this labyrinth, seeking clarity and self-reflection. Along the winding passages, they encounter whimsical illusions, symbolic statues, and hidden messages that guide them on their inner journey.	5♣
	Q♣
	3♥
	10♥

1. *What fragrances from the lush foliage and mystical flora accompany you as you enter the misty labyrinth?*
2. *As you wander the first twisting pathway, what sights appear through the mist?*
3. *Who crosses your path, seemingly lost in thought, and you feel drawn to walk together for a time?*

Mystic Alchemy Exhibition

	Date
The mist is a laboratory for the most ingenious experiments of the season. These creations are not simple potions, they are made with a complex combination of ingredients that have various effects on the mist, such as changing its color, density, temperature, or smell. Some creations make the mist glow, swirl, or ripple, while others make it emit sounds, scents, or sensations.	K♦
	9♣
	2♥
	J♠

1. *What smells of bubbling cauldrons and sizzling mixtures fill the air as island alchemists conduct their magical experiments on the mist?*
2. *As the first experiment begins, what do your eyes behold?*
3. *What strange yet intriguing tastes find your tongue as you sample an experimental vials?*
4. *Who catches your interest among the ingenious inventors?*

Seasons Scenario

These are just some examples of the stories you can create, the possibilities are endless. Craft your own adventures with these story hooks for the season:

• • • • • • • • • • • • • • • • • •

♦♣♥♠	Scenarios
A	A friendly ghost haunts your house, and tells you stories about its past life.
2	You forge a friendship with a shy villager after discovering you share a favorite hobby—birdwatching.
3	A daring explorer, long thought missing, stumbles out of the mist with tales of a hidden realm.
4	You witness a crime committed by a masked figure, and decide to investigate.
5	The lake at the heart of the island turns into a mirror, reflecting glimpses of the past and future.
6	A renowned painter unveils an ethereal masterpiece, rumored to come alive at night.
7	A mesmerizing traveling circus arrives, enchanting all with extraordinary performances under the moonlit mist.
8	Time seems to behave erratically when the mist rolls in.
9	Enchanted lanterns appear throughout the town, guiding islanders to secret gatherings.
10	Music and laughter can be heard within the mist, but no source is found.
J	A child claims their imaginary friend is real and lives within the mist.
Q	The mist muffles all sound, bringing an eerie silence until it passes.
K	Animals around town start behaving strangely as if under a spell.

• • • • • • • • • • • • • • • • • •

Determine if the this Season will repeat for, Draw a Card from the Fate Deck:
♦ ♣ :Proceed to the next Season of Glow
♥ ♠ :Play another session of The Season of Whispering Mist.

Last day of the Season

It's the final day of Whispering Mist season and a sense of calm settles over the islands. The mist begins to clear as you see the first fireflies emerge, their tiny lights flickering on and off in the dusk. You can hear their faint buzzing as they swarm through the air, dispelling the last wisps of mist with their wings.

The season of Whispering Mist is drawing to a close. You have spent the last few months braving the cold and foggy weather. As night falls, the fireflies dance in synchrony, illuminating the trees in a golden glow.

The first fireflies of the year are emerging from their hibernation, and filling the air with their soft glow. These are not ordinary fireflies, but a special kind of insect that has magical properties. They are able to disperse the mist with their fluttering wings, and warm up the atmosphere with their bioluminescence.

Return Home
Page.86

Season of Glow

An Enigmatic Embrace

The Season of Glow is one of the most anticipated and celebrated seasons. The Mists provide cover for the various insects to metamorphose as they hibernate. They will emerge in the Season of Glow with glowing properties, creating a dazzling spectacle of light and color. This Season comes with a unique event at the Last Day of the Season (*Pg. 168*) that correspond to the Glowing Magic weather (*Pg. 165*). Make sure to check it out and don't miss out on this magical dates.

Length of Season: 2 Deck

The Legend
Islanders believe the island with the most fireflies will receive the goddess's blessings. They concoct special syrups to attract swarms to their trees and plants. Each island glitters like a galaxy as residents compete for the most radiant display.

The Glow Insects
The Season of Glow begins when the first firefly emerges from its hibernation. It is a sign that the Mists are about to clear and the insects are ready to reveal their new forms. The fireflies come in many shapes and sizes, from tiny sparks to large lanterns, and they have different colors and patterns that reflect their personalities and abilities.

Some fireflies can produce heat, others can emit sounds, and some can even create illusions. As the fireflies fly out of their cocoons, they light up the Mists and make them glow with their own hues. The floating islands become illuminated as they get swarmed by the fireflies, creating a stunning contras.

Weather

Season of Glow												
♦ **Clear**			*Crisp blue skies provide a perfect backdrop for your island adventures.*									
A	2	3*	4	5	6*	7*	8	9	10	J	K	Q*
Glittering Dewdrops*			Playful Sunshower		Crystal-Clear Skies			Hints of Sunlight		Sparkling Raindrops		
♣ **Drizzle**			*Light raindrops create a shimmering effect, adding a touch of magic.*									
A*	2	3	4*	5*	6	7*	8	9	10	J	K	Q
Glowing Droplet of Water			Glistening mist covering islands			Rainbows arching between Islands			Misty Veil		Gentle rain showers	
♥ **Foggy**			*A thick blanket of fog descends upon the floating island.*									
A*	2*	3	4*	5	6*	7*	8	9*	10*	J	K*	Q*
Dancing Lights in the Fog			Thick Mist Blanket		Flickering Lights		It's a clear sunny day instead			Luminous Glow within the Fog		
♠ **Storm**			*Thunder booms and lightning crackles across the sky.*									
A	2	3	4	5*	6	7*	8*	9*	10*	J*	K*	Q
Luminous Rain Curtain*				Gusty Winds		It's a cloudy day instead		Radiant Lightning		Icy Storm		

///////////////////////

Glittering Dewdrops: Each morning, the dewdrops shimmer like tiny stars, reflecting the glow of the fireflies from the night before.

Playful Sunshower: The sun and rain coalesce, creating a playful dance of light and water, infusing the air with a sparkling charm.

Crystal-Clear Skies: The mist momentarily parts, revealing clear skies that showcase the brilliance of the floating islands in all their splendor.

Hints of Sunlight: The mist lets in gentle rays of sunlight, casting a soft glow on the landscape and hinting at the radiant beauty to come.

Sparkling Raindrops: Raindrops glisten like diamonds as they fall through the mist, adding a magical glimmer to the season.

Glowing Droplet of Water: The fireflies' magic infuses raindrops, causing them to glow like tiny orbs of enchantment.

Glistening Mist Covering Islands: The mist wraps the floating islands in a shimmering embrace, transforming them into ethereal havens.

Rainbows Arching Between Islands: As the mist blends with sunlight, rainbows arch between the islands, painting the sky with a kaleidoscope of colors.

Misty Veil: The mist swirls, forming a mysterious veil that conceals and reveals the wonders of the Season of Glow.

Gentle Rain Showers: Soft rain showers caress the land, bringing a soothing melody of tranquility.

Dancing Lights in the Fog: The fireflies' glow dances with the mist, creating an enchanting display of dancing lights.

Thick Mist Blanket: The mist wraps the world in a thick, cocoon-like embrace, imbuing an aura of mystique.

Flickering Lights: Fireflies flit and flicker through the mist, creating a dreamlike ambiance.

It's a Clear Sunny Day Instead: On rare days, the mist recedes, allowing the sun's brilliance to bathe the islands in golden light.

Luminous Glow within the Fog: The fireflies' glow permeates the mist, casting an otherworldly luminosity.

Luminous Rain Curtain: Rainfall takes on a radiant glow, as if each drop carries a touch of the fireflies' magic.

Gusty Winds: The winds carry the whispers of the fireflies, creating a symphony of rustling leaves and gentle gusts.

It's a Cloudy Day Instead: The mist intensifies, shrouding the islands in a soft, luminescent embrace.

Radiant Lightning: Rarely, bolts of lightning illuminate the mist, adding an awe-inspiring spectacle to the season.

Icy Storm: As the season progresses, a rare icy storm blankets the islands, creating an enchanting yet chilly atmosphere.

Special Feature

Glowing Magic		
The weather of ***Glittering Dewdrops*** and ***Luminous Rain Curtain*** is a rare and magical phenomenon. You are lucky to witness it and receive a random bonus from its enchantment, you feel a surge of energy and ***gain a random bonus***.		**Bonus Result**
	♦	Another Islander received +1 Bonus to Season Finale
	♣	Recover +1 Energy
	♥ ♠	+1 Bonus to Season Finale
Draw a Card from the Fate Deck and check the Result table to determine the result of the bonus you received.		
Record in Bonus Sheet.To gain an edge in the final scoring, add the Season Finale Bonus to your score on the "***Last day of the Season***" in ***Page.168***. If another Islander received it, use the ***Randomize Islander Ritual*** to find out who gets it instead.		

Naming Ritual
Every year, new fireflies are born on the island. The islanders have a tradition of giving names to these fireflies. If you encounter, receive, or acquire a firefly, you should also name it. However, you do not have to record it on the Islander Sheet. The fireflies on the Islander Sheet will only reappear in the next Season of Glow, after the current season ends.

Festivals

Note: Each season has a Date for its seasonal festivals. You will see four options for each Date. When you draw a card from the Main Deck that matches the Date of the current season, you can choose to celebrate the festival or skip it. If you skip it, you can celebrate it later if you draw the same Date again. But you can only celebrate each festival once per season.

The Firefly Fishing Festival

	Date
A unique and thrilling tradition, the Firefly Fishing Festival challenges islanders to catch the a Queen Firefly, a rare firefly. Using special concoctions and baits, islanders lure the fireflies to their fishing rods, hoping to reel in the prized catch. The Queen is then placed in a special nest, where she attracts more fireflies.	7♦
	7♣
	7♥
	K♥

If you decide to join the festival, **Draw a card from the Main Deck**. If you've drawn any **Q** "Queen" Card, you've obtained a queen too. **Add +1 Bonus** to the score during "**Final Day of the Season**" event. **Record** this bonus in the **Bonus Sheet**.

Twilight Theater

	Date
As the sun sets and the fireflies emerge, islanders gather in open-air amphitheaters to enjoy captivating performances during the enchanting Twilight Theater. Illuminated by fireflies and the soft glow of mystical crystals, actors bring mythical tales and fables to life, transporting audiences to realms of wonder and imagination. From comedy to tragedy, romance to adventure, Twilight Theater offers something for everyone.	6♦
	7♠
	8♠
	9♠

1. *As you take your seat, what story do you hope the actors will bring to life tonight under the firefly lit sky?*
2. *Who is sitting next to you? What are they wearing?*
3. *What characters and adventures unfold before your eyes this enchanting evening at twilight theater?*
4. *Who was most visibly and emotionally impacted by the stories?*

Bioluminescent Boat Parade

	Date
One of the most breathtaking events of the season, the Bioluminescent Boat Parade showcases the creativity and craftsmanship of islanders. Gliding along the tranquil clouds of floating islands, intricately decorated boats adorned with glowing motifs participate in the parade, creating a stunning procession. The boats' reflections shimmer on the cloud's surface, echoing the mesmerizing display of the fireflies above.	3♦
	5♣
	10♥
	J♠

1. *What creation has your own skilled hands fashioned this evening?*
2. *What creation did you witness today? How do you feel about it?*
3. *Who crafted the best boat?*

Luminary Light-Off

	Date
A celebration of beauty and elegance, the Luminary Light-Off is a fashion show like no other. Islanders dress up in their finest outfits, accessorized with their collected fireflies. They then strut their stuff on a runway, dazzling the judges and spectators with their luminescent style. The winner is crowned as the Luminary of the Season.	A♣
	2♥
	5♠
	10♠

1. *What colorful decorations do you see hanging from the trees and lamp posts?*
2. *Which delicious smells waft towards you on the night air, making your mouth water?*
3. *Who do you see in the crowd as you move closer, and what are they wearing that catches your eye?*
4. *Which outfit stands out to you the most as they strut down the lit pathway, and why does it captivate you so?*
5. *Who is the next contestant to catch your eye, and what do they do to really "wow" the audience and judges*
6. *How do the fireflies floating around the contestant's costumes make you feel as they twinkle and dance in the air?*

Glittering Glow Games

	Date
A series of friendly and fun-filled games are organized, celebrating the radiant energy of the fireflies. Games such as glow-in-the-dark archery, firefly tag, and luminescent scavenger hunts bring islanders of all ages together, fostering a spirit of camaraderie and joy. The games are not only entertaining, but also educational, teaching islanders about the fireflies' habits and habitats.	A♥
	4♥
	9♥
	K♠

1. *What colorful decorations do you see glowing faintly in the dusk?*
2. *Who do you notice smiling and laughing as they welcome you?*
3. *Who do you team up with for the scavenger hunt?*
4. *Which glow-in-the-dark clothing and accessories really stand out to you as the firefly tag game begins?*

Firefly Flight Race

	Date
A test of speed and skill, the Firefly Flight Race pits islanders against each other in a thrilling aerial competition. Using their collected fireflies as propulsion, islanders navigate through a challenging race track, dodging obstacles and outsmarting opponents. The winner is rewarded with a trophy and a special firefly lantern.	Q♦
	4♣
	6♥
	Q♥

To join this event, you need a firefly with a name. In each round, you will compete with three other fireflies. Before the race starts, you have to assign one of the four suits (♦,♣,♥,♠) to the fireflies. Then, shuffle the Fate Deck.

1. First, you draw a card from the Fate Deck and look at its number. This number is the length of the race, which represents how many "Distance" the fireflies have to travel to reach the finish line.
2. Then, you draw another card from the Fate Deck and look at its suit. The firefly with the same suit as the card moves one space forward. You keep drawing cards and moving fireflies until one of them reaches the finish line.

The first firefly to do so wins the round. The top two fireflies from each round advance to the next round. The Champion of the Firefly Flight Race is crowned after 3 rounds.

Seasons Scenario

These are just some examples of the stories you can create, the possibilities are endless. Craft your own adventures with these story hooks for the season:

♦ ♣ ♥ ♠	Scenarios
A	A firefly with an extraordinary glow captures the curiosity of the islanders.
2	A reclusive islander is rumored to possess a unique gift of communicating with fireflies.
3	A firefly festival is interrupted by a swarm of giant wasps.
4	A young firefly whisperer asks for your help in finding a lost firefly.
5	Your town is visited by a famous firefly researcher, and they offer you an opportunity to join their team.
6	A new breed of bioluminescent firefly is discovered, one that glows brighter than any seen before.
7	One island's fireflies all disappear overnight. No one knows why or where they went.
8	A child befriends a firefly that seems to understand wishes. Strange coincidences occur around the firefly.
9	You are interrupted by a firefly swarm that forms alarming shapes and words.
10	A Travelers arrive showing never-before-seen firefly species in bottles.
J	A breathtaking migration of bioluminescent butterflies fills the skies
Q	A firefly queen emerges with a hypnotic glow. The swarm is drawn away from the islands.
K	A legendary glowing comet is rumored to pass over the floating islands.

Last day of the Season

The Season is over and it's time to find out **who has the most fireflies** on their island. Your effort during the Glowing Magic weather will influence the outcome. **Check in *Page. 165*** and your **Bonus Sheet** for any bonus received. To do this, you will perform a special ritual with the following steps:

1. **Shuffle** the Islander cards and ***draw one*** at random.
2. ***Draw a Fate card from the Fate deck*** for the Islander you picked. This is the **Islander's Score**. Add the points from the Fate card to the Islander's score.
3. Check your **Bonus Sheet** for any extra points.
4. Repeat steps 1 to 3 until every Islander has a Fate card and a score.
5. The Islander with the **highest score** has the most fireflies on their island.

On the final night of the Season of Glow, all the islanders gather at the individual islander's floating island believed to possess the most fireflies. As the Goddess appears to bless the island, the fireflies rise into the night sky, creating a luminescent vortex that ascends toward the galaxy. The islanders watch in awe and wonder, cherishing the fleeting beauty of the fireflies becoming one with the stars. As the fireflies drift away, islanders bid them a fond farewell, knowing they'll return when the Season of Glow descends again next year.

Return Home
Page.86

Oracles

Oracles are a special feature that allows you to play the game solo, without needing a group of friends or a pre-written story. Before you start, it's essential to understand what you're trying to achieve. Ask yourself what you want to know or what goal you'd like to reach.

What can you do with an Oracle?

Whether it's a question about or a situation, or you're looking to drive the narrative, you need to have a clear idea of what you're seeking. For example:

- Create a new character to interact with in the island. Or you can let the oracle decide for you, and see who you meet by chance.
- You want to visit a new location in the world. You can use an oracle to generate a random location, such as a forest, a cave, or an Island. You can also use an oracle to determine what you find there, such as animals or plants.
- You want to start a new quest or a challenge. You can use an oracle to generate a random quest, such as finding a lost item, rescuing someone in danger, solving a mystery, or defeating an enemy. You can also use an oracle to determine the rewards and risks of the quest, such as money, allies, or enemy.
- You want to have some fun or romance with another character. You can use an oracle to generate a random event, such as a festival, a party, a date, or a wedding. You can also use an oracle to determine the outcome of the event.

Oracles can help you add more variety and surprise to your game. You can find oracles for almost any situation in this game, such as weather, quests, locations, enemies, allies, and more. You can also customize the oracles to suit your style and preferences.

Oracles are a great way to enjoy the game solo, without having to create everything from scratch. They are like your personal storyteller, who can guide you through an exciting and unpredictable adventure.

How to use an Oracle?

You never know what will happen next when you use oracles. The only limit is your imagination. ***To use an Oracle:***

1. Choose an Oracle
2. Ask a Question
3. Draw a Card from the Main Deck
4. Consider the Result
5. Craft your Story
6. Return the Card card drawn during this generation session to the Main Deck

If you're not satisfied with the result, you can always roll again or choose a different table to find the inspiration you're seeking.

Important Note: Only cards that you draw during an action are discarded. This means that if an action asks you to draw a card and refer to an Oracle, those cards are put in the Fate Deck.

Table of Content: Oracles

Name Oracles (Masculine/ Feminine)

A♦: Matteo/ Aiko	A♣: Rowan/ Stella	A♥: Grayson/ Ashlyn	A♠: Heath/ Emily
2♦: Charlie/ Chihiro	2♣: Jude/ Violet	2♥: Harvey/ Grace	2♠: Thatcher/ Olivia
3♦: Elijah/ Clara	3♣: Asher/ Maya	3♥: Arthur/ Madelyn	3♠: Hope/ Aubrey
4♦: Finn/ Emma	4♣: Clark/ Penelope	4♥: Bennett/ Isla	4♠: Finnegan/ Rin
5♦: Lucas/ Riley	5♣: Felix/ Lila	5♥: Everett/ Taylor	5♠: Everest/ Suki
6♦: Jasper/ Sophia	6♣: Elliot/ Paisley	6♥: Lochlan/ Sadie	6♠: Valentine/ Akiko
7♦: Caleb/ Abigail	7♣: Silas/ Aurora	7♥: Wells/ Nevaeh	7♠: Robin/ Yumi
8♦: Milo/ Valentine	8♣: Forest/ Ellis	8♥: Arlo/ Cecilia	8♠: Klaus/ Sayuri
9♦: Levi/ Isabelle	9♣: Griffin/ Ella	9♥: Dorian/ Skyler	9♠: Mistel/ Sakura
10♦: Ezra/ Madison	10♣: Blake/ Leah	10♥: Brooks/ Delaney	10♠: Raeger/ Kimiko
J♦: Theodore/ Minami	J♣: Jude/ Gracie	J♥: Miles/ Paige	J♠: Hiro/ Juliette
Q♦: Leo/ Savannah	Q♣: Poe/ Brielle	Q♥: Lachlan/ Emily	Q♠: Nori/ Miki
K♦: Caleb/ Caroline	K♣: Myles/ Eliza	K♥: River/ Emerald	K♠: Rune/ Hitomi

Family Name

A♦: Wang/ Crimson	A♣: Huang/ Firebrand	A♥: Yamada/ Shadow	A♠: Sakai/ Wood
2♦: Zhang/ Azure	2♣: Lin/ Brightoak	2♥: Mori/ Oakheart	2♠: Tamura/ Wright
3♦: Lee/ Hawthorn	3♣: Yang/ Brightsun	3♥: Matsuda/ Hills	3♠: Kubo/ York
4♦: Li/ Sterling	4♣: Liu/ Streambend	4♥: Takeda/ Claude	4♠: Kubo/ Shaw
5♦: Kim/ Willowby	5♣: Kimura/ Sundust	5♥: Ando/ Krest	5♠: Ohta/ Rosales
6♦: Chung/ Everglade	6♣: Ono/ Wingforge	6♥: Kaneko/ Briar	6♠: Kamata/ Rogers
7♦: Park/ Kestrel	7♣: Yamamoto/ Aurora	7♥: Hirai/ Wynd	7♠: Sasaki/ Rivera
8♦: Chen/ Windrose	8♣: Murakami/ Twili	8♥: Matsui/ Cecilia	8♠: Abe/ Ryes
9♦: Tanaka/ Ember	9♣: Ito/ Morningstar	9♥: Okada/ Schwartz	9♠: Aster/ Reyes
10♦: Nguyen/ Madison	10♣: Sato/ Throne	10♥: Honda/ Smith	10♠: Tokunaga/ Owens
J♦: Wu/ Stembane	J♣: Kato/ Sage	J♥: Inoue/ Turner	J♠: Sasahara/ Palmer
Q♦: Pham/ Riversong	Q♣: Fukuda/ Crest	Q♥: Maeda/ Wells	Q♠: Miyazaki/ May
K♦: Tran/ Highcastle	K♣: Nagase/ Leaf	K♥: Shimizu/ Wilson	K♠: Shita/ Little

Age

A	2	3	4	5	6	7	8	9	10	J	Q	K
1	2-5	6-10	11-20	21-30	31-40	41-50	51-60	61-70	71-80	81-100	>100	>1000

Floating Island Name

A♦: Nimblum	**A♣**: Fallup Isle	**A♥**: Cloudknoll	**A♠**: Airsail
2♦: Clovancia	**2♣**: Galavant Isle	**2♥**: Skybay	**2♠**: Skyswell
3♦: Flotazon	**3♣**: Hoverport	**3♥**: Driftwood	**3♠**: Wisp
4♦: Cloudhaven	**4♣**: Celuma	**4♥**: Highheft	**4♠**: Highridge
5♦: Skyhoven	**5♣**: Skyleft	**5♥**: Soarpoint	**5♠**: Nimblemead
6♦: Levitas	**6♣**: Casca Isle	**6♥**: Wander Isle	**6♠**: Ascant
7♦: Nimble Isle	**7♣**: Oave Isle	**7♥**: Airstudy	**7♠**: Cirro
8♦: Driftcrest	**8♣**: Zephyre	**8♥**: Summit Isle	**8♠**: Cirre
9♦: Maridale	**9♣**: Taloft	**9♥**: Skyraise	**9♠**: Flotica
10♦: Sky Drifts	**10♣**: Shiver Isle	**10♥**: Fjoat Isle	**10♠**: Aerisle
J♦: Airlift Isle	**J♣**: Paradroft	**J♥**: Flighat Isle	**J♠**: Skyloftia
Q♦: High Heavens	**Q♣**: Isle Aloft	**Q♥**: Dreambay	**Q♠**: Cloudview
K♦: Cirronia	**K♣**: Skilly Isle	**K♥**: Flasca	**K♠**: Ascanta

Species

Solitaria is populated by four different species. You have the freedom to randomize the species you meet.

♦	♣	♥	♠
Fleshlings	**Angelkin**	**Beastkin**	**Aviankin**
Carbon-based bipeds with dexterous hands and curious minds. They seek meaning, create art, and ponder the nature of reality.	spiritual beings of light and love, with wings of sublime radiance. They spread joy, mercy and peace wherever they fly.	intuitive creatures of fang and claw who live in sacred harmony with nature's rhythms. They defend the web of life with tooth and nail.	Versatile avians with wings of silk and bone. They soar the skies searching for adventure and sharing tales of their journeys.
Human, Dwarf, Halflings, Hobbits	Seraph, Cherub, Demon, Gargolye	Otterkin, Bearfolks, Kitsune, Mousefolk	Owlfolk, Harpy, Tengu, Drakekins

Traits

A♦: Imaginative	**A♣**: Idea-driven	**A♥**: Refined	**A♠**: Rebellious
2♦: Holistic	**2♣**: Curious	**2♥**: Ingenious	**2♠**: Brave
3♦: Fearless	**3♣**: Meticulous	**3♥**: Energetic	**3♠**: Honest
4♦: Enthusiastic	**4♣**: Wise	**4♥**: Intentional	**4♠**: Reliable
5♦: Innovative	**5♣**: Hyper-focused	**5♥**: Cynical	**5♠**: Humble
6♦: Reflective	**6♣**: Confident	**6♥**: Determined	**6♠**: Resourceful
7♦: Perceptive	**7♣**: Conceptual	**7♥**: Analytical	**7♠**: Charming
8♦: Outgoing	**8♣**: Playful	**8♥**: Artistic	**8♠**: Humorous
9♦: Eclectic	**9♣**: Scattershot	**9♥**: Grumpy	**9♠**: Romantic
10♦: Versatile	**10♣**: Unpredictable	**10♥**: Quirky	**10♠**: Idealistic
J♦: Inspiring	**J♣**: Methodical	**J♥**: Adventurous	**J♠**: Clumsy
Q♦: Optimistic	**Q♣**: Fast-paced	**Q♥**: Athletic	**Q♠**: Sarcastic
K♦: Bold	**K♣**: Thoughtful	**K♥**: Hardworking	**K♠**: Impulsive

Hobbies

A♦: Tend to your garden	A♣: Write letters by hand	A♥: Roll out dough for pastries	A♠: Cook on an open fire
2♦: Knit by the fireside	2♣: Make hot cocoa	2♥: Create flower pressed art	2♠: Visit a farmers market
3♦: Adopt a cat or dog	3♣: Draw pictures	3♥: Rearrange your bookshelves	3♠: Listen to vinyl records
4♦: Make homemade jam	4♣: Learn to play an instrument	4♥: Chop wood	4♠: Host dinner parties
5♦: Bake an apple pie	5♣: Collect vintage cameras	5♥: Collect tea cups	5♠: Curl up with a blanket
6♦: Watch the sunset	6♣: Plant bulbs for spring	6♥: Watch the clouds	6♠: Bathe in a hot spring
7♦: Play in the rain	7♣: Pop corn on the stove	7♥: Feed birds in the garden	7♠: Have picnics in the park
8♦: Grow herbs in pots	8♣: Cook old family recipes	8♥: Join a local hiking group	8♠: Camp in the backyard
9♦: Read mystery novels	9♣: Grind your own spices	9♥: Knit sweaters	9♠: Make puzzles
10♦: Play board games with friends	10♣: Carve wood	10♥: Catch up with old friends over tea	10♠: Create shadow puppets
J♦: Make flower arrangements	J♣: Collect postcards	J♥: Take care of houseplants	J♠: Paint flower petals falling
Q♦: Go for country walks	Q♣: Chase fireflies at dusk	Q♥: Write in a journal	Q♠: Watch the squirrels play
K♦: Star gaze at night	K♣: Practice calligraphy	K♥: Brew your own beer	K♠: Cloud Watching

Actions

A♦: Conceive/Invent	A♣: Take apart	A♥: Comprehend	A♠: Rewrite/ Trim
2♦: Design/Blueprint	2♣: Deconstruct	2♥: Theorize	2♠: Edit/ Transform
3♦: Build/Construct	3♣: Repurpose/Notice	3♥: Propose/ Suggest	3♠: Expand Boundary
4♦: Experiment/Test	4♣: Make do/Observe	4♥: Pitch/Advocate	4♠: Blend/ Manifest
5♦: Refine/Iterate	5♣: Analyze/Examine	5♥: Challenge/ Warn	5♠: Remix/ Intersect
6♦: Amplify/Magnify	6♣: Think through	6♥: Confront/ Alert	6♠: Improve/ Remix
7♦: Visualize/Hone	7♣: Model/Simulate	7♥: Advice/ Envision	7♠: Live out
8♦: Imagine/ Narrow	8♣: Investigate/	8♥: Recommend	8♠: Leave a Legacy
9♦: Sharpen/Focus	9♣: Inquire	9♥: Offer/ What if?	9♠: Foster/ Nurture
10♦: Perfect/Craft	10♣: Seek Pattern	10♥: Alternatives	10♠:Propel/ Push
J♦: Connect/Link	J♣: Put into context	J♥: Set free/ Change	J♠: Influence
Q♦: Synthesize/Fuse	Q♣: Frame/ Speculate	Q♥: Let go/ Morph	Q♠: Shift Paradigms
K♦: Merge/Combine	K♣: Understand	K♥: Revise/ Polish	K♠: Spark/ Ignite

Relationships

A♦: Classmate	A♣: Neighbour	A♥: Godchild	A♠: Flatmate
2♦: Acquaintance	2♣: Roommate	2♥: Club Members	2♠: Half Siblings
3♦: Supporter	3♣: Enemies	3♥: Rival	3♠: Playmate
4♦: Apprentice	4♣: Regular	4♥: Step Parent	4♠: Guardian
5♦: Friend	5♣: Parent	5♥: Warden	5♠: Siblings
6♦: Mutual Friends	6♣: Child	6♥: Idol	6♠: Instructor
7♦: Mentor	7♣: Coworker	7♥: Twins	7♠: Nemesis
8♦: Patron	8♣: Grandparents	8♥: Assistant	8♠: Crush's Parents
9♦: Relative	9♣: Fan	9♥: Step Children	9♠: Bro
10♦: Parental Figure	10♣: Bad Neighbour	10♥: Co-worker	10♠: Student
J♦: Companion	J♣: Like a Family	J♥: In-Laws	J♠: Godparent
Q♦: Caretaker	Q♣: Step Siblings	Q♥: Mentee	Q♠: Pupil
K♦: Admirer	K♣: Role Model	K♥: Protege	K♠: Casual Friends

Romantic Relationships

A♦: Just dating casually	A♣: Desperate attempts	A♥: Taking the relationship slowly	A♠: Co-parents
2♦: Young love	2♣: Long time coming	2♥: Taking our time	2♠: Smitten
3♦: High school sweethearts	3♣: Trapped in feelings	3♥: Planning forever togethe	3♠: Best friends
4♦: Long-distance lovers	4♣: Shy admiration from afar	4♥: Figuring it out together	4♠: Graying together
5♦: Meeting up in secret	5♣: Built on compromise	5♥: Committed partners	5♠: Still madly in love
6♦: Whirlwind romance	6♣: Hearts set on each other	6♥: Upsetting family dynamics	6♠: Second chance at love
7♦: Opposites attract	7♣: Reluctant partnership	7♥: Lifelong companions	7♠: Meeting again after years apart
8♦: Convenience	8♣: Secret admirers	8♥: Magnetic pull	8♠: Growing together
9♦: Engaged to be married	9♣: Forced into romance	9♥: Struggling to keep the spark alive	9♠: Rekindled romance
10♦: Newlyweds	10♣: Flirty friends	10♥: Intense passion	10♠: Meant to be
J♦: Growing resentment	J♣: Friendship turned romantic	J♥: Settled comfort	J♠: Breaking up and getting back together
Q♦: Soulmates	Q♣: Overdue	Q♥: Inseparable	Q♠: Bound for life
K♦: Passionate affair	K♣: Enemies to lovers	K♥: Through thick and thin	K♠: Staying together for the kids

Scenes/ Moods

A♦: Victorious	A♣: Animated	A♥: Heartwarming	A♠: Curious
2♦: Optimistic	2♣: Hysterical	2♥: Melancholy	2♠: Overwhelming
3♦: Intriguing	3♣: Hopeless	3♥: Touching	3♠: Serious
4♦: Gloomy	4♣: Stagnant	4♥: Startling	4♠: Solemn
5♦: Hectic	5♣: Romantic	5♥: Ingenious	5♠: Lighthearted
6♦: Hurried	6♣: Threatening	6♥: Graceful	6♠: Affectionate
7♦: Determined	7♣: Chaotic	7♥: Brave	7♠: Wondrous
8♦: Frantic	8♣: Calm	8♥: Dramatic	8♠: Adventurous
9♦: Vengeful	9♣: Furious	9♥: Witty	9♠: Instinctual
10♦: Thoughtful	10♣: Violent	10♥: Lively	10♠: Harmonious
J♦: Dramatic	J♣: Peaceful	J♥: Scholarly	J♠: Uplifting
Q♦: Grim	Q♣: Eventful	Q♥: Arduous	Q♠: Resolute
K♦: Hilarious	K♣: Unexpected	K♥: Painful	K♠: Awkward

Descriptor

A♦: Wondrous	A♣: Multidimensional	A♥: Various	A♠: Suspicious
2♦: Vibrant	2♣: Optimized	2♥: Trendsetting	2♠: Distant
3♦: Energized	3♣: Evolving	3♥: Forward-thinking	3♠: Soothing
4♦: Thrilling	4♣: Adaptive	4♥: Novel	4♠: Rich
5♦: Futuristic	5♣: Fluid	5♥: Thoughtprovoking	5♠: Overheating
6♦: Innovative	6♣: Collaborative	6♥: Perplexing	6♠: Untouched
7♦: Developing	7♣: Limitless	7♥: Campy	7♠: Illuminating
8♦: Emerging	8♣: Burgeoning	8♥: Cursed	8♠: Sleek
9♦: Growing	9♣: Expansive	9♥: Comprehensive	9♠: Nostalgic
10♦: Refined	10♣: Abundant	10♥: Crumbling	10♠: Broad
J♦: Polished	J♣: Nuanced	J♥: Overgrown	J♠: Welcoming
Q♦: Complex	Q♣: Profound	Q♥: Developmental	Q♠: Familiar
K♦: Interconnected	K♣: Sophisticated	K♥: Unsettling	K♠: Handmade

**Return Home
Page.86**

A♦: A secret garden hidden within a bamboo grove	**A♣**: An eternal springtime park filled with flowers	**A♥**: An old Museum with ancient artifacts	**A♠**: Post Office
2♦: A windswept grassy hill overlooking the town	**2♣**: A cluttered workshop filled with inventions	**2♥**: A towering gazebo offering a panoramic view	**2♠**: A secret room hidden behind a bookcase
3♦: A sleepy fishing village by the sea	**3♣**: An ever-changing maze garden	**3♥**: An isolated lighthouse by the sea	**3♠**: An endlessly rolling prairie
4♦: An orchard of fruit trees in full blossom	**4♣**: A grand library lined with ladders and staircases	**4♥**: An endless sky full of colorful kites	**4♠**: An imposing terraced temple complex
5♦: An enchanted forest filled with fairy rings	**5♣**: A whimsical teahouse high up in the treetops	**5♥**: Enchanted hedge maze that seems to shift and change	**5♠**: The base of the mountain
6♦: A windswept mountaintop monastery	**6♣**: A traditional ryokan inn	**6♥**: A majestic treehouse	**6♠**: An open meadow by a tranquil lake
7♦: A hidden magical grotto	**7♣**: An endless field of lavender at dusk	**7♥**: A ramshackle country mansion	**7♠**: An overgrown ruin
8♦: A winding river path lined with cherry blossoms	**8♣**: An improbable windmill perched atop a high peak	**8♥**: Atelier studio covered in paintings and sculptures	**8♠**: A towering library full of tomes
9♦: An open air market filled with vendors	**9♣**: An ancient shrine nestled in the mountains	**9♥**: A lively cafe with a stage for performances	**9♠**: Rambling country manor house with ivy-covered walls
10♦: An isolated cabin in the woods	**10♣**: A maze of hidden city streets	**10♥**: An eternally twilit forest	**10♠**: A bustling dockside
J♦: A windswept beach with rugged cliffs	**J♣**: An immense network of cavern tunnels	**J♥**: A hot air balloon floating lazily overhead	**J♠**: Park/ Garden
Q♦: A bustling town square	**Q♣**: A moonlit bamboo forest	**Q♥**: An elegant imperial palace	**Q♠**: Rock climbing spot
K♦: A rustic farmhouse surrounded by fields of crops	**K♣**: An mysterious observatory high up on a cliff	**K♥**: Hiking Trail in the Wilderness	**K♠**: An Well filled with water.

Backlash

A♦: Cursed into animal form	A♣: Irked ancient golem	A♥: Unleashed plague of insects	A♠: Trigged destructive storm
2♦: Stuck in enchanted maze	2♣: Disturbed sleeping monster cave	2♥: Accidentally freed bound spirit	2♠: Called down elemental wrath
3♦: Lost in faerie realm	3♣: Disturbed enchanted ruins	3♥: Crossed threshold	3♠: Plagued by vengeful ghost
4♦: Stricken by fairy fever	4♣: Unknowingly sat in faerie ring	4♥: Unwittingly broke sacred oath	4♠: Cursed farmland
5♦: Plagued by nightmares	5♣: Cursed by trickster spirit	5♥: Tripped magical alarm	5♠: Isolated from everyone
6♦: Under villain's spell	6♣: Crossed paths with vampires	6♥: Broke protective ward	6♠: Divided by misunderstanding
7♦: Kidnapped by shadows	7♣: Trespassed on sacred ground	7♥: Disturbed nature spirit's slumber	7♠: Broken family relationships
8♦: Trapped within haunted painting	8♣: Unknowingly insulted an elder	8♥: Bad Harvest due to imbalance	8♠: Estranged from friends
9♦: Drank forgetful potion	9♣: Disrespected local custom	9♥: Released hoard of creatures	9♠: Activated destructive golem
10♦: Took wrong turn	10♣: Damaged tree	10♥: Spilled potion	10♠: Violated taboo
J♦: Upset local spirits	J♣: Irritated jealous rival	J♥: Trapped in Time Loop	J♠: Collapsed magic barrier
Q♦: Made enemy of witch	Q♣: Upset balance of forces	Q♥: Cursed by witch	Q♠: Awakened malign spirit
K♦: Disturbed resting dragon	K♣: Separated from Body	K♥: Upset faerie blessings	K♠: Lost protective talisman

Purpose/ Quest

Your character has reasons for their behavior. What are they seeking / challenge that drives them?

A♦: Wisdom	A♣: Rescue	A♥: Seek	A♠: Knowledge
2♦: Growth	2♣: Discover	2♥: Inspire	2♠: Fear
3♦: Rebuild	3♣: Freedom	3♥: Search	3♠: Memory
4♦: Roam	4♣: Empower	4♥: Pursuit	4♠: Passion
5♦: Journey	5♣: Community	5♥: Pilgrimage	5♠: Greater Good
6♦: Peace	6♣: Connect	6♥: Hunt	6♠: Premonition
7♦: Healing	7♣: Coexist	7♥: Collect	7♠: Ambition
8♦: Belonging	8♣: Persevere	8♥: Wander	8♠: Bravery
9♦: Explore	9♣: Share	9♥: Travel	9♠: History
10♦: Restore	10♣: Revive	10♥: Self-discovery	10♠: Lack of Info
J♦: Learn	J♣: Renew	J♥: Disire	J♠: Confusion
Q♦: Hope	Q♣: Understanding	Q♥: Intuition	Q♠: Unknown
K♦: Escape	K♣: Aid	K♥: Reality	K♠: Truth

Requests 1

A♦: Catch a rare fish	**A♣**: Fix a broken machine	**A♥**: Make jam/wine/cheese	**A♠**: Prank someone
2♦: Clean the town hall	**2♣**: Give a haircut to someone	**2♥**: Help someone practice their hobby	**2♠**: Rescue someone from danger
3♦: Collect seashells	**3♣**: Give a massage to someone	**3♥**: Make jewelry/pottery/candles	**3♠**: Sell something at the market
4♦: Cook a special dish for someone	**4♣**: Give a speech at the festival	**4♥**: Organize a party/picnic/barbecue	**4♠**: Set up a campfire
5♦: Craft a gift for someone	**5♣**: Grow a giant vegetable	**5♥**: Paint a mural/portrait/landscape	**5♠**: Solve a mystery/riddle/puzzle
6♦: Deliver a letter to someone	**6♣**: Help a ghost find peace	**6♥**: Perform in a play/concert/circus	**6♠**: Take care of a sick/injured person
7♦: Design a new outfit for someone	**7♣**: Help a lost child/creature	**7♥**: Plant flowers/trees/crops	**7♠**: Take photos of the scenery/people
8♦: Dig up fossils	**8♣**: Feed the animals	**8♥**: Gather mushrooms	**8♠**: Harvest honey
9♦: Find a hidden treasure	**9♣**: Help a stranded alien	**9♥**: Help someone with their homework	**9♠**: Teach someone how to dance/sing
10♦: Find a magic ingredient	**10♣**: Help an inventor test their invention	**10♥**: Help someone propose to their partner	**10♠**: Make friends with an animal/monster/spirit
J♦: Find a missing person	**J♣**: Help someone confess their love	**J♥**: Learn a new skill from someone	**J♠**: Join a band for a day
Q♦: Find a secret passage	**Q♣**: Help someone overcome their fear	**Q♥**: Help someone remember their past	**Q♠**: Tell stories/jokes/riddles
K♦: Find out somcone's birthday	**K♣**: Learn how to fly a kite	**K♥**: Play hide and seek/tag/chess	**K♠**: Trade something with someone

Requests 2

A♦: Deliver package	**A♣**: Prune garden	**A♥**: Promote business	**A♠**: Tend sick person
2♦: Water plants	**2♣**: Weed garden	**2♥**: Model clothing	**2♠**: Scout new area
3♦: Find ingredient	**3♣**: Give advice	**3♥**: Spread word	**3♠**: Lead meditation
4♦: Plant flowers	**4♣**: Feed animals	**4♥**: Join expedition	**4♠**: Maintain tools
5♦: Cook dinner	**5♣**: Write letter	**5♥**: Chase animal	**5♠**: Negotiate trade
6♦: Visit friend	**6♣**: Train animal	**6♥**: Protect crops	**6♠**: Interpret dream
7♦: Fix leaking pipe	**7♣**: Name new baby	**7♥**: Collect data	**7♠**: Test machinery
8♦: Pick fruit	**8♣**: Revive forest	**8♥**: Urgent delivery	**8♠**: Clear branches
9♦: Test recipe	**9♣**: Hold concert	**9♥**: Repair roof	**9♠**: Spread hay
10♦: Babysit kids	**10♣**: Rescue animal	**10♥**: Survey new land	**10♠**: Record Data
J♦: Fix broken tool	**J♣**: Clean up debris	**J♥**: Locate lost item	**J♠**: Fortify defenses
Q♦: Redecorate room	**Q♣**: Host even	**Q♥**: Unearth artifact	**Q♠**: Gather team
K♦: Mend clothes	**K♣**: Translate text	**K♥**: Exorcise ghost	**K♠**: Illuminate paths

Plot Twist

A♦: Villain revealed as a kidnap victim	**A♣**: Unlocks power from within	**A♥**: Loses memory of past	**A♠**: Prank backfires badly
2♦: Artifact summons spirits	**2♣**: Discovers true identity	**2♥**: Must choose between duty & desire	**2♠**: Misunderstanding snowballs
3♦: Main character swaps bodies	**3♣**: Hidden danger lurks nearby	**3♥**: The illness has a cure	**3♠**: Couple breaks up
4♦: Amnesia blocks the truth	**4♣**: Forced into an alliance	**4♥**: Forbidden doorway opens	**4♠**: Unexpected friendship formed
5♦: Trapped in a time loop	**5♣**: Confronting childhood bully	**5♥**: Criminal accusations made	**5♠**: Town tradition threatened
6♦: Rescued from a curse	**6♣**: Backfires good intentions	**6♥**: Plagued by ghostly visions	**6♠**: Mystery ailment strikes livestock
7♦: Secrets in a family tree	**7♣**: Quest for a stolen item	**7♥**: Kitten causes trouble	**7♠**: Proposal goes awry
8♦: Newcomer shakes up town	**8♣**: Pursued by an ancient curse	**8♥**: Task goes horribly wrong	**8♠**: Competition heats up
9♦: Wedding plans go awry	**9♣**: Mistaken identity trouble	**9♥**: Important harvest ruined	**9♠**: Item needed urgently found
10♦: A lost sibling returns	**10♣**: Facing a difficult decision	**10♥**: Secret admirer revealed	**10♠**: Hired help causes problems
J♦: Someone isn't who they seem	**J♣**: Uncovers shocking past	**J♥**: Legendary creature appears	**J♠**: Past comes knocking
Q♦: Rivalry turns to romance	**Q♣**: Race against the seasons	**Q♥**: Stranger comes to town	**Q♠**: Inherits unwanted pet
K♦: Someone returns from the dead	**K♣**: Journey to another world	**K♥**: Unexpected storm hits	**K♠**: Found diary reveals past

Landmark

Small	Medium	Big	Large
A♦: Small Pond	**A♣**: An old ruin	**A♥**: Big Garden	**A♠**: An old ruin
2♦: A termite mound	**2♣**: Hollowed Tree	**2♥**: Forgotten Park	**2♠**: Old Library
3♦: Natural Arch	**3♣**: Wishing Well	**3♥**: Oasis	**3♠**: Old Watch Tower
4♦: A Clearing	**4♣**: Tree Tunnel	**4♥**: Canyon	**4♠**: Waterfall
5♦: Groove	**5♣**: Old Well	**5♥**: Giant Tree	**5♠**: Broken Bridge
6♦: Spring	**6♣**: A Clearing	**6♥**: Ravine	**6♠**: Old Tree House
7♦: Old Fountain	**7♣**: Small Garden	**7♥**: Valley	**7♠**: Bamboo Grove
8♦: Spring	**8♣**: Wildflower Field	**8♥**: Volcano	**8♠**: River
9♦: Stone Circle	**9♣**: Hut	**9♥**: Rock Sculpture	**9♠**: Cliff
10♦: A bird's nest	**10♣**: Ruined Temple	**10♥**: Rapids	**10♠**: Lake
J♦: Mushroom circle	**J♣**: Remain of Bridge	**J♥**: Stream	**J♠**: Crater
Q♦: A flower patch	**Q♣**: Dead Tree	**Q♥**: Boulder	**Q♠**: Hills
K♦: Beehive	**K♣**: Big Spiderweb	**K♥**: Old Lighthouse	**K♠**: Village Ruins

Mail

You can create a mail that was sent to you with the help of the Mail Oracle. It will use the parts of a mail, such as "I went/ did, someone else", and the content theme, such as "someone confessed their love, an animal came up to me, saw an old friend", to give you a mail to work with.

♦	I went/ did ...
♣	I saw/ experience ...
♥	Someone else ...
♠	Someone close to me ...

A:	... someone conffessed their love to me.
2:	... an animal came up to say hello.
3:	... something funny happened that made me laugh.
4:	... tasted something delicious.
5:	... saw an old friend.
6:	... helped someone in need.
7:	... nature was especially stunning.
8:	... a challenge taught an important lesson.
9:	... life gave a pleasant surprise.
10:	... joy bubbled up from within.
J:	... a treasured memory came to mind.
Q:	... hope filled heart anew.
K:	... for simple pleasures and love that makes life worth living fully.

You can also use the words oracles below to get some keywords for the mail content and combine them. You can also use other oracles, such as request, purpose/quest, scenes, or descriptors oracles, to make your mail more lively and appealing.

A♦: Adventure	**A♣**: Crystal	**A♥**: Artisan	**A♠**: Magic
2♦: Airship	**2♣**: Garden	**2♥**: Festival	**2♠**: Chicken
3♦: Creature	**3♣**: Chocolate	**3♥**: Fruit	**3♠**: Dream
4♦: Bakery	**4♣**: Cheese	**4♥**: Love	**4♠**: Track
5♦: Balloon	**5♣**: Farm	**5♥**: Fairy	**5♠**: Cherry blossom
6♦: Beach	**6♣**: Cooking	**6♥**: Jewelry	**6♠**: Goals
7♦: Cake	**7♣**: Bridge	**7♥**: Cloud	**7♠**: Fish
8♦: Goddess	**8♣**: Friend	**8♥**: Market	**8♠**: Craft
9♦: Crop	**9♣**: Firefly	**9♥**: Heart	**9♠**: Harvest
10♦: Flower	**10♣**: Forest	**10♥**: Castle	**10♠**: Nature
J♦: Wind	**J♣**: Island	**J♥**: Wilderness	**J♠**: Journey
Q♦: Rest	**Q♣**: Clinic	**Q♥**: Contest	**Q♠**: Market
K♦: Future	**K♣**: Gift	**K♥**: Hangout	**K♠**: Pride

Rumours 1

To generate rumours, you can use the tables below that provide elements such as who, what, where, when, why, how, consequence, and reaction. You can mix and match any row from each table to create a rumour, or you can use your own imagination. You can also use the randomize islander ritual to choose a random who from the list of characters.

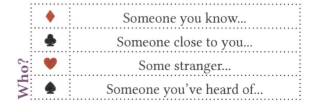

Who?	
♦	Someone you know...
♣	Someone close to you...
♥	Some stranger...
♠	Someone you've heard of...

What?

A: Is secretly a witch

2: Has a crush on someone

3: Found a treasure map

4: Is hiding a rare book

5: Is making a legendary tools

6: Is a spy for another realm

7: Has a talking creature

8: Is experimenting on Islanders

9: Is stealing clothes from another

10: Is haunted by a ghost

J: Is a famous singer in disguise

Q: Has a secret garden with exotic plants

K: Has visions of the future

When?

A: Every full moon

2: Every morning

3: Last week

4: For years

5: Every night

6: During classes

7: All the time

8: Every weekend

9: Every day

10: Every midnight

J: Every evening

Q: Whenever he feels inspired

K: Every dawn

Why?

A: To cast spells on the townsfolk

2: To impress her and win her heart

3: To find hidden treasure and become rich

4: To protect it from thieves & collectors

5: To fulfill a prophecy

6: To gather information and sabotage

7: To keep it as a pet and a friend

8: To find a cure for a rare disease

9: To make more money and expand business

10: To get rid of it and find peace

J: To escape fame and enjoy simple life

Q: To create beautiful art and share it

K: To enjoy nature and escape from society

How?

A: By using a hidden book of magic

2: By baking her delicious pastries

3: By following the clues on the map

4: By locking it in a secret vault

5: By using a rare metal

6: By pretending to be friendly

7: By feeding it special grass

8: By using unethical methods and drugs

9: By altering the clothes' color & size

10: By hiring an exorcist

J: By wearing a disguise

Q: By caring for the plants and animals

K: By letting them escape from jail

Consequences

A: The Islander are becoming more obedient

2: Flattered but confused by the intention

3: Discovers an ancient dangerous curse

4: The book contains powerful knowledge

5: Imbued with magic

6: Vulnerable to an attacks

7: Has a witty personality

8: Suffering from side effects & mutations

9: Customers are unhappy and dissatisfied

10: Causes more trouble for everyone

J: Makes new friends in the town

Q: More confident and bold in their raids

K: Discovers a lost island

Reactions

A: Suspicious and want to expose it all

2: Becomes jealous and angry

3: Ready to confront

4: Worried about the dissapearance

5: Determined to steal and use for self

6: Amazed and wants to learn

7: Doesn't suspect his true identity

8: Annoyed by the loud noise

9: Horrified and wants to report it

10: Scared by the presence

J: Impressed and proud

Q: Becomes worried and lonely without him

K: Naive and unaware of the betrayal

Topic of Conversation

A♦: Why did you come to Solitaria?	**A♣**: How do you deal with stress or anger?
2♦: What is your favorite animal or creature in this world?	**2♣**: What are some of the traditions or festivals that you celebrate or enjoy?
3♦: How do you feel about magic and its effects on society?	**3♣**: What are some of the stories or legends that you know or believe in?
4♦: What is the most beautiful place you've ever visited or want to visit?	**4♣**: What are some things that make you happy or unhappy?
5♦: What is your dream in life?	**5♣**: How do you express your love?
6♦: How do you cope with the challenges and dangers of living in Solitaria?	**6♣**: What are some of the things that you are afraid of or excited about?
7♦: What is the most interesting or unusual thing you've ever found or made?	**7♣**: What are some of the things that you are curious or passionate about?
8♦: How do you cope with loss or grief?	**8♣**: How do you handle criticism?
9♦: How do you get along with the other people or races in this world?	**9♣**: What are some of the things that you are proud of or ashamed of?
10♦: What are some of the hobbies or skills that you have or want to learn?	**10♣**: What are some of the things that you regret or wish for?
J♦: How do you communicate with others?	**J♣**: How do you decide and solve problems?
Q♦: What is the most valuable lesson you've learned in your life?	**Q♣**: What are some of the things that you admire or despise in others?
K♦: How do you balance your work and leisure time?	**K♣**: What are some of the things that you agree or disagree with in this world?
A♥: How do you learn or teach new things?	**A♠**: How do you spend or save your money?
2♥: What are some of the things that you enjoy or dislike doing in your spare time?	**2♠**: What are some of the things that you are loyal to or betray?
3♥: How do you relax or have fun?	**3♠**: How do you trust or doubt others?
4♥: What are some of the things that you find easy or difficult to do?	**4♠**: What are some of the things that you are thankful for or resentful of?
5♥: How do you plan or organize your day?	**5♠**: How do you forgive or hold a grudge?
6♥: What are some of the things that you are good at or bad at?	**6♠**: What are some of the things that you are optimistic or pessimistic about?
7♥: How do you show or hide your emotions?	**7♠**: How do you dream or face reality?
8♥: What are some of the things that you are interested in or bored by?	**8♠**: What are some of the things that you are confident or insecure about?
9♥: How do you lead or follow others?	**9♠**: How do you create or destroy things?
10♥: What are some of the things that you are generous or stingy with?	**10♠**: What are some of the things that you are adventurous or cautious about?
J♥: How do you explore or settle in a place?	**J♠**: How do you change or resist change?
Q♥: What are some of the things that you are curious or indifferent about?	**Q♠**: What are some of the things that you are friendly or hostile to?
K♥: How do you cooperate or compete with others?	**K♠**: What are some of the things that you are proud of or ashamed of?

Topic of Conversation: Social Gathering

A: How do you feel about the recent changes in the island's altitude?

2: What are some of the best and worst things about living on a floating island?

3: How do you get along with the other residents of your island?

4: What are some of the skills that you have or want to learn on your island?

5: How do you celebrate or enjoy the seasons on your island?

6: Do you have any traditions or festivals that mark the changes in the weather, the crops, or the animals?

7: How do you travel or explore other islands?

8: How do you entertain or have fun on your island?

9: What are some of the places that you have visited or want to visit?

10: How do you protect or defend your island from threats or dangers?

J: How do you maintain or improve your island's condition and appearance?

Q: Do you have any tools, machines, or magic that help you repair, enhance, or decorate your island?

K: How do you communicate or trade with other islands?

Creature Feature Creator

A♦: Hollow bones	**A♣**: Hibernates	**A♥**: Auditory warnings	**A♠**: Spikes
2♦: Webbed feet	**2♣**: Sharp teeth	**2♥**: Nocturnal	**2♠**: Fur
3♦: Feathers	**3♣**: Armored hide	**3♥**: Cold-blooded	**3♠**: Shell
4♦: Fur	**4♣**: Spots	**4♥**: Regenerates limbs	**4♠**: Fins
5♦: Gills	**5♣**: Bioluminescence	**5♥**: Glowing Lure	**5♠**: Snout
6♦: Quills	**6♣**: Pincers	**6♥**: Flashes colors	**6♠**: Beak
7♦: Lays eggs	**7♣**: Compound eyes	**7♥**: Adapted mimicry	**7♠**: Whiskers
8♦: Exoskeleton	**8♣**: Retractable claws	**8♥**: Rely on teamwork	**8♠**: Mane
9♦: Breathes fire	**9♣**: Prehensile tongue	**9♥**: Elaborate nest	**9♠**: Floppy Ears
10♦: Roars	**10♣**: Venomous sting	**10♥**: Antennae	**10♠**: Slimy
J♦: Camouflage	**J♣**: Changes color	**J♥**: Scales	**J♠**: Hooves
Q♦: Night vision	**Q♣**: Stripes	**Q♥**: Horns	**Q♠**: Multiple Tails
K♦: Flies	**K♣**: Makes cocoon	**K♥**: Tentacles	**K♠**: Vines

Adverts

Do you want to know more about the adverts that you just got? Use the oracle to discover what they are offering you in the mail.

♦ ♥	♣ ♠
A: Flowers By Aurora: Discover magical floral arrangements created by the first light of dawn.	**A**: Whimsy Toys and Oddments : Novelty items and enchanted tokens to stir the spirit of fun and wonder within.
2: Airship Tours By Sunrise: Spectacular scenic tours of the island chain from the sky. Limited seats available.	**2**: Dreamweavers: Unique furnishings and textiles imbued with comfort and ease woven from the cloth of dreams.
3: Life Elixirs By Twilight: Potions to enliven your spirit and renew your zest for life. Now open for business!	**3**: Radiant Healing Center: Holistic treatments using the life energy of nature to restore balance and tranquility.
4: Breezy Bakery: Freshly baked goods using ingredients grown by the beams of sun and moon. Open 24/7.	**4**: Cloudrunners: Urgent deliveries to anywhere - the spirit realms, the world of mortals or the heavens above!
5: Fairy Lights Decor: Brightening living spaces with shimmering lighting and effects inspired by fireflies.	**5**: Crimson Leaf Winery: Fine wines crafted from sacred grapes blessed by the harvest spirits for rich body and spirit.
6: Cloud Dreams Airbnb: Stay in cozy floating cottages tethered to the islands, offering unobstructed views of the horizon.	**6**: Arcane Ink Tattoos and Body Art: Embellish your soul's vessel with mystical sigils and symbolism using indelible inks.
7: Isle Animal Rescue: Seeking donations and volunteers to care for displaced forest creatures. Every bit helps!	**7**: Sage's Almanac: Guidance on moon phases, planting by the signs, spiritual readings and more - delivered quarterly!
8: Wayfinder Holistic Services: Custom dream interpretations and vision quest guidance to find your purpose.	**8**: Moonlight Meadery: World renowned mead crafted from blossom honey harvested by lunar light for sweet euphoria.
9: Lullaby Music Studios: Lessons on all mythic folk instruments from flutes to string harps and more.	**9**: Everwood Outfitters: Unique apparel created from fine fabrics woven by spirits of the wood for comfort and charm.
10: Spirit Tea Company: Fine teas harvested by benevolent spirits to unlock your higher self. Free samples!	**10**: Sunlit Masonry: Exquisitely crafted stoneworks imbued with light, peace and bucolic charms by artisans of the sky.
J: Lotus Spa: Holistic treatments including herbal soaks, aura cleansings and alchemical facials. Renew your spirit!	**J**: Spirit League Lending: Loans for worthy projects to nurture souls, spread joy and serve common good - good rates
Q: Twilight Forge: Handcrafted magical odds and ends including spoons that never scald, compasses that point homewards.	**Q**: Soft Landing Inn: Simple accommodations with panoramic views and morning teas infused with good dreams.
K: Wanderlust Tours: Tickets for grand adventures to realms unreachable by ordinary means! Now selling for Spring.	**K**: Fable Grove Publishing: Seeking submissions of original stories, poems and songs to delight future generations for years to come!

Creature Oraclepedia: Tiny

Name (♦ ♥)	Worth	Description
A: Flooferball	3	Fluffy sphere creatures with one large eye, they bounce around joyfully and love to play catch.
2: Brook Toggle	2	Tiny turtles that activate streams and brooks in gardens by pulling lever 'toggles' with their heads.
3: Hummilie	7	Hummingbird-like fairies that collect pollen and carry it to flowers with their songs.
4: Fuzzspore	5	Mushrooms that release 'good mood' spores when sung or played music too.
5: Gnomelet	4	Tiny toddler gnome-like creatures that enjoy helping in the gardens.
6: Glowcap	6	Mushrooms that glow soothing rainbow colors at night and provide just enough light for reading.
7: Whispter	2	Miniature whisp creatures that flit around and emit quiet whispering sounds at night.
8: Treeblet	1	Miniature maple tree creatures that emit crunchy falling leaf sounds when walked by.
9: Ladyhop	5	Graceful ladybug-like creatures that ride on leafs enjoying the wind.
10: Peep	3	Tiny owl-eyed creatures that make soft 'peeping' sounds and enjoy being cradled.
J: Burrowbud	7	Flower buds that burrow underground in winter and reemerge in spring.
Q: Click	15	A little mouse who clicks to open secret doors in the forest.
K: Wispleaf	8	Delicate floating leaf creatures that emit soft colorful glows at night.

Name (♣ ♠)	Worth	Description
A: Roostingun	13	Tiny winged creatures that joyfully fire tiny seeds from their 'roosting guns' into gardens.
2: Acornling	9	Tiny acorn creatures with deeprooted family trees that help other acorns grow.
3: Weevilite	12	Miniature friendly metallic weevil creatures that cheerfully maintain tools and machines.
4: Nestling	6	Tiny soft feathered creatures that invite other tiny beings to nest with them.
5: Droplet	18	Miniature water creatures that delight in riding on leaves and vines during rains.
6: Mossclinger	12	Tiny mossy creatures that enjoy climbing boots and then wave cheerfully from them.
7: Tuftrabbit	4	Miniature tufted rabbits that enjoy nibbling on clovers and flowers.
8: Wigglegrub	2	Tiny pink grubs that serenely 'wiggle' and emit pleasant smells as they feed.
9: Dewdropper	1	Tiny creatures that live in dewdrops and emit rainbows as they move between drops
10: Cloverkin	7	Miniature clover creatures that enjoy sharing news with other tiny beings.
J: Seedsprite	5	Tiny sprites that live in and protect plants seeds, ensuring new growth.
Q: Littledrummer	9	Miniature drumming beetle creatures that march joyfully, drumming on everything.
K: Wingleap	1	Miniature grasshopper-like creatures that enjoy launching into the air with fluttering wings.

Creature Oraclepedia: Small

Name (♦ ♥)	Worth	Description
A: Snugmus	2	Tiny snails with shells radiating warm glow that follow you around your garden.
2: Cloudfluffer	5	Floats above gathering clouds into soft shapes to make residents smile.
3: Gingerbun	5	Orange rabbit-like creatures that hop around gardens and cheer residents up with their energy and antics.
4: Leafwisp	6	Made of leaves and nature magic, they protect and tend gardens from invasive pests.
5: Pollenpip	4	Tiny fairy-like beings covered in yellow pollen that bring joy, good luck and new ideas.
6: Tundrapup	1	Fluffy white dogs that live in snowy areas and accompany residents on adventures.
7: Islandgull	8	Seagulls that deliver letters, parcels and gifts between the various floating islands.
8: Twigstrider	2	Long-legged creatures made of twigs that patrol the forests and keep them safe.
9: Mossrabbit	4	Rabbits covered in moss that tend gardens and orchards leaving them more fertile.
10: Nutmouse	2	Tiny squirrel-like mice that gather nuts, seeds and fruit to help residents with their chores.
J: Sproutfairy	6	Tiny fairy helpers that sprinkle seeds and growth magic to nurture plants.
Q: Breezebird	7	Birds that ride winds to bring news from around the realm.
K: Glinter	3	Tiny colorful fish that swim in ponds and rivers, glittering in the sunlight.

Name (♣ ♠)	Worth	Description
A: Leafhopper	1	Insect with long limbs that hops from leaf to leaf caring for plants and assisting residents.
2: Twigmonkey	2	Playful tree-dwelling monkeys that enjoy lightheartedly teasing residents.
3: Glowbee	4	Bees with glowing abdomens that illuminate gardens at night like living lanterns.

4: Mosspuma	3	The puma-like guardian of the mossy forest who keeps it safe and tranquil.
5: Scatterlamb	6	Fluffy lambs that wander carefreely through fields and meadows bringing cheer.
6: Spottedpaw	5	The loyal guardian dogs of the realm, covered in spots that glow in darkness.
7: Fuzzwing	8	Bats with fluffy wings that emerge at night to gently spread their pollen.
8: Fieldfrog	6	Frogs that sing joyful melodies from ponds to salute the new day.
9: Glowhare	19	Golden jackalope-like creatures whose antlers glow as they forage through fields at night.
10: Skyfinch	12	Colorful songbirds that signal hopeful change with their uplifting melodies.
J: Chirpsquirrel	7	Tiny squirrels that chirp cheerfully as they gather nuts and seeds to help residents.
Q: Twigling	5	Child-like creatures made of twigs who explore the realm with wide-eyed curiosity.
K: Cloudkitten	4	Playful kittens made of clouds who love to ambush and surprise residents.

Creature Oraclepedia: Medium

Name (♦ ♥)	Worth	Description
A: Mosscub	4	Bear cubs covered in soft moss who love tumbling and playing through grassy fields.
2: Nuthedge	3	Hedgehogs who collect and shape nuts, seeds and twigs into useful items for residents.
3: Cloudpup	2	Puppy-like clouds that drift across the sky spreading joy and comfort.
4: Moss Sprite	4	Tiny fairy-like creatures made of moss and mushroom that live in gardens and orchards.
5: Sky Mole	6	Round fluffy mole-like creatures with large ears that flutter around the island seeking trinkets and treasures.
6: Stilt Goat	5	Goats with long stick-like legs that balance delicately on floating branches and stones in the ponds.
7: Gleam Beetle	4	Large iridescent green beetles that feast on the nectar of blossoming flowers at dusk, coating their shells in bright colors.
8: Wisp Salamander	7	Tiny salamanders with glowing orbs along their backs that live within lanterns and lamps illuminating homes at night.
9: Bloom Butterfly	3	Beautiful winged pollinators with petal-like patterns along their wings that travel from flower to flower spreading nectar.
10: Slumber Snail	1	Large snails with spiraling shells that rest for months beneath the soil, awakening when new crops and plants breakthrough the earth.
J: Cloud Minnow	5	Tiny fish with feather-like fins that drift on the breezes between the floating islands, raining down when it storms.
Q: Dew Toad	8	Small pixel-like toads with bulging eyes that emerge from the grass to feast on insects after the morning dew falls.
K: Hiss Spider	6	Large spiders with metallic carapaces that spin iridescent webs between trees and scare off unwanted pests with loud hisses.

Name (♣ ♠)	Worth	Description
A: Mist Otter	3	Playful semi-aquatic otters with long whiskers and thick fur that slide down misty hills and swim between waterfalls.
2: Leaf Monkey	6	Curious monkeys with prehensile tails that swing from tree to tree, collecting colorful leaves to adorn their fur.
3: Drift Boar	4	Large semi-aquatic pigs with fins instead of ears that float listlessly down rivers, snorting bubbles as they doze.
4: Flutter Moth	1	Colossal moths with patterns like stained glass that emerge from their cocoons at night, fluttering slowly and awing all who see them.
5: Tumble Hedgehog	2	Little hedgehogs with upturned quills that somersault playfully down grassy hills and nap in curled-up balls in meadows.
6: Hover Bunny	7	Tiny bunnies with membranous paddle-like limbs that glide lightly on warm air currents, waving as they float past.
7: Swirl Eel	9	Transparent eels with iridescent fins that create swirling currents as they dance within ponds and puddles.
8: Circle Worm	2	Large worms that emerge after rain to create huge spiral patterns on lawns and gardens with their passage before burrowing back below.
9: Slumber Lamb	4	Lambs with velvety wool and lolling tongues that doze beneath fruit trees through the day, awakening at dusk to graze.
10: Tree Stoat	8	Long bodied Mustelids that climb trees searching for bird nests to eat from, curling up in hollows to sleep.
J: Still Slug	5	Large slugs that adhere themselves to tree trunks and walls, only moving occasionally after rains.
Q: Dew Newt	11	Salamanders that emerge from the fields after rains to feast on prey washed up by the receding waters.
K: Flap Moth	8	Gigantic nocturnal moths with intricate patterns that emerge from their cocoons, their leisurely fluttering bringing beauty to the night.

Creature Oraclepedia: Big

Name (♦ ♥)	Worth	Description
A: Cloud Sloth	4	Huge fluffy sloths that live on the cuffs of clouds, making them puff and swirl with their slow movements.
2: Wisp Deer	13	Glowing deer with antlers made of lights that roam the islands at dawn and dusk, giving trails of luminosity where they walk.
3: Living Floating Reefs	11	Large coral reef creatures that form living barriers to protect the island's cliffs.
4: Treecko	8	Tree lizard creatures that live in the branches of the ancient trees on the islands, keeping the forests alive.
5: Gem Dragons	17	Tiny dragons with gemstone horns and scales that collect shiny objects to adorn their nests.
6: Mist Vultures	11	Old wise vultures that ride the misty clouds between islands, sharing stories and knowledge with those they meet.
7: Moonglow Flits	6	Miniature moth like creatures that flutter about in the moonlight, giving off a soft glow as they dance through the silvery air.
8: Geyser Gremlins	5	Playful mischievous creatures that live in the hot springs and geyser fields, up to harmless tricks.

9: Glass Antelopes	6	Delicate antelopes with fur like glass that tinkle when they move, giving a sense of serenity and beauty.
10: Summer Sprites	9	Tiny, colorful sprites that live in the flowers and long grasses, filling the warm air with tingles of magic and joy.
J: Fallen Maple Fawns	6	Adorable twin fawns born from leaves of the maple trees, bringing renewal and hope at the beginning of each season.
Q: Dust Jackals	4	Jackal like creatures that drift through the dusty lands between islands, guardians of secrets.
K: Tide Turtles	7	Large turtles that ride the currents between the floating island clouds, their ancient shells holding memories of history and wisdom.

Name (♣ ♠)	Worth	Description
A: Dirigible Sea Serpents	4	Patchwork bears sewn together from many different fur types.
2: Patchwork Bears	3	Patchwork bears sewn together from many different fur types.
3: Air Eagle Lions	5	Majestic winged lions that soar the skies above the islands, protecting the creatures below.
4: Coral Butterflies	6	Beautiful butterflies with wings of iridescent coral, their flight turning the shores into a kaleidoscope of color and wonder.
5: Visage Foxes	7	Shapeshifting fox creatures that walk between the floating islands.
6: Luminous Fennecs	5	Glowing fennecs that live on the islands, their delight at simple things.
7: Ember Hornets	3	Tiny hornets with fiery bodies that pollinate the volcanic gardens, spreading new life.
8: Echo Harpies	4	Winged creatures that live high in the mountains, singing songs that echo across the islands.
9: Wind Whales	10	Gentle whale -like creatures that swim the breezes high above.
10: Spirit Deers	9	Deers with ethereal glowing antlers who bring messages of hope and comfort wherever they walk.
J: Woolly Mice	6	Hedgehog-like mice who live in burrows between roots.
Q: Mist Owls	7	Owls who watch over the islands through cold and misty nights.
K: Miyumi Koi	14	Protective koi fish who live in island ponds, guarding the inhabitants with patience, wisdom, and compassion.

Creature Oraclepedia: Fish

Name (♣ ♠)	Worth	Description	Name (♣ ♠)	Worth	Description
A: Skyfin	1	Translucent wings let it soar through the air.	A: Nimbusfish	1	Manipulates tiny clouds and creates drizzles.
2: Blinkfish	5	Teleports short distances by blinking its eyes.	2: Orbiter	2	Has a ring of smaller fish circling around it.
3: Coraline	4	Looks like a coral reef and hosts symbiotic algae.	3: Petaline	1	Looks like a flower and releases pollen or nectar.
4: Flasher	1	Stuns its prey with bright flashes of light.	4: Quillfish	3	Has sharp quills on its body and shoots them out.

5: Echofish	1	Navigates the murky waters with echolocation.	5: Rippler	1	Creates waves and currents with its tail fin.
6: Icebit	2	Freezes the water around it with its breath.	6: Sirena	1	Sings a hypnotic melody to enchant other creatures.
7: Shimmer	4	Changes its color and pattern to blend in.	7: Tangler	2	Has long tentacles and ensnares its prey or foes.
8: Hydron	6	Regenerates its body parts and splits into clones.	8: Umbrine	4	Manipulates shadows and hides in the dark.
9: Inkfish	3	Squirts ink to create a smokescreen.	9: Vortexa	1	Creates whirlpools and sucks in anything nearby.
10: Zapper	2	Generates electric shocks to defend itself.	10: Goblinfish	1	Has green skin and a big nose, loves shiny objects.
J: Kelpie	4	Shape-shifts into a horse-like creature on land.	J: Starfish	1	Has star-shaped body and can glow in the dark.
Q: Lanternfish	1	Lures prey with a bioluminescent organ on its forehead.	Q: Goldfish	1	Has golden scales and can float above water with magic.
K: Magmarine	2	Survives in extreme heat and spews fireballs.	K: Sunfish	6	Has a round body and can emit heat and light.

Harvest: Livestock

If you want to know how much produce you can get from a livestock, pick a card and consult the oracle that matches your creature's size. Also, use the Worth table to find out how valuable the produce is.

Worth			
♦: 1	♦: 2	♦: 3	♦: 4
♣: 2	♣: 3	♣: 4	♣: 5
♥: 3	♥: 4	♥: 5	♥: 6
♠: 4	♠: 5	♠: 6	♠: 7
Tiny	**Small**	**Medium**	**Big**
A: Insect silk	A: Wool	A: Leather	A: Fertilizer
2: Honey	2: Feathers	2: Eggs	2: Wool
3: Wax	3: Silkworm silk	3: Rendered fat	3: Hair
4: Allantoin	4: Eggs	4: Meat	4: Manure
5: Natural dyes	5: Shells	5: Skin	5: Skin
6: Dyes	6: Peptides	6: Bones	6: Bones
7: Pigments	7: Musk	7: Sinew	7: Sinew
8: Venom	8: Pheromones	8: Oils	8: Oils
9: Larvae	9: Polymers	9: Horn	9: Dairy
10: Pesticides	10: Bioplastics	10: Feather	10: Tendons
J: Enzymes	J: Scales	J: Dairy	J: Leather
Q: Mucus	Q: Cosmetics	Q: Honey	Q: Rendered fat
K: Preservatives	K: Vitamins	K: Tendons	K: Meat

Name (♦ ♥)	Worth	Description
A: Flower Bud Teacup	4	A delicate china teacup painted with blossoming flower buds, perfect for cozy evenings spent with loved ones.
2: Friend Bracelet	6	A woven bracelet that strengthens friendships the more it is worn.
3: Memory Jar	7	An old jam jar filled with trinkets and treasures that invoke fond memories.
4: Book Collection	2	A collection of pages bound together that contains written or printed information or stories.
5: Magic Music Box	4	A music box that plays a beautiful melody that fills the listener with wonder.
6: Gratitude Tea	1	Tea leaves that brew a special brew that fills the drinker with thankfulness.
7: Happiness Pin	7	A ornamental pin that fills the wearer with joy and contentment.
8: Lullaby Bell	5	A silver bell that produces a restful chime to ease one into peaceful sleep.
9: Dreamcatcher	6	A woven hoop decorated with feathers and beads that hangs above the bed.
10: Flower Crown	4	A wreath of fresh flowers that can be worn on the head.
J: Starry Night Lamp	9	A lamp that projects a soothing starry sky onto the ceiling to ease one to sleep.
Q: Moon Jar Nightlight	8	An old glass jar filled with glitter and water which casts a glow of starlight on the walls when lit, calming the spirit.
K: Garden Blessing Bell	2	A chime that rings to summon helpful faeries when rung in the garden at dusk.

Name (♣ ♠)	Worth	Description
A: Story Acorn	5	An acorn that contains a new fairy tale when planted and cared for with love.
2: Harmony Wind Chime	9	A chime that plays a soothing tune that induces peaceful feelings.
3: Warm Hug Bear	7	A stuffed teddy bear that seems to give a real comforting hug to those who need one most.
4: Heart Telescope	8	A looking glass that allows one to see the good in all things.
5: Kind Act Amulet	4	An amulet that glows warmly each time the bearer performs a selfless deed.
6: Faith Ring	5	A ring that fills the wearer with reassurance during times of doubt.
7: Gratitude Candle	6	A candle that gives off a sweet, reassuring scent when lit with thoughts of thanks.
8: Family Tree Seed	4	A seed that, when planted and cared for, grows into a symbolic tree representing one's loved ones and roots.
9: Magic Umbrella	7	An umbrella that protects the holder not only from rain but also from worries and fears.
10: Beanbag Chair	9	A soft warm cushion filled with dried beans that molds to the user's body shape.
J: Warm Fuzzy Slippers	8	Well-worn but comfy slippers that feel like walking on a sunny meadow on a spring day.
Q: Thimble Full of Hopes	5	A silver thimble filled to the brim with wishes for the future carried in a pocket.
K: Flower Bud Teacup	4	A delicate china teacup painted with blossoming flower buds, perfect for cozy evenings spent with loved ones.

Item Oraclepedia: Rare

Name (♦ ♥)	Worth	Description
A: Timeless Hourglass	21	An hourglass that instead of measuring seconds, counts some of life's most precious moments.
2: Hearthstone	17	A small rounded stone that when held, transports the holder's mind to a cozy fireside in an bygone era.
3: Locket of Memories	15	A golden locket containing a single photo that magically updates to remind its owner of loved ones
4: Bouquet Eternal	16	An enchanted bouquet that never wilts, infusing the room with the scents of spring and new beginnings.
5: Lucky Coin	18	A small copper coin that magically grows to fill its owner's hand whenever hope or courage is needed most.
6: Woven Scarf	13	A rainbow-hued scarf that warms the body and spirit, filling the wearer with nostalgic comfort.
7: Book of Wisdom	11	An endlessly refilling book that pens advice tailored for any situation, filled with serenity and insight.
8: Gardenia Brooch	15	A silver brooch in the shape of a gardenia flower, imbuing the wearer with patience and kindness.
9: Crystal Unicorn	14	A figurine carved from pale blue crystal, bringing good dreams and fortune to its owner
10: Everlasting Flute	22	A wooden flute that plays any song the owner thinks of, the music lingering in the air for minutes after.
J: Worn Journal	12	A journal filled with stories of loved ones, recipes, and a lifetime of memories.
Q: Glowing Seed	9	A tiny seed that when planted, grows into a cottage-sized tree that glows softly at night.
K: Magic Quill	17	An enchanted quill that permanently writes in gold ink, spelling out feelings of joy and wonder.

Name (♣ ♠)	Worth	Description
A: Warm Woolen Shawl	10	A knitted shawl that chases away both winter's chill and feelings of loneliness with its cozy embrace.
2: Baby Blanket Bear	11	An aging teddy bear that brings comfort and familiarity when gripped in its well-worn blanket.
3: Moonstone Phone	22	A phone that only connects the caller to those they most need to speak with, cutting through all else.
4: Fairy Figurine	24	A tiny figurine of a fairy that looks after her owner, bestowing random acts of good fortune and happiness.

5: Yarn Nest	18	A pile of leftover yarn that somehow finds its way into just the right patterns for gifting to loved ones.
6: Magic Carpet	25	A colorful and soft carpet that can fly in the air. It can carry one or more passengers, or travel to any destination.
7: Time Flower	20	A rare and mysterious flower that blooms once every hundred years. It can manipulate time or travel to different eras.
8: Fairy Wing	17	A delicate and colorful wing that comes from the playful creature of the forest. It can fly in the air or manipulate nature.
9: Mermaid Pearl	19	A smooth and lustrous pearl that comes from the beautiful creature of the sea. It can breathe underwater or control water.
10: Storybook Compass	15	A compass that always points the way to those one seeks to reconnect with, loved ones near and far.
J: Lucky Penny Bank	23	A cast iron bank that overflows with coins whenever its owner is in need of hope or opportunity.
Q: Angel Feather	22	A white and soft feather that comes from the heavenly being of grace. It can bless anyone or anything, or protect from evil.
K: Traveling Tiara	14	A transforming tiara that adjusts to fit any who wear it

Item Oraclepedia: Divine Items

Name (♦ ♣ ♥ ♠)	Worth	Description
A: Divine Enchantment	45	Grants you a +/- 1 bonus for your next Fate Step in the Blessing Ritual.
2: Celestial Aura	52	Bestows a +/- 2 bonus for your next Fate Step in the Blessing Ritual.
3: Blessed Token	60	Provides a +/- 1 bonus for your next Fate Step in the Blessed Union Ritual.
4: Sacred Relic	34	Offers a +/- 2 bonus for your next Fate Step in the Blessed Union Ritual.
5: Divine Blessing	33	Gives you a +1 bonus for your next Fate Step in the Blessed Union Ritual.
6: Cursed Talisman	46	Imparts a -1 penalty for your next Fate Step in the Blessed Union Ritual.
7: Graceful Charm	51	Grants a +1 bonus for your next Fate Step in the Blessing Ritual.
8: Ominous Amulet	47	Inflicts a -1 penalty for your next Fate Step in the Blessing Ritual.
9: Favored Trinket	48	Provides a +/- 1 bonus for your next Fate Step in any action.
10: Guiding Emblem	35	Grants a +1 bonus for your next Fate Step in any action.
J: Fading Medallion	43	Imposes a -1 penalty for your next Fate Step in any action.
Q: Enchanted Sigil	35	Enables you to gain an ability of your choice during the Blessed Union: Blessing Ritual.
K: Mirrored Talisman	41	Allows you to gain an ability that costs the same as the one you've chosen during the Blessed Union: Blessing Ritual.

Crop Oraclepedia 1

Name (♦ ♥)	Worth	Description: (Produce)	Maturity Duration
A: Joy Berry	4	Sweet crimson berries that spark a feeling of elation when tasted: **Happiness Jam**	2 Cards
2: Wind Chime Vine	6	A vine heavy with tiny silver chimes that tinkle softly in the breeze: **Melodies of Peace**	1 Card
3: Warm Hearth Mint	7	Fragrant mint leaves that emit a cozy fireplace smell when crushed: **Comfort Tea Leaves**	1 Cards
4: Be Well Blossom	9	An abundant white daisy like flower with purple centers: **Wellbeing Drops**	2 Cards
5: Sun Shine	4	A burst of tiny yellow trumpet shaped blossoms that track the sun: **Ray of Light Extract**	1 Card
6: Fire Balm	11	Smooth red leaves that give off a warm golden glow when rubbed: **Warmth Infusion**	1 Card
7: Unity Vine	7	A fast growing vine dotted with star shaped pink and yellow blooms : **Togetherness Fruit**	1 Card
8: Friend Fern	5	A gently curving fern with heart shaped fronds in varying tones of green: **Amity Leaves**	1 Card
9: Moon Lily	16	A night blooming flower with wide white petals and a pleasant silver glow: **Lunar Essence**	3 Card
10: Luck Leaf	14	A cloverlike plant with seven rounded leaves of soft green: **Lucky Charms**	3 Card
J: Heart Bloom	9	A radiant crimson flower shaped like an open lotus with soft pink stamens: **Love Nectar**	2 Cards
Q: Star Blossom	8	A delicate flower with pale yellow petals that resemble a five-pointed star: **Wish Petals**	2 Cards
K: Aurora Tulip	12	A shimmering tulip that glows a soft blue reminiscent of the aurora borealis: **Dream Catcher Bulbs**	2 Cards

Crop Oraclepedia 2

Name (♣ ♠)	Worth	Description: (Produce)	Maturity Duration
A: Hope Bulb	2	A sprout with broad foliage: **Optimism Stems**	1 Card
2: Kindness Clover	4	Four leaf clover that emits a pleasant sweet aroma: **Goodwill Petals**	1 Card
3: Peace Lily	7	A white bloom with wafting fragrance that evokes feelings of tranquility: **Serenity Pollen**	1 Cards
4: Caring Candlebush	3	This plant's glowing crimson buds are said to ignite love and compassion in all who see them: **Care Pods**	1 Card

5: Gladsome Gourd	4	Sturdy vines bearing large orange gourds said to lighten spirits and lift moods: **Cheer Seeds**	1 Card
6: Solace sage	13	Soft wooly silver foliage that releases a scent soothing to both body and spirit: **Tranquility Leaves**	1 Card
7: Happily ever herb	14	Fragrant sprigs that emit a sweet floral scent associated with joyful endings: **Contentment Spice**	1 Card
8: Phoenix Feather	18	A fiery red plants that looks like a feather. Legend says that it originates from a Phoenix: **Fire Spice**	2 Card
9: Everafter Elderberry	7	Bushes bearing berries said to induce visions of destiny and future joys: **Contentment Juice**	3 Card
10: Warm Embrace	8	Woody shrub with branches that seem to lovingly enfold and shelter what lies beneath: **Affection Leaves**	1 Card
J: Cheery Cherry	5	Trees bearing fruit that boosts cheer and whose fruits are said to ward off melancholy and sadness: **Joy Jam**	1 Card
Q: Unicorn Horn	3	A spiral-shaped horn that comes from the mythical creature of purity: **Sharp Fruit**	3 Cards
K: Starlight Bonsai	9	Miniature tree with delicate silver leaves that only fully bloom under a moonlit sky:Serenity Pollen	2 Cards

Forage

Name (♦ ♥)	Worth	Name (♣ ♠)	Worth
A: Fragrant Fern Fronds	2	**A**: Peaceful lichen	2
2: Warm cloves	3	**2**: Scented pine needles	1
3: Sweet clover blossoms	4	**3**: Joyful lady's mantle	4
4: Red maple keys	1	**4**: Hopeful mullein	5
5: Ruby rose hips	5	**5**: Spirit lifting lamb's ears	2
6: Soothing Thyme	2	**6**: Grounding mushroom mycelium	3
7: Lavender leaves	3	**7**: Witch Hazel twigs	4
8: Healing comfrey roots	4	**8**: Witch Hazel twigs	1
9: Bracing ginger roots	2	**9**: Brave pennyroyal	5
10: Happy daisies	5	**10**: Cherished snapdragons	2
J: Gold thread pods	1	**J**: Chiming bluebells	3
Q: Sunny dandelion roots	3	**Q**: Wispy willow bark	1
K: Tranquil moss	6	**K**: Serene sorrel	4

Craft Oraclepedia: Raw Materials

Name (♦ ♥)	Worth	Description
A: Leaf Circlet	3	Wreath made from autumnal foliage.
2: Fey Dust	2	Sparkling particles that fall from the wings of fairies.
3: Gold Bee Honey	9	Viscos gold liquid that hardens into steel.
4: Root Vine	5	Long woody tendril that winds.
5: Field Daisy	1	Simple yellow wildflower that fills the air.
6: Everburn Flame	7	Tiny orb of light and heat that never fades or spreads.
7: Shell Mist	3	Crystallized essence of the sea that glitters.
8: Silver Feather	2	A single iridescent feather from a rare forest bird.
9: Songroot	6	White roots that emit a soothing melody when rubbed.
10: Moss Agate	7	Green stone with wisps of pale moss trapped within.
J: Spring Blossom	4	Fragrant white and pink flower petals shimmering.
Q: Faerie Thread	3	Translucent gold string spun from faerie wing membranes.
K: White Wood	4	Pale, almost glowing lumber with a smooth texture.

Name (♣ ♠)	Worth	Description
A: River Pebble	2	Smooth orb borne from a cool, clear mountain stream.
2: Star Clovers	7	Four-leaf clovers infused with twinkling starlight.
3: Acorn Cup	5	Minuscule wooden bowls crafted from hollow acorn caps.
4: DandelionFluff	3	White fibrous seed heads.
5: Creek Stone	4	Water-worn pebble filled with the sounds of burbling.
6: Memory Sand	5	Shifting grains that re-form into past scenes.
7: Glow Moss	2	Pale vegetation that shines with an inner light.
8: Maple Syrup	3	Rich amber fluid.
9: Winter Glaze	4	Sheen of rime frost that solidify.
10: Heartwood	6	Oak beams permeated with warmth and steadfastness.
J: Crystal Dew	3	Tiny shard of frozen water that refracts the light.
Q: Twilight Berry	4	Midnight purple fruit accented with silver speckles.
K: Star Bloom	8	Exotic flower that glows softly at night.

Return Home
Page.86

+1: Fleshling	Quill of Infinite Tales
Draw 2 Raw Materials + 1 Produce.	
A magical quill that never runs out of ink. Each stroke brings forth captivating stories and vivid imagery.	

+1: Aviankin	Eye of Vision
Draw 3 Raw Materials + 1 Rare Item	
An enchanted decorative orb that grants visions of possibilities beyond the ordinary sight.	

+1: Beastkin	Gauntlets of Strength
Draw 2 Raw Materials + 1 Produce + 1 Common Item	
Forged from hide and beast, these gauntlets magnify the wearer's physical might.	

+1: Beastkin	Boots of Swiftness
Draw 1 Raw Materials + 1 Produce + 1 Common Item	
Races are easily won while wearing these speed-enhancing leather boots cushioned with grass and leaves.	

+1: Angelkin	Clockwork Bug
Draw 3 Raw Materials + 1 Produce.	
A tiny mechanical insect that delivers messages upon command with clockwork precision.	

+1: Angelkin	Dust of Vanishing
Draw 1 Raw Materials + 1 Produce.	
A pinch of powder that renders anything coated with it invisible for a short time.	

+1: Beastkin	Scroll of Protection
Draw 2 Raw Materials + 1 Produce + 1 Common Item	
An enchanted parchment scroll imbued with ancient runes that ward away evil beings.	

+1: Angelkin	Oil of Healing
Draw 2 Raw Materials + 2 Produce.	
Restore vigor and mend wounds with this potent herbal infusion in olive oil.	

+1: Angelkin	Crystal Key
Draw 1 Produce + 1 Item + 1 Forage	
A key fashioned from precious semi-precious stones that unlocks doors.	

+1: Aviankin	Belt of Weightlessness
Draw 1 Raw Materials + 2 Produce + 1 Rare Item	
A simple yet magical leather belt that allows the wearer to defy gravity at a whim.	

+1: Aviankin	Sapphire Compass
Draw 2 Raw Materials + 1 Forage + 1 Rare Item	
A delicate navigational tool with a sapphire point that always points to one's desired destination.	

+1: Fleshling	Wand of Wonder
Draw 2 Raw Materials + 1 Produce.	
A whimsical wooden wand with a rainbow spinel gem that casts amusing yet harmless magical effects.	

+1: Fleshling	Helmet of Thought
Draw 1 Raw Materials + 2 Produce.	
Wear this finely wrought helmet set with lapis lazuli to sharpen insights, trigger epiphanies and unleash creative thought.	

+1: Fleshling	Journal of Ideas
Draw 3 Raw Materials + 1 Produce.	
A blank journal bound in veg-tanned leather, its pages fill with inspiration and actionable concepts upon command.	

+1: Aviankin	Gloves of Archery
Draw 3 Raw Materials + 1 Produce.	
These unassuming yet enchanted gloves allow their wearer to notch, draw and loose any projectile with unmatched precision.	

+1: Beastkin	Gauntlets of Mining
Draw 2 Raw Materials + 2 Produce.	
Forged for strength and durability, these gauntlets grant superhuman abilities when hacking, digging and chiseling stone.	

+1: Fleshling	Slippers of the Swamp	+1: Angelkin	Amulet of Far Sight
Draw 2 Raw Materials + 2 Produce + 1 Common Item		*Draw 2 Raw Materials + 2 Produce.*	
Easy and lightweight, these leather slippers enchanted with mud and moss allow silent, swamp-like movement.		Crafted from hawk feathers and amber stones, this amulet grants visions of things far away when one gazes into it.	

+1: Angelkin	Ring of Fire	+1: Fleshling	Pot of Growth
Draw 1 Raw Materials + 1 Produce + 1 Rare Item		*Draw 1 Raw Materials + 1 Produce + 1 Rare Item*	
A simple red garnet ring that grants fiery powers to its wearer such as the ability to summon and control small flames.		A simple yet enchanted earthenware pot, when planted with a seed it nurtures explosive, supercharged growth.	

+1: Aviankin	Pinwheel Wind Charm	+1: Beastkin	Flower Patch Sachet
Draw 2 Raw Materials + 2 Produce.		*Draw 2 Raw Materials + 2 Produce.*	
Spin this colorful paper pinwheel on a breeze to usher in good tidings and excite daydreams of faraway adventures.		Fill your room with the sweet aroma of this sachet filled with dried wildflower petals to lift your spirits and renew your energy.	

+1: Fleshling	Patchwork Quilt	+1: Angelkin	String of Friendship
Draw 2 Forage + 1 Produce + 1 Common Item		*Draw 1 Raw Materials + 2 Produce.*	
Snuggle under this one-of-a-kind heirloom quilt, each piece representing a story, a place and a face that warms your heart.		Treasured homemade bracelets tied around wrists, each knot representing a cherished connection that enriches your life.	

+2: Aviankin	Hand Warmers	+2: Aviankin	Windchime of Hope
Draw 2 Forage + 1 Raw Material + 2 Favor.		*Draw 1 Forage + 1 Raw Material + 2 Favor + 1 Rare Item*	
Warm your hands by this basket filled with soft wool infused with the soothing scent of lavender to lift your spirits.		The melodic chiming of this windchime recalls a distant happy place in your thoughts.	

+2: Fleshling	Clay Flower Pot	+2: Beastkin	Painted Rock Collection
Draw 2 Forage + 1 Produce + 2 Favor + 1 Common Item		*Draw 1 Produce + 2 Raw Material + 2 Favor.*	
Tend to this simple handcrafted pot as you witness the wonder of new life taking root.		Decorating smooth rocks with vivid colors seems a small act yet brings joy in sharing these shiny tokens of happiness.	

+2: Fleshling	Bookmark of Beginnings	+2: Angelkin	Homemade Origami Figures
Draw 3 Forage + 1 Raw Material + 1 Favor.		*Draw 2 Produce + 2 Raw Material + 1 Favor.*	
A meaningful bookmark marks the start of a hopeful journey through new stories.		Each neatly folded paper shape brings back fond memories of a patient teacher and hazy afternoons filled with giggles.	

+2: Beastkin	Rainstick Rhythm	+2: Angelkin	Solar Powered Lantern
Draw 1 Forage + 1 Raw Material + 1 Favor + 1 Rare Item		*Draw 2 Forage + 1 Favor.*	
The joyful shaker rattles of this rainstick crafted with loving care evoke thoughts of better times.		Although simple, the gift of this reliable source of light imbues a sense of security, hope and warmth.	

+1: Fleshling	Blossom's Sweetbread
Draw 2 Produce + 1 Forage	
Baked goods made with flour enchanted by fairy dust, giving it an ethereal quality and natural sweetness.	

+1: Aviankin	Rosehip Cream Cake
Draw 2 Produce + 2 Forage	
A small cake baked with rosehip cream filling and topped with rose petals, bringing to mind summer picnics.	

+1: Angelkin	Elderberry Fizz
Draw 3 Produce + 1 Forage	
A bubbly, refreshing drink made from elderberries picked by friendly forest spirits, imbuing it with their good cheer.	

+1: Beastkin	Broomstick Candy
Draw 1 Produce + 3 Forage	
Hard candy sticks made from autumn maple syrup that grant a feeling of soaring freedom when tasted.	

+1: Aviankin	Spirit of the Forest Stew
Draw 3 Produce + 2 Forage	
A hearty stew made with ingredients foraged from the forest and blessed by woodland spirits.	

+1: Angelkin	Calamari Rings
Draw 2 Produce + 3 Forage	
Fried calamari rings made from crisp flour.	

+1: Angelkin	Koi Pond Kale Chips
Draw 2 Produce + 2 Forage	
Kale chips seasoned with flavored"pond water" made from enchanted spring.	

+1: Aviankin	Everlasting Pastry Dough
Draw 2 Produce + 2 Forage	
A self-kneading dough blessed with longevity, able to rise and bake into pastries.	

+1: Beastkin	Gemstone Muffins
Draw 4 Produce + 1 Raw Material	
Muffins speckled with glittering gemstone chips that fill one's thoughts with childhood memories.	

+1: Aviankin	Sea Salt Caramels
Draw 1 Produce + 1 Forage + 1 Raw Material	
Caramels infused with delectable sea salt harvested from an enchanted shoreline.	

+1: Aviankin	Featherlight Waffles
Draw 2 Produce + 1 Forage + 1 Raw Material	
Waffles impossibly light and crispy, made by woodland elves during their merriest revelries	

+1: Fleshling	Golden Tea Biscuits
Draw 1 Produce + 2 Forage + 1 Raw Material	
Buttery shortbread biscuits imbued with the magic of lazy summer afternoons	

+1: Angelkin	Spirited Egg Nog
Draw 1 Produce + 1 Forage + 2 Raw Material	
A creamy, spicy egg nog made with milk blessed by winter spirits, filling the imbiber with warmth.	

+1: Fleshling	Summer Sprite Pie
Draw 3 Produce + 1 Forage + 1 Raw Material	
A sweet pie filling made with berries and fruits grown under the watchful gaze of summer sprites.	

+1: Aviankin	Wisher's Bread
Draw 1 Produce + 3 Forage + 1 Raw Material	
Baked goods made with flour enchanted by those who wish upon falling stars.	

+1: Beastkin	Melodie' Tea Biscuits
Draw 1 Produce + 3 Forage + 1 Raw Material	
Buttery shortbread biscuits flavored with the sweet music of marsh melodies.	

Craft Oraclepedia: Food Recipe 2

+1: Angelkin	Stardust Macarons
Draw 3 Produce + 2 Raw Material	
Macarons filled with stardust-infused buttercream that sparkles and shines.	

+1: Aviankin	Gnome Gingersnaps
Draw 4 Forage + 1 Raw Material	
Gingersnaps baked by hardworking garden gnomes during their celebrations, imparting a spirit of joy.	

+1: Beastkin	Fairy Frond Spoon Bread
Draw 3 Forage + 2 Raw Material	
Cornbread laced with fairy fronds that bring to mind sunlit glades and laughter of fairies at play, filling one with wonder.	

+1: Fleshling	Everbloom Tea Cakes
Draw 4 Produce	
Small cakes made with self-refreshing blossoms that smell of spring renewal and fresh beginnings.	

+1: Fleshling	Twinkletale Pie
Draw 3 Produce	
A magical pie filled with fruit that trigger stories upon eating.	

+1: Angelkin	Acorn Stew of Wisdom
Draw 3 Forage	
A hearty stew made from ingredients foraged by wise forest creatures.	

+1: Angelkin	Waffle of Joy
Draw 3 Raw Materials + 1 Favor.	
A crispy waffle that is drizzled with maple syrup and butter.	

+2: Beastkin	Xocolatl of Wisdom
Draw 2 Raw Materials + 2 Favor.	
An ancient drink that is made with cacao beans, chili peppers, honey, and vanilla.	

+2: Angelkin	Songbird Sugar Cookies
Draw 3 Forage + 2 Favor.	
Cookies baked to the tune of songbirds during springtime, filled with memories of happier times.	

+2: Aviankin	Moonbeam Muffins
Draw 3 Produce + 2 Favor.	
Muffins dotted with dewdrops collected under a full moon, evoking feelings of wonder and magic.	

+1: Beastkin	Spirit Grove Salad
Draw 3 Forage + 1 Favor.	
Lettuce grown with care from nature spirits, filled with peaceful energy that uplifts the spirit.	

+2: Fleshling	Starshine Lemonade
Draw 1 Forage + 1 Produce + 2 Favor.	
A lemonade made from lemons that fell to earth from the heavens, instilling hope in those who drink it.	

+2: Beastkin	Everclover Tea Biscuits
Draw 2 Forage + 2 Raw Material + 1 Favor.	
Shortbread cookies that bring to mind frolicking in fields of endless clover, filling one's heart with contentment.	

+2: Angelkin	Dandelion Wine
Draw 2 Raw Material + 2 Produce + 1 Favor.	
Wine made from eternal dandelions, transporting drinkers back to carefree days of youth.	

+2: Aviankin	Gladegather Stew
Draw 3 Forage + 1 Raw Material + 1 Favor.	
A potage made from forest offerings that leaves the eater filled with a sense of belonging and oneness with nature.	

+2: Fleshling	Snowglobe Ice Cream
Draw 2 Forage + 2 Produce + 1 Favor.	
Ice cream packed with mini gifts that trigger nostalgic memories perfect for quiet wintry evenings.	

Power:	**Stroke of Luck**	**Divine Favor Cost:**	12

With a mere stroke of luck, you can elevate the outcome of a Fate Draw. Move a result up a single tier. *Note this sequence: Critical Failure > Failure > Success > Plot Twist > Critical Success.*

Power:	**Physical Enhancement**	**Divine Favor Cost:**	12

Engage in physical activities such as adventures, fishing, or field work with enhanced prowess. Gain an additional +1 to your attribute bonus during Fate Draw.

Power:	**Joker's Blessing**	**Divine Favor Cost:**	12

The Joker's Blessing bestows upon you exceptional fortune. Double your attribute bonus during Fate Draw, amplifying your chances of success.

Power:	**Angel's Touch**	**Divine Favor Cost:**	14

In times of need, the Angel's Touch grants rejuvenation. Recover 2 Energy, replenishing your vitality and allowing you to continue your endeavors.

Power:	**Chrono Cross**	**Divine Favor Cost:**	16

Harness the manipulation of time itself through the Chrono Cross ability. Move your Time Token backward by 1 Time Section (TS), enabling you to gain more time.

Power:	**Fortune's Blessing**	**Divine Favor Cost:**	14

With Fortune's Blessing, increase your odds of success in Fate Draw. Gain an additional +1 bonus to your Fate Draw, allowing you to achieve favorable outcomes more frequently.

Power:	**Fateful Intuition**	**Divine Favor Cost:**	12

Tap into your intuition and make calculated decisions. Draw another Fate Card and use your instincts to select the more advantageous result.

Power:	**Fate Manipulation**	**Divine Favor Cost:**	12

As a master of fate, you can bend the outcome to your advantage. Choose a card from the Fate Deck and replace it with a card from the Main Deck, giving you greater control over your destiny.

Power:	**Serendipitous Encounter**	**Divine Favor Cost:**	12

Serendipitous Encounter grants you the power of synchronicity. Trigger a Scenario or Seasonal Scenario to embark on unexpected and delightful adventures.

Power:	Inner Resilience	Divine Favor Cost:	20

Unlock your inner resilience to overcome adversity. A Critical Failure now turns into a Plot Twist, allowing you to embrace challenges and find silver linings.

Power:	Harmonious Balance	Divine Favor Cost:	14

Achieve a Harmonious Balance with nature and the world around you. Change the weather to any condition you desire, creating a tranquil and harmonious environment.

Power:	Abundant Harvest	Divine Favor Cost:	18

Tap into the bountiful energies of the land. Increase the worth of your harvested items by +1, allowing you to reap greater rewards from your efforts.

Power:	Joyful Celebration	Divine Favor Cost:	12

Embrace the spirit of celebration and camaraderie. Trigger a Seasonal Festival and indulge in the joyous festivities with your fellow islanders.

Power:	Everlasting Bond	Divine Favor Cost:	14

Forge an Everlasting Bond with the islanders. A Critical Success during the Blessed Union: Blessing now grants an additional +2 bonus, deepening your connections.

Power:	Pristine Exchange	Divine Favor Cost:	16

With Pristine Exchange, reduce the required craft ingredients by 1 card, making crafting simpler and more efficient.

Power:	Respite of Nature	Divine Favor Cost:	14

Immerse yourself in the Respite of Nature. Resting now grants an additional +1 Energy replenish, restoring your vitality and energy.

Power:	Masterful Artistry	Divine Favor Cost:	18

Unleash your Masterful Artistry to transform the ordinary into the extraordinary. Instantly complete a crafted item, showcasing your artistic prowess.

Power:	Divine Providence	Divine Favor Cost:	14

With Divine Providence, gain insight into the mysteries of fate. Draw 2 cards from the top of the Fate Deck and select the most favorable one for your situation.

Ability Oraclepedia

Power:	**Renewed Vigor**	**Divine Favor Cost:**	*14*

Reinvigorate your spirit with Renewed Vigor. Gain a +/-1 bonus during the Blessed Union: Blessing, increasing the likelihood of a successful outcome.

Power:	**Essence of Serenity**	**Divine Favor Cost:**	*16*

Channel the Essence of Serenity to harmonize with the world around you. Instantly reverse the Action's Critical Success to Critical Failure, and Success to Failure.

Power:	**Dreamweaver's Blessing**	**Divine Favor Cost:**	*12*

With the Dreamweaver's Blessing, gain the power to alter dreams and destinies. Trigger a Seasonal Scenario to shape the course of fate.

Power:	**Celestial Bounty**	**Divine Favor Cost:**	*20*

Unleash the blessings of the heavens with Celestial Bounty. Double a Bonus in your Bonus Sheet, amplifying its effects.

Power:	**Spirit Guide Item Swap**	**Divine Favor Cost:**	*18*

Embrace the guidance of the Spirit Guide. Change an Item from your inventory with an item of your choice, allowing you to equip yourself for upcoming challenges.

Power:	**Arcane Craft**	**Divine Favor Cost:**	*14*

Preserve the mystical energy within Arcane Preservation. Draw a Card from the Main Deck and choose an Oracle to generate a random item and add it into your inventory.

Power:	**Enchanted Forging**	**Divine Favor Cost:**	*18*

Tap into Enchanted Forging to enhance your crafting prowess. Increase the worth of crafted items by +2, creating valuable creations.

Power:	**Harmonic Symphony**	**Divine Favor Cost:**	*12*

Unleash the Harmonic Symphony to orchestrate your fate. Rearrange the top 5 cards of the deck during a mini-game, optimizing your chances of success.

Power:	**Radiant Embrace**	**Divine Favor Cost:**	*14*

Radiant Embrace infuses you with divine energy. Use 1 Power instead of using 2 Energy when performing any ability or action that requires 2 Energy.

| *Power:* | Twilight Whispers | Divine Favor Cost: | 12 |

Embrace the serenity of nature's whispers. Add -1 Bonus to your Fate Draw, granting you a moment of tranquility and focus.

| *Power:* | Lucky Trinket | Divine Favor Cost: | 14 |

Carry a Lucky Trinket that enhances your chances. Add +2 Bonus to your Fate Draw, attracting good fortune to your endeavors.

| *Power:* | Cursed Talisman | Divine Favor Cost: | 14 |

Beware the Cursed Talisman's influence. Add -2 Bonus to your Fate Draw, testing your resilience in the face of adversity.

| *Power:* | Rich Harvest | Divine Favor Cost: | 18 |

Nurture your crops with care. Increase Item Worth by +2, reaping bountiful rewards from your harvest.

| *Power:* | Charismatic Aura | Divine Favor Cost: | 14 |

Radiate a natural charm that endears you to others. You gain an additional +1 Favor when receiving Favor, fostering strong bonds with the community.

| *Power:* | Spirit's Embrace | Divine Favor Cost: | 16 |

The Spirit's Embrace grants divine support. You gain a +-1 Bonus during the Blessed Union: Blessing, connecting you to the spiritual realm.

| *Power:* | Celestial Benediction | Divine Favor Cost: | 20 |

Seek blessings from the heavens. You gain a +-2 Bonus during the Blessed Union: Blessing, drawing upon celestial favor.

| *Power:* | Reversal of Fate | Divine Favor Cost: | 12 |

Unravel the threads of fate itself. At any time if you -1 Favor, void that event, granting you a chance to rewrite your destiny.

| *Power:* | Divine Intervention | Divine Favor Cost: | 14 |

Call upon the divine for assistance. At any time if you -1 Divine Favor, void that event, invoking the Goddess's benevolent guidance.

Ability Oraclepedia

Power:	**Favorable Winds**	**Divine Favor Cost:**	20

Harness the winds of change. At any time if you -1 Favor, you gain +1 Favor instead, guiding your fate toward positivity.

Power:	**Divine Grace**	**Divine Favor Cost:**	18

Embrace the Goddess's grace. At any time if you -1 Divine Favor, you gain +1 Divine Favor instead, drawing her blessings to your side.

Power:	**Fortunate Twist**	**Divine Favor Cost:**	16

Unravel the threads of destiny. A Critical Success turns into Plot Twist, opening up new possibilities amidst your journey.

Power:	**Fortune's Gamble**	**Divine Favor Cost:**	16

Embrace the thrill of chance. A Critical Failure turns into Plot Twist, offering a glimmer of hope even in moments of misfortune.

Power:	**Twist of Fate**	**Divine Favor Cost:**	14

Bend the rules of destiny. A Success/Failure turns into Plot Twist, revealing unexpected outcomes in the course of your adventures.

Power:	**Elemental Command**	**Divine Favor Cost:**	12

Command the skies and the seas. You can change the weather to any weather you want, influencing the world's climate.

Power:	**Fate's Reversal**	**Divine Favor Cost:**	18

Twist the fabric of reality. Reverse the Action's Critical Success to Critical Failure and Success to Failure, reshaping the course of events.

Power:	**Master Artisan**	**Divine Favor Cost:**	16

Embrace the skills of a master craftsman. Instantly complete a Craft item, showcasing your craftsmanship and expertise.

Power:	**Master of Chronos**	**Divine Favor Cost:**	22

At any time, Pay 2 Power to unlock 5-Section Clock for a single day.

General Scenario Oracle

A♦: A young child discovers a baby bird that fell from its nest on a passing island. You help reunite them.	**A♣**: Island children convince you to join their make-believe adventures around the island as a brave knight.
2♦: You find a message in a bottle that floated from a faraway island. It contains a secret map.	**2♣**: You stumble upon a grove of rare singing flowers. Their haunting melodies draw in villagers.
3♦: Your friend is lovesick for someone who lives on another island. You help them arrange a meeting.	**3♣**: An important barge delivery is delayed. You volunteer to help distribute goods to villagers in need.
4♦: A famous pastry chef opens a new bakery on your island. Long lines form as villagers eagerly await a taste.	**4♣**: Your friend twists their ankle foraging in the Wilderness. Bring them home safely.
5♦: A traveling circus arrives, bringing wondrous acts and performances to dazzle the villagers.	**5♣**: A talented violinist arrives from a faraway island. You help organize a welcoming concert.
6♦: You discover a hidden grotto beneath your island, filled with bioluminescent plants and glowing crystals.	**6♣**: You nurse an injured baby creature back to health after finding it in the forest. Its parents watch over you.
7♦: An important island holiday is approaching. You help villagers prepare celebrations and decorations.	**7♣**: A young entrepreneur opens a popular seamstress shop using rare silks traded from passing islands.
8♦: A mysterious stranger arrives, claiming to be from a legendary lost island. You are skeptical of their far-fetched tales.	**8♣**: A painter arrives seeking an apprentice. With practice, you find you have talent capturing the beauty around you.
9♦: You find a forgotten library on an uninhabited island filled with rare books. You begin restoring it to share with others.	**9♣**: You join a group of islanders who are planning a surprise party for their friend's birthday. Help them bake cake, decorate the venue, and prepare some games
10♦: Two islands collide during a storm! Thankfully no one was hurt, and you help reroute foot traffic afterwards.	**10♣**: You suspect someone is stealing eggs from the communal creature coop. You decide to investigate.
J♦: Your friend invites you to a moon viewing party on their island's highest hill to gaze at the night sky.	**J♣**: An elderly neighbor asks you to deliver a heartfelt love letter to their childhood sweetheart.
Q♦: A kindly widow teaches you how to brew homemade ciders and wines using island fruits.	**Q♣**: You discover a forgotten lighthouse and restore it to help guide passing ships. Its beacon shines once more.
K♦: You discover the island's bees have escaped from their hive! Working together, you safely capture them.	**K♣**: A renowned chef opens a new restaurant on your island, drawing visitors from across the sky.

Return Home
Page.86

General Scenario Oracle

A♥: You volunteer at the island animal rescue to help care for orphaned and injured creatures.	**A♠**: A renowned singer arrives from a distant land. You organize impromptu performances around the island.
2♥: Your friend gets lost in a dense fog. You organize a search party to find them.	**2♠**: You recruit volunteers to help build a community greenhouse to share crops.
3♥: The island children convince you to tell stories around a campfire. Their favorite is how the islands came to float.	**3♠**: Your cousin gets married on a faraway island. You help arrange travel for attending relatives.
4♥: On a moonless night, you witness mysterious glowing lights dancing above the forest.	**4♠**: On a market trip, you find rare spices traded from exotic islands. You buy some to experiment with.
5♥: You counsel an anxious friend who wants to confess their feelings to their crush.	**5♠**: An old widow needs help repairing her roof. You and your friends spend the day fixing it.
6♥: A package accidentally falls from a passing hot air balloon onto your doorstep.	**6♠**: You find a stray puppy during a storm. No one claims it, so you bring it home.
7♥: You discover an overgrown stone labyrinth and decide to restore it as a meditative space.	**7♠**: You find a rare seashell washed up from a distant ocean. You donate it to the island museum.
8♥: You volunteer at a clinic providing healthcare to those on remote islands.	**8♠**: You volunteer to run the children's crafts booth at the harvest festival.
9♥: An eager young inventor asks you to invest in their design for airship propellers.	**9♠**: Your neighbor invites you to join a star gazing party on their roof to witness a comet.
10♥: You take up birdwatching and document sightings from migrating flocks travelling between islands.	**10♠**: You discover an abandoned orchard and revive it to provide fresh fruit for the village.
J♥: Your friend sprains their wrist, so you help out by tending their garden.	**J♠**: The island matchmaker invites you and your friends to a singles mingling event.
Q♥: Your neighbors surprise you with a housewarming party in your new home.	**Q♠**: You take up carpentry and build custom furniture for fellow villagers.
K♥: You discover a hidden hot spring beneath a waterfall's cave. It becomes a popular gathering place.	**K♠**: A sickness spreads quickly across neighboring islands. You volunteer delivering medicine.

Strange Scenario Oracle

A♦: You spot an abandoned hot air balloon caught in the branches of a tree on your island. Upon inspection, you find the initials of a country engraved on its side.

A♣: You rescue a team of scientists whose weather balloon crashed onto your island. They reward you with data on conditions far below.

2♦: A piece of a billboard slogan floats up from the world below. You puzzle over what the full advertisement was.

2♣: You stumble upon an odd metallic orb. When you touch it, holograms of major cities flicker around you.

3♦: You discover a solar-powered satellite phone washed up on the lake. When you answer, a confused voice asks your location.

3♣: Your friends dare you to leap onto a passing low-flying plane using a parachute. You successfully land inside the cargo hold.

4♦: Loud sonic booms shake your island, and in the distance you see strange jet trails in the sky below.

4♣: You discover a discarded personal diary. Passages describe living in poverty in an unfamiliar world you've never seen.

5♦: A capsule floats up containing a crying baby inside. You search for clues to locate its parents far below.

5♣: You comfort two children who cling to the wreckage of a strange vehicle known as a "hot air balloon".

6♦: You uncover a hidden radio receiver picking up broadcasts from a major city on the ground. Snippets of news filter up.

6♣: A printed sheet blows by bearing unfamiliar faces titled "Wanted by the FBI." You puzzle over what law they broke.

7♦: A pigeon with a message capsule tied to its leg lands on your island. The note contains coordinates and a cry for help.

7♣: Lightning strikes an object falling from the sky, embedding odd silicon wafers onto your landscape.

8♦: You spot an offshore oil rig far below. That night your island is showered with debris when it catastrophically explodes.

8♣: While camping you witness a fireball crashing into the distant earth. Tracking its impact point, you set out to find the meteorite.

9♦: A suitcase washes up the lake containing jewelry, business cards, and a gun. Just what happened to its owner?

9♣: You discover a waterlogged duffel bag stuffed with gold bars and casino chips worth a fortune below.

10♦: You discover a discarded astronaut helmet containing photos of distant earth and a cryptic message inside.

10♣: Exploring a cave, you find a skeleton clutching a briefcase handcuffed to its wrist.

J♦: A crumpled and singed paper floats by bearing a faded but legible breaking news headline about a major disaster.

J♣: You rescue a team of smugglers when their plane sputters and crashes onto your island.

Q♦: You comfort a man who parachuted onto your island, claiming his plane was hijacked during flight.

Q♣: You rescue two children clinging to a small house ripped from its foundation during a major storm far below.

K♦: Sightseeing on a low island, you witness a massive multicar collision unfold on a highway far below.

K♣: You come upon a crashed spacecraft from a distant world. Inside you find only dust and cobwebs.

Strange Scenario Oracle

A♥: While stargazing, you witness a brilliant flash. Tracking the disturbance, you find a crashed probe filled with photos of other worlds.

A♠: You decipher the notes of a deceased islander, detailing their exploration of a wrecked submarine at the bottom of the clouds.

2♥: You comfort a cruise ship survivor found adrift in a lifeboat. They describe glimpsing a mythical floating island after their ship sunk.

2♠: You discover a camera encased in a waterproof drone. Reviewing the footage reveals striking aerial views of bustling cities in a strange world.

3♥: Your friend dares you to leap onto a passing zeppelin using a parachute. You become stranded when it immediately changes course.

3♠: You find an odd pair of infrared goggles that lets you witness stunning images of volcanic eruptions, missile launches, and meteor impacts far below.

4♥: Your island is showered with pamphlets depicting faraway places and bearing a single word: "Wish you were here!"

4♠: You come upon a makeshift grave with a helmet engraved "Lost Astronaut - dies returning from Mars 2032".

5♥: You discover a working mobile phone dropped from the cargo of a passing airplane. You ponder whether to keep it.

5♠: A message in a bottle directs you to a hidden cave containing DNA samples of extinct creatures like dinosaurs.

6♥: You watch in awe as a rocket launches into space from a site far below. Tracking its orbit, you find a discarded component, still warm from its journey.

6♠: A espionage drone falls onto your landscape bearing warning signs in unfamiliar languages. You suspect it was monitoring activity far below.

7♥: You pull a waterlogged suitcase from the lake containing ornate relics and jewelry dating back centuries.

7♠: You come upon a forgotten cemetery holding generations of bodies from a surface city.

8♥: Your nets snag an experimental underwater drone. It contains footage of coral cities, shipwrecks, and mythical ocean creatures.

8♠: You help an injured pilot whose fighter jet crashed after encountering a strange distortion in the sky. No record exists of the craft originating anywhere.

9♥: You comfort two children found adrift in a life raft. Between sobs, they describe fleeing a war-torn country far below.

9♠: A message in a bottle contains a hand-drawn map of a seemingly utopian island nation thriving deep under the ocean waves.

10♥: A frozen capsule washes up containing ancient plant matter. You cultivate the species, rediscovering fruits and flowers not seen in generations.

10♠: You rescue a team of architects when their experimental airship splutters and crashes on your land. Their blueprints depict wondrous floating cities.

J♥: You comfort two elders found adrift who describe fleeing rising waters consuming their island home.

J♠: A message in a bottle warns of a new World War brewing among powerful nations. You hope wiser voices prevail far below.

Q♥: You come upon a wrecked sailboat. The hull contains odd artifacts from a legendary lost continent mentioned in vague rumors.

Q♠: You happen upon a crashed spacecraft bearing symbols matching those of ancient ruins on your island. Exploring further reveals you are all interlinked.

K♥: Exploring a cave, you find a forgotten bunker stocked for doomsday by a long-deceased survivalist.

K♠: You discover a cache of cryogenically frozen seeds from extinct plants.

Favor Scenario Oracle

A♦: They ask you to stargaze with them and confide their dreams of exploring space one day.	**A♣**: They share their favorite constellation and stargazing memories growing up.
2♦: They reveal their passion for painting and ask if you'd pose for a portrait to hang in their home.	**2♣**: They ask what home means to you and confide their difficulty finding where they truly belong.
3♦: They confide their worries about being good enough and ask you to help them see their strengths.	**3♣**: They reveal their passion for volunteering and invite you to join them at the local food bank.
4♦: They teach you a family recipe that's been passed down generations and ask you to cook it together.	**4♣**: They surprise you with a cake on your birthday and wish for you to make a meaningful wish.
5♦: They surprise you by decorating your farmhouse with flowers and ask you on a picnic date.	**5♣**: They ask you to help pick their outfit for their first school dance and confide their nerves.
6♦: They invite you hiking and at the summit, they thank you for inspiring them to face their fear.	**6♣**: They invite you to meet their beloved childhood pet and share what that pet means to their family.
7♦: They reveal their childhood dream of being a writer and ask you to brainstorm story ideas with them.	**7♣**: They confide their stage fright before a musical recital and ask you to cheer them on.
8♦: They share their favorite book with you and ask what novel impacted you profoundly.	**8♣**: They teach you a few chords on their favorite instrument and ask you to jam together.
9♦: They confide their sadness over a friend moving away and ask you to send that friend well wishes.	**9♣**: They share their favorite fairy tales from childhood and ask you to recount your own favorites.
10♦: They ask your advice on overcoming heartbreak after a tough breakup.	**10♣**: They confide feeling homesick and ask if you'll build a blanket fort for comfort like when they were young.
J♦: They invite you to meet their childhood best friend visiting town.	**J♣**: They reveal their acceptance to their dream college and happily make plans for the future with you.
Q♦: They teach you to skip rocks and share how the rhythmic waves inspire them.	**Q♣**: They express feeling lost about what career path to take and ask your advice.
K♦: They ask you to watch the sunset with them and reveal their dream of traveling the world.	**K♣**: They surprise you with concert tickets to your favorite band and joyfully express their love.

Favor Scenario Oracle

A ♥: They ask you to dance in the rain with them like when they were young and carefree.	**A ♠**: They surprise you with cooking lessons as a meaningful gift to grow together.
2 ♥: They confide their parents' divorce and ask if you'll accompany them while they tell their sibling.	**2 ♠**: They confide feeling depressed lately and ask you to encourage them to see their inner light.
3 ♥: They share their favorite family traditions and ask you to partake in them together.	**3 ♠**: They express frustration in learning a new skill and seek your guidance to persevere.
4 ♥: They express having a traumatic nightmare and ask you to hold them until they fall back asleep.	**4 ♠**: They nervously reveal their singing talent through a song written for you.
5 ♥: They confide their grief over a grandparent's passing and ask you to reminisce together about happy memories.	**5 ♠**: They ask to cuddle under the stars and ruminate on the meaning of life together.
6 ♥: They surprise you with a promise ring and ask you to promise your love will last.	**6 ♠**: They express their sorrow over an ill parent and ask you to visit them in the hospital together.
7 ♥: They nervously rehearse proposing to you, then ecstatically ask for your hand in marriage once ready.	**7 ♠**: They share their deepest regrets and ask you to help them forgive themselves.
8 ♥: They express anxiety about having kids and ask you to soothe their worries.	**8 ♠**: They surprise you with adoption paperwork, overjoyed to start a family together.
9 ♥: They proudly show you ultrasound photos after finding out they are expecting.	**9 ♠**: They reminisce happily about raising children together and express pride in the adults they've become.
10 ♥: They fondly reminisce about the day they first met you.	**10 ♠**: They recount the ups and downs of your relationship and thank you for sticking by their side.
J ♥: They recount falling in love with you and thank you for your steadfast support.	**J ♠**: They ask you to renew your vows on a sunset beach, promising their friendship.
Q ♥: They express feeling overwhelmed with life and ask you to escape to the beach together and unwind.	**Q ♠**: They ask you to accompany them on a trip to another island
K ♥: They share their childhood dream of flying and ask you to fly a kite with them.	**K ♠**: They give you a nickname

**Return Home
Page.86**

Favor Scenario Oracle: Drama

A♦: Your childhood sweetheart returns to your island after years abroad. You learn if absence really makes the heart grow fonder.

A♣: A childhood friend you grew up with proposes marriage. You are unsure if your platonic affection could become romantic love.

2♦: Your best friend reveals they have feelings for you. You weigh possibly risking the friendship for romance.

2♣: Your new partner pressures you to take the relationship further, faster than you expected.

3♦: You comfort a heartbroken neighbor after their lover departed for another island.

3♣: Your lover gets an opportunity on a distant island, but wants you to leave everything behind and come too.

4♦: A passionate summer romance cools when your partner returns home. Was it meant to last?

4♣: Your partner pressures you to introduce them to your family, but you suspect they won't approve.

5♦: You discover two villagers secretly dating despite their families' generations-long feud.

5♣: You learn your new love interest left someone heartbroken when they fled their last island home.

6♦: A new villager arrives, and multiple islanders compete for their affection.

6♣: Your lover surprises you with a secret romantic hideaway on a secluded island.

7♦: Your partner seems distracted. You suspect they may be growing close to another.

7♣: An elder you care for shares their story of losing their true love years ago. You are moved by their heartbreak.

8♦: Your friends convince you to meet them at a singles event on a nearby island.

8♣: Your partner forgets your anniversary. They scramble to plan a belated surprise.

9♦: You learn your new love interest is arranged to marry someone on their home island.

9♣: Sailing alone, you meet eyes with a stranger passing by on another ship. Was it love at first sight?

10♦: You and your partner can't agree on whether to settle down or keep exploring the islands.

10♣: Your partner is jealous of the time you spend with a new villager on the island.

J♦: Your lover gifts you a rare flower that blooms once every decade.

J♣: You discover your lover has a child from a past relationship on another island.

Q♦: An ex-partner tries to rekindle your expired relationship. You hesitate to risk getting hurt again.

Q♣: A former lover returns and tries to rekindle your relationship. You hesitate to tell your current partner.

K♦: Your crush awkwardly confesses their feelings for you - but are they genuine?

K♣: Your lover picks a fight with your best friend. You mediate between them.

Favor Scenario Oracle: Drama

A♥: Your partner forgets your birthday. You argue when they give you a thoughtless, last-minute gift.	**A♠**: An old friend declares their love. You don't reciprocate, straining the friendship.
2♥: You suspect your lover is getting bored with you. They deny it when you ask.	**2♠**: You catch your lover flirting with someone else. Harsh words are exchanged.
3♥: Your new relationship falls apart when your lover returns home to care for an ailing parent.	**3♠**: Your lover gets cold feet about raising children and questions your future together.
4♥: The new villager you're dating hides your relationship from their disapproving friends.	**4♠**: Sorting belongings of a deceased villager, you find passionate love letters from an anonymous writer.
5♥: You learn a friend has strong unspoken feelings for you when they try to sabotage your new relationship.	**5♠**: Your lover asks if you see yourself ever leaving the island. You hesitate, realizing your paths may differ.
6♥: Your partner pressures you to grow closer before you are ready. You ask them for more time.	**6♠**: A widow(er) you begin seeing still wears their ring and speaks of their late partner. You feel uneasy.
7♥: The villager your lover left you for returns to the island begging for another chance.	**7♠**: Your partner wants marriage and children soon. You don't feel ready to settle down and begin that new chapter.
8♥: Your crush agrees to a secret rendezvous - but will they actually show up?	**8♠**: You discover your lover embellished their humble origins to impress you. You must decide if you truly know them.
9♥: An old flame returns to the island wanting to pick up where you left off years ago.	**9♠**: On a romantic picnic, your lover surprisingly proposes. You froze up and respond poorly.
10♥: Your partner wants you to choose between them and pursuing your dream of island exploration.	**10♠**: Your lover gets an incredible opportunity on a faraway island. The long distance strains your relationship.
J♥: After a fight, your lover stops responding. Days of silence pass as you worry the relationship is over.	**J♠**: Your new relationship causes a rift in your family when your parents forbid you from seeing them.
Q♥: Your crush agrees to meet up together alone for a picnic. You spend all night worried if you are ready.	**Q♠**: As months pass, your partner stops saying "I love you." You don't know how to rekindle lost passion.
K♥: Your new romance faces scrutiny when locals gossip about you and your family's reputation.	**K♠**: Right before your wedding, your fiance begins acting aloof and cold. You worry they are getting cold feet.

Favor Scenario Oracle: Romance

A♦: They surprise you with a private dinner under the stars and moonlight serenade to express their love.	**A♣**: They surprise you with adoption paperwork, thrilled to start a family together.
2♦: They reveal their childhood fear of the ocean but ask you to teach them to swim so you can share more adventures.	**2♣**: They ask you on a hot air balloon ridedate so you can escape together and enjoy the views.
3♦: They confide their dream of having children someday and ask what it would be like raising a family together.	**3♣**: They express wanting more quality time together and ask you to take a couples cooking class date.
4♦: They nervously ask if they can kiss you for the first time under the fireworks at the summer festival.	**4♣**: They plan a romantic sunset sailboat ride complete with champagne to toast your love.
5♦: They surprise you with a scrapbook of your relationship milestones and thank you for the memories.	**5♣**: They surprise you with tickets to your favorite musician's concert and backstage passes to meet them.
6♦: They confide their desire to be more affectionate and ask to practice cuddling together.	**6♣**: They create a special scrapbook of your most precious memories to look back on when you're both old.
7♦: They share their favorite poetry and prose about love and recite an original piece written for you.	**7♣**: They nervously surprise you with an extravagant cross-world trip tailored exactly to your bucket list dreams.
8♦: They reveal a hidden grove filled with your favorite flowers and lovingly crown you with a flower ring.	**8♣**: They fully open their heart, confessing you're their soulmate and they can't imagine life without you.
9♦: They express feeling insecure in the relationship and ask how they can be a better partner for you.	**9♣**: They plan a secret romantic dinner on the beach, complete with candles and flowers.
10♦: They plan a scavenger hunt date ending in a romantic candlelit dinner outdoors.	**10♣**: They surprise you with a promise ring, hoping you'll promise to be faithful and cherish their love always.
J♦: They surprise you by filling your home with paper hearts, each with a loving message written for you.	**J♣**: They surprise you with a romantic tropical vacation and dreamily plan your future together.
Q♦: They confess their fear of losing you and ask you to promise your eternal love.	**Q♣**: They express concern about growing apart over time and ask to renew your vows.
K♦: They nervously ask your parents/family for blessing of your relationship and proposal.	**K♣**: They ask you on a romantic camping trip date under the stars away from daily stresses.

Favor Scenario Oracle: Romance

A♥: They ask you to dance under the full moon, like you did on your first date.	**A♠**: They plan a private slow dance lesson culminating in a moonlit dance together.
2♥: They plan a fun day date full of your most favorite activities culminating in a romantic dinner.	**2♠**: They surprise you with a private fireworks show at sunset choreographed to romantic music.
3♥: They nervously share their deepest secrets, fully trusting and opening themselves up to you.	**3♠**: They ask you to live out romantic movie scenes together and create your own happily ever after.
4♥: They surprise you with a personalized song or poem expressing their eternal love for you.	**4♠**: They surprise you with a horse drawn carriage ride under the stars culminating in a proposal.
5♥: They ask you to move in together, excitedly planning how you'll decorate your shared home.	**5♠**: They confess you helped them find the courage to come out and proudly proclaim their love for you.
6♥: They confess you're their first love and nervously ask to experience intimacy together.	**6♠**: They nervously ask you to move to a new city together and embark on new adventures.
7♥: They express their happiness being with you and desire to grow old together.	**7♠**: They reminisce fondly about your first kiss and ask to recreate that magic moment.
8♥: They surprise you by proposing at the location of your first date down on one knee.	**8♠**: They ask you on a hot air balloon ride so you can escape daily life and be alone together.
9♥: They express their dreams of starting a family together and ask how many kids you'd like to have.	**9♠**: They plan a romantic treasure hunt ending with a proposal and promise of forever.
10♥: They look deeply into your eyes and confess you're the love of their life.	**10♠**: They nervously ask you to meet their family and ask for their parents' blessing.
J♥: They plan a romantic hike to a waterfall and ask you to go skinny dipping together.	**J♠**: They lovingly care for you when you're sick and reaffirm how much you mean to them.
Q♥: They lovingly reminisce about the highlights of your relationship so far.	**Q♠**: They plan a romantic treasure hunt ending with a moonlit proposal and promise of forever.
K♥: They surprise you by recreating your first date, reminding you how lovestruck they were from the start.	**K♠**: They lovingly surprise you with breakfast in bed, an intimate song, and a slow dance in the kitchen.

Special Thanks

A huge thank you goes to the wonderful team who poured their love and care into building Solitaria. Your tireless work has given life to this magical world with its floating islands, endearing islanders, and curious creatures. Your attention to detail and dedication have truly made Solitaria a captivating experience:

Yojiico: Creative Director

Aru: Digital Artist

Colijiyo: Layout Artist

Ischiron: Writer

Yoone: Editor

We send a warm hug to all of you venturing into Solitaria for the first time! Your curiosity and smiles motivate us to create even more moments of wonder and coziness. Every time you step into the game, your imagination helps our world grow in exciting and unexpected ways.

Thank you from the bottom of our floaty little hearts. Thank you for playing Solitaria, the game where you can explore and create your own island paradise. I am the lead designer of this game, and I want to express my gratitude to you for downloading and enjoying our game. Your support means a lot to us, and we are always happy to hear your feedback and suggestions.

Solitaria is a game that we created with passion and love, and we hope that you can feel that in every detail of the game. We wanted to give you a relaxing and fun experience, where you can unleash your creativity and imagination. We also wanted to give you a sense of adventure and discovery, where you can find new things and surprises on your island.

We are not done yet, though. We have more exciting plans for Solitaria, and we want to share them with you. For our loyal customers, we are working on an expansion pack, which will introduce a different island for Solitaria, with new features, items, and challenges. This way, you can enjoy playing on unique islands, each with its own personality and charm.

We will keep you updated on our progress and release date. In the meantime, we hope that you continue to have fun with Solitaria, and we thank you again for your support.

Sincerely,

Creative Director

Player Sheet

.... Spend 1 Power to Upgrade ....

3-Section Clock

4-Section Clock

.... Requires Blessing ....

5-Section Clock

Name: Pronoun: Age:

Gender: Species: DOB: Refer to Page.47

Dreams :

Passion:

Energy	Power	Ability Cap		♦	♣	♥	♠

Name	Power	Ability

Island Estate Sheet

Name: Produce Worth:
Produce:
Notes   :

Name: Produce Worth:
Produce:
Notes   :

Name: Produce Worth:
Produce:
Notes   :

Name: Produce Worth:
Produce:
Notes   :

Name: Produce Worth:
Produce:
Notes   :

Islander Sheet

Name: Pronoun: Age:

Gender: Species: DOB:

Dreams :

Passion:

Hidden Gift: Favor:

Description:

Name: Pronoun: Age:

Gender: Species: DOB:

Dreams :

Passion:

Hidden Gift: Favor:

Description:

Name: Pronoun: Age:

Gender: Species: DOB:

Dreams :

Passion:

Hidden Gift: Favor:

Description:

Goal Sheet

Why? :

Detail:

Bonus/ Note Sheet

Name	#	Note

Inventory Sheet

Name	Worth	Description

Ability Sheet

Name	Power	Note

Made in the USA
Monee, IL
30 August 2023

41841418R00125